On the Back of an Envelope

PETER HENNESSY

On the Back of an Envelope

A Life in Writing

With Polly Coupar-Hennessy

First published by Haus Publishing in 2024
4 Cinnamon Row
London SW11 3TW

Copyright © Peter Hennessy, 2024

The right of the author to be identified as the author of this work has been asserted in accordance with the Copyright, Designs and Patents Act 1988

A CIP catalogue record for this book is available from the British Library

ISBN: 978-1-913368-85-2
eISBN: 978-1-913368-86-9

Typeset in Garamond by MacGuru Ltd

Printed in the UK by Clays Ltd (Elcograf S.p.A.)

All rights reserved.

Jacket image: Copyright © Charlie Bibby/*Financial Times*
The Listener extracts reproduced with kind permission of RadioTimes/Immediate Media Co Ltd
The Independent extracts courtesy of Independent Digital News & Media Ltd
The Times extracts, and the photos on pages 45 and 53, courtesy of *The Times*/News Licensing
With thanks to *The Tablet* for their kind permission to reproduce published material

A note from the publisher: All published articles have been reproduced in accordance with the house styles of the original publications. Errata have been corrected.

For Enid, with love and gratitude

Foreword

Polly Coupar-Hennessy

There's a family story, told many times to many people, that my dad, Peter, got his first break in journalism because he got drunk with the editor of *The Times Higher Education Supplement* at a party. It's a story I enjoy, because it's revealing of a number of things: the chummy, boys'-club nature of journalism in the seventies, Dad's gregariousness, the absolute centrality of luck in all of our lives. The party in question – at Lancaster House in 1971 – was for the Kennedy Scholars, a small group of bright young academics setting out on their Ivy League adventure, paid for by a foundation set up in memorial of John F. Kennedy. Dad was among them, twenty-three, newly married, living in Luton with his wife and mother-in-law. He's an excitable man, my dad, and not terribly cautious after a few drinks, which makes him both lots of fun, and occasionally a bit of a liability. I can imagine that the grand surroundings, mixed with high-quality booze, interesting company, and the sunlit prospect of a year at Harvard put him at his most Tiggerish.

The story goes that Dad got drunk with the aforementioned editor, Brian MacArthur, who told him to send back some pieces from Harvard when he got there. And when – now in Boston – Dad began work on his first piece, my mum said, 'Don't be silly Pete, he was pissed. He'll have forgotten all about it by now.'

Like a lot of such stories, however, it is the framing in family lore that is as revealing as the event itself. It's tempting to see Dad as successful in large part because he bounces through life, relentlessly agreeable, working like a Stakhanovite, and infecting all those around him with his positive energy. There is a lot in this, to be fair. Who could fail to be charmed by a man so easily enthused, so quick to make a joke, so ready to (literally) burst into song at any given opportunity?[1] In a way, we've come to portray him as almost totally guileless, which is both a bit dishonest and does him a great disservice.

The real story of the big break in journalism doesn't turn out to be so very different, when I ask about it, but it's always the details that are the most illuminating. 'Like all students when the drink is free and of high quality, you just hit it,' he says, with a remark about not leading the blameless life that he does now. 'And so I hit the G & T, I think, and Enid [his wife] was getting slightly anxious about that, as she didn't drink in those days. Especially with me getting louder and louder. Brian MacArthur came up, who I knew of, because he was on *The Times* as their education correspondent. And I got *The Times*, we got the cheap student edition every day. I knew what Brian looked like, because in those days they had pictures of the correspondents. Brian introduced himself and said, "tell me how you get one of these scholarships."' Dad goes on to recount how, gin-loosened, he explained his success. 'I remember talking to a friend of mine, who got one a couple of years earlier than me. And he coached me on how to conduct the interview. He said "Lord Harlech, the chairman, wants you to be an all-rounder – a good chap, a bit of good works here, a bit of sports, a bit of work on the books. If it's Lord Sherfield, former ambassador to Washington, you can be fairly radical about foreign policy but you mustn't dump on NATO. There will probably be the cultural attaché from the American Embassy in Grosvenor Square, who will expect you to be up on the latest literature. And Isaiah Berlin, who hates people to be boring. So don't be boring. And you mustn't be overawed." So

---

1 I'm not making this up – he sang during his own wedding speech, in countless lectures, on Radio 4, on the odd occasion at board meetings of learned institutions, and too many times to mention just walking down the street. To my great disappointment, he has not yet burst into song in the chamber of the House of Lords. But there is time.

I prepared with that in mind, and it worked.' MacArthur was very tickled by this, and also perhaps sensed that a man who could do his research and press the right buttons with people might be quite a good journalist. Tiggerish? Yes. Guileless? Certainly not.

In the strictest sense, this little vignette marks the beginning of Dad's 'Life in Writing'. When we first started this project, I expected that it would form the beginning of a jolly little pen-portrait of Fleet Street in the 1970s, written by Dad on the back of conversations with me to jog his memory. It hasn't quite worked out like that; instead, I wrote the 'memoir' parts of the book on the back of interviews with Dad. We decided to do it this way for a number of reasons. The most important, to my mind, is Dad's discomfiture about writing about himself. Don't misunderstand, this is not a question of modesty. He will happily recount many amusing anecdotes featuring himself without compunction or fear of 'showing off'. Showing off is one of his core skills. It is – I think – a generational reticence to discuss anything personal, taken to almost ludicrous extremes in my father. This book is not going to be a deep dive into the soul of its subject – that would take a far more skilled interlocutor than me. But I hope to have drawn out something that gives the reader a sense of the man.

The second reason is his recent diagnosis with Parkinson's disease, which causes him pain and fatigue, and also makes it physically much harder to write (especially with one of his beloved fountain pens).

The third – and most important – reason is love. It's taken me a lot longer than most to realise that my parents are not, in fact, immortal. This, again, is due in part to family lore surrounding Hennessy longevity (my grandfather died aged 100, his mother made 103). It's also because of a strong Hennessy tendency to avoid facing up to difficult things. The Parkinson's diagnosis, and the concomitant weakening of his body, if not spirit, was like a bucket of cold water over the head for me: unpleasant but energising. All any of us has is now, and talking to Dad about his life, mulling over the patterns and meanings, chatting about the past, and delving into all those family stories has been a source of great joy, and I think comfort, to both of us. Perhaps it's vain to think that it will be of interest to anyone else. I hope it is; Dad's has been an interesting life, and a life that, in its way, reveals something of the post-war Britain that he has lived through and written about. A classic grammar-school boy, teetering on the edge of the British establishment, he is in some ways the insider's outsider, never quite part of the system or the group that he chronicles, never quite separate from it either. As anyone who has met him knows, he has a prodigious memory, a talent for mimicry (sadly irreproducible here), and an abiding love of a good story. Or as he would call it, gossip. Hopefully, these qualities will be enough to hold the reader's attention as they have held mine. If not, then I am content that this project has brought great happiness to me and to Dad, and helped us to make the most of our time together.

Contents

Preface: (North) Circular thoughts ... xv

Part One: Formations
'A nostalgist with a purpose': Early life in North London and Nympsfield ... 5
'You never quite leave your first university': Cambridge, 1966–9 ... 16
Establishment and meritocracy (Queen Mary valedictory lecture, 7 October 2014) ... 23
'Do I detect a note of flattery in your voice?': Becoming a journalist, Boston and London, 1971–3 ... 37
Growing up on *The Times*, 1974–84 ... 47
'A bloody nuisance but in the end he's on the side of the Queen': Working the Whitehall beat, 1975–92 ... 60
The fraction of the curve: Journalism and contemporary history ... 72

Part Two: Crown and Constitution
The Queen as a Heineken-lager monarch: The parts of the constitution that only she can reach (Jubilee Lecture series, Dulwich Picture Gallery, 3 January 2012) ... 87
The National Royal Service ... 105
A UK state of mind ... 112
Britain and Europe: The emotional deficit (Lecture given to the University of Iceland/British Embassy, Reykjavik, 18 May 2007) ... 122

Keeping calm and carrying on: British crises since 1945 and
  the special case of Brexit (Vice-Chancellor's Lecture,
  University of Birmingham, 12 June 2017)   129
On the Shelf: On Walter Bagehot's *The English Constitution*
  (*The Sunday Times*, 3 December 1995)   143
Speech on the Rwanda Bill (House of Lords, 29 January 2024) 146

Part Three: Prime Ministers, Parliament, and Politicians

Never did so many talk such drivel: On the quality of political
  language today (*The Independent*, 25 September 1989)   152
What are prime ministers for? (Lecture at the Cheltenham
  Literature Festival, 6 October 2017)   158
How to build a prime minister   174
The incomparable Clem (Lecture to mark the unveiling of the
  statue of Clement Attlee, Queen Mary, 2011)   185
Harold Macmillan: Healer of the nation's scars (*The Listener*,
  8 January 1987)   196
Whitehall brief: Shades of a Home Counties Boudicca
  (*The Times*, 17 May 1983)   200
Exit the Tigress (*The Tablet*, 13 April 2013)   203
The rise of Napoleon Blair (*The Times*, 25 September 2000)   208
Tony's signature: The Blair style of government since 1997
  (The Alistair Berkley Lecture, Robinson College,
  Cambridge, 2006)   215
The undoing of prime ministers   230
Parliament and the state (The Speaker's Lecture, Houses of
  Parliament, 18 November 2014)   238

Part Four: On Crown Service

Why the best job in the Civil Service involves carrying the
  prime minister's bag (*The Times*, 10 November 1976)   252
The Cabinet Office: A magnificent piece of powerful
  bureaucratic machinery (*The Times*, 8 March 1976)   259

Whitehall brief: How public servants keep it private (*The Times*, 22 September 1981)	266
No 10 in the Jay-Lynn eye: The megaphone theory of 'Yes Minister' (*The Listener*, 19 and 26 December 1985)	269
The Treasury: Bank manager and probation officer rolled into one (*The Times*, 28 March 1977)	274
The Good and the Great: The most elevated and distinguished casualties of the Thatcher years (*The Listener*, 7 February 1985)	283
Lord Franks: The lord who sits in judgement (*The Times*, 17 January 1983)	292
Royal commissions: New social foundations lack crucial commissions (*The Independent*, 25 April 1988)	297
Afterthoughts	301
Acknowledgements	303
Also by Peter Hennessy	305

PREFACE

(North) Circular thoughts

As a long, freezing snowbound winter crept into a thaw, I came into the world on the evening of Friday 28 March 1947 in the North Middlesex Hospital alongside the North Circular Road in Edmonton. I arrived courtesy of a caesarean section cut into my mum, Edith, by a surgeon, Mr Purdy, whose name she often gratefully invoked as part of one of her most highly polished stories across the years until she died aged eighty in 1986. She was over forty, unwell and suffering from high blood pressure, when she had me. It was a close-run thing, which mercifully for me and my three older sisters – Kathleen, Terry, and Maureen – she survived. She discovered later that my dad, Bill, and our parish priest in Whetstone, Father Gerry Ryan (a glorious man and great friend of our family) had discussed who should be saved in the event of a catastrophe – Mum or me. That they did so without consulting her naturally scarred her memory of an event which otherwise would always bring on a huge beaming smile (she rather specialised in these) when she recalled it, particularly when I passed through the stages in life she had not expected to see: primary school; secondary school; university; marriage; children of my own. I'm curious still about certain aspects of my arrival. Did Dad and Father Ryan decide that if it came to it, I should survive? I rather think they did (and I have a faint memory of Mum telling me so many years later).

As the (almost) site of my birth, the A406 acquired a special place in our family history. The North Circular Road has a permanent niche in the map room of my mind as a kind of British equivalent of Route 66, the legendary gateway to the American West (though its poetry seems lost on those to whom I have mentioned this comparison). Over those years I have travelled in an arc of about four and half miles round the sacred A road to Walthamstow, where I have lived since 1973. Now, as I write, I am being treated for an old man's complaint in that very same North Middlesex hospital. A beautiful symmetry in its own north-east London-ish way.

What kind of Britain was I born into? What was it the heavens were telling the night Mr Purdy did his stuff for Mum and me? A quick reading of *The Times* for Saturday 29 March 1947 (then the proud paper of record – a claim it still sustained when I joined it in 1974) throws up still more symmetries that have run through my span living on our cherished damp islands in the cold northern seas.

As Britain thawed, the Cold War was chilling in Moscow, where a foreign ministers' conference was falling out over the future of Germany in the early stages of the great, forty-year East–West confrontation which so shaped my early and middle years – and now, in my twilight years, the new cold war has turned hot in Ukraine.

The perpetual anxiety about the productivity and performance of the British economy was reflected in those pages as *The Times* strove to be cheerful about the Labour government's creation of a new Central Economic Planning Staff headed by Sir Edwin Plowden, a businessman with wartime Whitehall experience. The eternal row about the boundary between the public and private sectors found its niche in an advert paid for by the Big Four railway companies – the Great Western; the London and North Eastern; the London, Midland and Scottish; and the Southern – plus the Road Haulage Association:

<u>DANGER</u>
Is THIS the time
to
Nationalize
Transport?

It was. British Railways came into existence on 1 January 1948.

Imperial stresses were felt in the pages of *The Times* too. Disposing of the huge territorial Empire was to be bound up with the life of the country of my birth for the next thirty years. The paper reported growing and bloody tensions in the Punjab in soon-to-be-partitioned India. Yet the dash for the exit in Africa, South-East Asia, and the Caribbean was plainly not in the forefront of the Whitehall minds who were, as reported that day, preparing to purchase the old Westminster Hospital site opposite Westminster Abbey on which to build a new Colonial Office, where the QEII Centre stands today (the cuts following the 1949 devaluation of the pound took care of that project).

But the lead story in what *The Times* then called its 'Imperial and Foreign' pages involved another figure who was to be a continuous presence throughout the bulk of my life: Princess Elizabeth, who, with her sister, Margaret, and her father and mother, the King and Queen, were on their celebrated tour of South Africa aboard the White Train. The paper's 'Special Correspondent' (no by-lines in those days) reported, in language that was of its time and place, from Westaffin, where some 2,000 labourers from the local fruit farms waited to greet the royal party in a hollow semi-circle facing the railway line along which the White Train was to roll:

> about 50 dancers, including a few women, all wearing the gayest possible costumes with ostrich feathers dyed brilliant colours, the men carrying shields and brandishing knobkerries, went tirelessly through a long succession of native dances. Hour after hour they kept it up, stimulated by a steady rhythm of a tom-tom.

Later the royal party visited a tropical-fruit research station. The special correspondent's taste buds lost all control at this point and his pen hymned the praise of 'this great fruit-growing area, whose citrus, tomato and mango, guava and pawpaw, and other fruit do so much to make this whole country seem to visitors from rationed England a land incredibly flowing with milk and honey.'

Rationed Britain, though still an imperial nation, was much more obsessed with its alimentary canal than it was with the Suez Canal. The slightest change in the food regime would get into the paper. Here's the bit that did as *The Times* sub-editors shaped the paper on the evening of 28 March 1947, as I prepared to make an entrance:

> The Minister of Food has made an Order, which comes into force tomorrow, revising prices for imported tinned meats, home-packed meat paste in 3oz and 6½oz tins, and imported salami sausages. The amending order also makes provision for the use of fat of vegetable origin in the manufacture of beef sausage, beef sausage meat and beef slicing sausage.

This then was the gloriously drab Britain into which I was born. Glorious because the country had resolutely held firm throughout nearly six years of total war, for one of which we had stood alone with the British Empire against the Axis powers. I would later come to cherish a line from the great economist, John Maynard Keynes, that in 1940–1, Britain had 'thrown good housekeeping to the winds, but we saved ourselves and we helped save the world.'

No first-rank great power has ever shed the 'super' bit of its powerdom to such critical and enduring effect. We lost a third of our wealth in doing it and wore ourselves out – hence the noble drabness of the late 1940s, with its food rationing, its shabby clothes, its run-down railway system, its bomb-damaged streets, its fuel and power crises, the strain on its economy, its currency, and its balance of payments, which stretched the great Labour government of 1945–51 to its limits.

Yet to be one of Mr Attlee's children turned out to be a winning ticket in the lottery of life. No generation has been better cared for than mine – a source of profound and perpetual gratitude on my part. Though it is thankfulness tinged with regret that subsequent generations have not been so fortunate in terms of the investments the state put into them and the lives and life chances open to them.

We children of the early post-war period were better fed, housed, and kept healthy than any generation that had come before. The males of our cohort did not have to put on uniform and fight unless we became professional soldiers, sailors, or airmen (we were too young to do National Service). We were the first generation to grow up beneath the shadow of the nuclear mushroom cloud. We never entirely got used to that, but we coped and though brinks were sometimes reached, international tensions never slipped into the catastrophe of a third world war. We had a bias towards optimism and what seemed a well-founded belief in incremental improvement – we were, if not a golden generation, certainly a gilt-edged one.

One way of depicting a generation is to think in terms of the banner upon which were embroidered the shared aspirations that its parents and grandparents had for it. As part of my reflective state of mind as Brexit neared, I was powerfully struck by just how lustrous was the banner under which I grew up and, to be honest, beneath which I still live and breathe in my seventies. Savour its embroidery, for in my judgement it reflects a second finest hour in the 1940s to rank alongside the one that saved us in the Battle of Britain and the year of standing alone that followed. It was the result of a deliberate choice, and was not forced upon them as had been the great moment of shared endeavour following the fall of France in June 1940, which created perhaps the most glorious collective national endeavour in the nation's history. The second forties banner came out of the experience of total war and lay at the heart of the post-war consensus, which so powerfully shaped the lives of my generation:

- The 1942 Beveridge Report, blueprinting a comprehensive welfare state for the post-war period.
- The 1944 Full Employment White Paper, committing all the political parties to avoiding a repeat of the interwar economic slump.

- The Education Act 1944, providing secondary education to all for the first time.
- The National Health Service from 1948, free to all at the point of delivery.
- The creation of NATO in 1949, placing a roof of collective security over the UK and its Western allies in the Cold War.
- The start of the shift from Empire to Commonwealth.

All presided over by those most celebrated constitutional monarchs, George VI and Elizabeth II.

I have long felt favoured by my professional lives having given me two goes at making sense of the banner of my country's lived experience, both as it first unfurled (as a journalist) and later reliving many of the same events in relative tranquillity laced with a dash of perspective (as a historian).

For example, when preparing *Winds of Change*, my study of Britain in the early sixties, it was as if a past and, in many cases, long-dead generation had opened the door and invited me to come back and move in with them for a few years, greeting me with the words: 'How nice to see you again. Let's talk about the old days. There are certain things we couldn't tell you at the time. But take a look at these old, once top-secret papers, and here's a fragment of a diary you might be interested in.'

This volume will be an exercise in recapturing flashes of the history of a land I cherish profoundly through my scribbles as I have lived through it; a revisiting of the paper trail laid down in articles, columns, and lectures as I have researched its archives, written about it as a journalist and a historian, and talked to my fellow travellers on the road from March 1947, alongside new pieces on the themes that have preoccupied me throughout my professional life. I hope it will be a small addition to the written debris left behind as the generations pass into one another. Part One of this book, Formations, also includes autobiographical segues: recollections of my own experience as told to my daughter, Polly, who came up with the idea of a 'life in writing' as she began to collect the bits of my archive of newspaper articles, lectures, and talks spanning the three professions I have engaged in so far: journalism (since 1971); university teaching (1992–2014); and sitting in the House of Lords (since 2010). Writing has been the link between all these phases, especially the preparation of my trilogy of British history from 1945–64 (*Never Again: Britain 1945–51, Having It So Good: Britain in the Fifties,* and *Winds of Change: Britain in the Early Sixties*). There is more than a dash of narcissism in creating a volume of this kind and even a degree of embarrassment (a condition to which many British males reared in the 1950s have always been prone). Polly persuaded me to have a go nonetheless. One of the many pieces of good fortune that have come my way is that all three phases of my professional life have kept boredom at bay. My sincerest wish is that the words that follow will do the same for you.

An early attempt at piety: altar boy, Whetstone, 1954.

PART ONE

FORMATIONS

It may seem a touch idiosyncratic – as well as quite seriously vain – to include in a book largely devoted to writings on politics and history a whole section on one's own personal formation. If I were, for example, an ancient historian, it would be downright bizarre to intersperse writings on the bureaucratic structures of the Roman Republic with pieces about trolleybuses in Finchley. Please bear with me; my professional life has been largely devoted to writing about the country and society that made me and the times in which I live. In the 1980s there was a famous TV advert for Remington shavers in which Victor Kiam, the owner of Remington, would announce, 'I liked it so much, I bought the company.' Maybe I am the Victor Kiam of the historical profession. I liked my little corner of the world so much I decided to write about it for fifty-odd years.

It's not just solipsism though. There may well be an excessive tendency among historians to impose patterns on the past, but the early post-war years really do qualify by almost any standards to be one of those transitional moments. We who were born in those years – the baby boomers – are a kind of hinge generation. Our lives, especially our youth and early adulthood, were much less constrained than the lives of those born just a decade or so earlier. By the same token, we look almost unbearably anachronistic to those born a decade later.

I was born into a war-scarred Britain. We played soldiers in bomb sites and clambered on the roofs of air-raid shelters. Rationing had not yet ended. We celebrated Empire Day at school and my sisters went up to London to watch the coronation. Men wore hats and suits, even going to the pub. It was still a deferential society: class dominated our thinking and structured our political parties. Our status consciousness touched on the obsessional. We were still a nation of believers, although decreasing numbers went to church, except for the Catholic population. Many Catholic families still thought of offering one son up to the priesthood. The thought crossed my mind, strange as it seems now; I used to go to the Vocations exhibitions at Olympia and I remember being particularly attracted by the 'White Fathers' with their pristine habits topped off by a bright red fez. And even for those less keen, the priests had a ridiculous level of influence over Catholic family life. In these ways we were connected to ancient worlds, and in the immediate postwar it may not have been obvious that they were fast disappearing.

By the time I reached young adulthood, the tide of affluence was incoming and deference was ebbing, although it wasn't until the 1970s that the deeper transformations set hard. But we were rising on a different type of tide, and we knew it. Now, in the twenty-first century, those of my generation are old, and old people find much comfort in reflection. The world we made is unrecognisable to the one that made us. The world being shaped by the generations that followed us is faster, looser, and surrounded by technologies beyond what our young selves could have imagined. The years since 1945 have been, for good or ill, absolutely transformational and in writing about my own formations – personal and professional – and the themes that have shaped me, I hope I am able to reflect the experiences of others and capture something of a changing society. Anyone who has lived through this period has stories to tell. What follows is only a little example – a boy from North London who was fortunate enough to meet some interesting people, do some interesting things, and – somehow – make a living out of indulging a personal passion for writing about my own times.

Finchley, 1950.

'A nostalgist with a purpose':
Early Life in North London and Nympsfield

'I knew I could write,' Peter says, 'when I got three gold stars for an essay I wrote in primary school called "A Foggy Day in London Town". The title was a straight lift from the Frank Sinatra song, which my older sisters used to play on the record player, but it was about the smogs. I remember walking to school on my own in the last of them, which was a faintly terrifying experience because my route involved crossing several main roads that carried trolleybuses, which were huge and virtually silent. It carried a bit of a thrill too, because in the greatest conurbation in the country you were, in effect, isolated into about five square yards of space, and the rest of North London might as well not have been there. My teacher told me she'd shown the essay to the others in the staffroom.' He is clearly still delighted by the recognition from his beloved teacher, even nearly seventy years later, which says a lot for the importance of teachers – a theme to which Peter returns often. As he recalls this, it would be easy to imagine a young boy who was gregarious, confident, and precocious. But, Peter says, he wasn't quite like that. For the first decade of his life he grew up in requisitioned houses in Finchley and Whetstone, North London, with his parents and three sisters, Kathleen, Terry, and Maureen, who were twelve, ten, and eight years older than him. His first school, Our Lady of Lourdes Primary in Finchley, was a tougher place than one might expect, given the affluence of the area now. 'It was a very poor catchment, drawn from quite a wide area because it was a Catholic school. I hadn't grown up with other boys and I was quite frightened of them. There were lots of fights and I wasn't used to fighting.'

The family in the back garden of Allandale Avenue, Finchley.
From left to right: Terry, Kathleen, Dad, PH, Mum
(in her Brown Owl uniform), Maureen.

Mostly, he kept himself to himself. 'I was quite shy and didn't talk much. Hard to imagine now! The kindergarten I went to before Our Lady of Lourdes was attached to a convent and I was also rather terrified of the nuns.' Peter's sisters tell stories of him holding onto the railings and refusing to budge as they walked him to school. Some memories are gentler, however. 'At the kindergarten, there was an old nun from Holland who wore clogs. She was in charge of the greenhouses, and they'd sell the fruit. She used to give me an apple or a pear when I didn't have quite enough money. At the gatehouse of the convent the local tramps, as they were called then, would come for soup and bread, so I also picked up the notion of the charitableness of the nuns.'

It was, he says, an intensely Catholic childhood. 'A lot of the social life was centred around the church. We'd go to Catholic film nights to see terrible films like *Going My Way*, with Bing Crosby playing a priest. Mum and Dad's friendship circles were also very Catholic. Mum was a Brown Owl of the Catholic Brownies attached to the church in Whetstone and I used to tag along on their trips. They'd bung us all in the back of a furniture lorry – no seats of course – and take us to the seaside in Kent. Wherever I looked was Catholicism. School, home, the Cubs. We'd go once a year to the Tyburn Walk from Westminster Cathedral to Tyburn – the martyrs' walk.' This may have fostered a fairly strong Catholic identity, but it doesn't seem to have produced much religiosity. He says of the martyrs' walk: 'I loved it because going up to town was quite an event, even though we lived in London. And in Central London they'd just introduced those rubber things in the road that change the traffic lights when a car drives over them. We'd go and stamp on them and the lights would go bananas.' He smiles. 'And on the way back we used to go to the Lyons' Corner House for a cup of tea.'

What did Catholicism mean to him? 'It gave me a sense of belonging to a huge world organisation linked by the Mass, and the Mass in Latin at that. But there were parts of it that were absurd. I remember the girls coming back from their youth club laughing hysterically because one of the nuns had told them that they should never share a comb with a boy, as it might produce impure thoughts and therefore become an occasion of sin. Almost everything was a potential occasion of sin, which rather added drama to the whole business of living. Looking back, it made one feel much more raffish than one ever was. I remember when I was at college, when it was fashionable to be a Trotskyist, feeling that having been subjected to Catholicism in all these ludicrous forms had inoculated me against any kind of ism ever again.'

He says of writing his post-war trilogy that his memories of his early childhood helped him recapture the feel of post-war Britain. 'I can remember what it felt like. I remember rationing, I remember never being entirely warm in the winter. I remember Dad living off the state. We never had quite enough money for things. There's lots of laughter too – my sisters were extraordinarily jolly and I was so lucky to have them – but I can remember how drab it all was.' And even though Peter wasn't born until two years after the war ended, it's clear that the effects of the war were very present in his life. 'We lived in a big house in Finchley that had been requisitioned by the government during the war, which they then used as social housing. We shared it with a lovely family who'd been bombed out of the East End in the Blitz. I used to call them Auntie and Uncle. They were generous and warm-hearted and their children, who were slightly older, were really kind to me. Uncle Alf, as I'll call him, worked as a lorry driver at the newly nationalised British Road Services depot in Muswell Hill, where Mum was a copy typist in the evening. I loved Uncle Alf. There was a touch of Private Walker about him; he had Brylcreemed hair and he wore a hat and one of those huge, belted raincoats that were all the rage then. He would sometimes call in to have his lunch at the beginning of his outward journey from the depot in one of the BRS lorries, which he'd park outside the house. On one occasion he sat me on his knee and got me to turn the steering wheel as he drove the lorry down the road – a six-year-old boy in this *huge* lorry – it was absolutely thrilling! Some time later Uncle Alf disappeared, and I asked Mum and Dad where he'd gone and whether he was all right. Rather guardedly they told me he'd gone away on work of national importance. Years later, Mum told me he'd been convicted of stealing engines from the BRS. I wasn't aware then of the phrase "fell off the back of a lorry" but when I became aware of it I knew quite literally what it meant.'

Peter's mother was a great talker and he credits her with his love of listening to people's stories. 'We'd go and stay with my Auntie Molly in her flat above the pub she ran in Newport. Mum and Molly would gossip, usually about their husbands, and they'd forget the little boy playing on the floor. I loved all of that – it was my signals intelligence on the adult world. Talking, gossiping, is how people handle the unexpected, the familiar, the frightening. When you're writing history, if you can move in and do retrospective signals intelligence on whoever you're writing about it's a wonderful thing.'

Today, Peter is something of an insider–outsider: he sits in the House of Lords and seems to be the typical 'establishment' type, but went to a state school and lives in a part of East London that has only recently become sort of fashionable. He seems at home in lots of groups, but never quite *of* any of them. Is this down to his childhood? The only boy in a family of older girls, Catholic in a time when that was still considered, as he puts it, 'a bit odd', growing up quite poor but with a middle-class and quite well-educated father. 'Partly,' he says. 'I'm a bit of a social amphibian. I like it like that.'

Peter's amphibious tendencies were perhaps also on display when, in 1958, he was sent to St Benedict's in Ealing, a private Catholic day school. 'Mum and Dad had tremendous aspirations, they wanted me to be a young Catholic gentleman. Dad wanted me to be a "great man", though it's never clear what he was thinking of. I came in on the bottom stream because I hadn't done very well on the entrance exam. I was quite a late developer.' Did he enjoy it? 'I was quite pleased to go to that school because I thought it was rather smart. There were some good teachers. I liked the model railway club.' For such an enthusiastic and positive man, this is, at best, lukewarm. He says that the public-school atmosphere didn't suit him. The school also has a dark history. One of the priests used to invite Peter to come to his flat and do work for the scouts in the holidays. At first his parents were pleased, but then his mother sensed something was off. 'Mum said to Dad, "You've got to tell him, Bill, you've just got to tell him".' Certain things were explained to young Peter, and there were no more visits to the priest's house after that. It didn't get any further than being sat on the priest's knee, but it's clear that he had a narrow escape. 'In those days people were tremendously deferential to the priests. When we moved to Gloucestershire [after his first year at St Benedict's] Dad wanted me to go to Downside, which also turned out to be blighted by abuse. Fortunately Dad ran out of money so I didn't go. I occasionally wonder how my life might have been different if I'd gone to Downside.

In 1959 the family left London and moved to Nympsfield, a small village in Gloucestershire. Even the choice of village was related to religion. 'In the late nineteenth century, a rich Catholic family had bought Woodchester Park just down the hill and built this huge mansion in the hope that the pope would come and visit them. They built a chapel in the village, where there was a Catholic orphanage. So this tiny village had quite a lot of Catholic connections.' They moved into a late-sixteenth-century house which Peter's father found in the property ads in *The Universe*, a Catholic weekly paper. 'We rented it from another Catholic family. It had supposedly been a coaching inn on the old road from Bath to Gloucester, even though it was quite small. It had beautiful features and a wonderful ceiling, but it was absolutely freezing and the spiral staircases were death traps. Dad used to sleep in the attic. I remember taking him up a cup of tea on the first morning of the big snow of early 1963 to find about two feet of snow curling around the end of his bed.

'We were really quite poor when we first got to Gloucestershire,' he says. 'We were never hungry but there was no margin. Mum was always worried about money.' In other ways, though, the move was like winning the lottery for the twelve-year-old Peter. He got into the local grammar, Marling School in Stroud, and found that – perhaps for the first time – he really belonged. 'Marling could have been made for me,' he says. His demeanour noticeably changes when he talks about Marling and the friends he made there, a group of clever, slightly competitive boys who nevertheless looked after each other and brought each other on. It is also clear that the teachers had a profound and positive influence on him. 'There were three different streams of teachers at Marling in the early sixties. There were those – particularly in science and maths – who joined the profession in the interwar years, when it was very difficult for graduates to find jobs. They were hugely qualified people. Then there were the teachers who'd done the crash course in eighteen months after coming back from the war. One of them, "Windy" Windust, was a heroic figure to us because he'd lost a leg during his time in the RAF. And then there was the other stream of teachers who were the first beneficiaries of the 1944 Education Act, like my history master, Eric Pankhurst. He was the first beneficiary from Stoke-on-Trent to go to Oxford on a full scholarship. We were so fortunate. Eric, Michael Gray, Peter Young, Tony Thomas, Cyril Campbell, Oliver Wicks; they not only knew their subjects, they knew *us*.' His history teacher was particularly inspiring. 'Eric was full of vim and character and laughter. He could make the most prosaic things into pure fun. There was a sort of running patter alongside the "proper history". I've always liked people you could see as older brothers. Eric was one of those. In fact, Eric gave me what I can confidently declare was the best-ever after-school service imaginable. Right up until his death, every three months he would send me a brown envelope of cuttings of things from the papers he thought I might have missed and needed to know. At his memorial service I included this in my tribute to him. At the tea afterwards, his wonderful wife Shirley said, "You were wrong about Eric's last packet to you arriving just a few weeks before he died. One of the things he did in his last days was to keep adding pieces for you in the next envelope he was going to send".'

At Marling, Peter was clearly not a shy, quiet boy any more. 'In the fourth form I led a revolt against excessive homework and became a sort of unofficial shop steward. We were quite competitive boys and we'd work hard, but it got too much. There was also an element of survival: we were taught in big wooden huts left over from the Great War and in the winter it was utterly freezing. If you were near the top of the class you got to sit by the windows. The hot-water pipes ran along beneath the windows and we'd rest our elbows on them. It added a certain incentive in the cold winters of the early sixties.' He spoke to his form master Michael Gray, who tactfully sorted out the homework issue. Gray also quietly looked after Peter. 'I was subversive rather than difficult, but it could have gone either way. Michael took me to one side very quietly and said in his lovely Dorset voice, "you've got great gifts of leading the others now. You can use it in two ways: you can lead them into revolt or you can use it to make things better. It's up to you." I never forgot that. He was a bit like a dad to me, giving me the sort of chat you need as a fourteen- or fifteen-year-old.'

Peter's interest in politics and current affairs started early. 'Looking back, I was quite a consumer of the news. I'm pretty sure I acquired that in 1956 at the time of the Suez crisis and the Hungarian crisis. I was handicapped slightly by not having a television and also the fact that the one newspaper we had in the house was the *Express* and later *The Telegraph*. The *Express* was a formidable newspaper in those days, but it only gave you only one line in terms of comprehending what was going on. My dad's political prejudices were very strong so there was a kind of mutually reinforcing right-wing view of life that I was picking up, plus the Catholicism which was of course pre-Vatican II. The most important stimulus, though, was going to Liverpool for my grandma's hundredth birthday in 1963, just after Harold Wilson had become leader of the Labour Party. We all gathered at the house the night before and my aunties and uncles, all of whom were of the Right, were rubbishing the Labour Party going back to the 1930s, denouncing people like Jimmy Thomas, the railwaymen's union leader, picking out particular hates of theirs from figures of the past. They were polishing each other's prejudices up and passing them on reinforced, whipping each other up into a frenzy. I've never liked that, instinctively. I remember thinking it can't be that simple, even though everyone was saying much the same thing with varying degrees of venom and passion. They were particularly scathing about the Attlee government. So I went to Stroud Public Library and started reading about it; I think I started with Hugh Dalton's diaries. I began to realise there was a bigger picture. They were terrible reactionaries, but I owe them a lot; the seeds of my interest in post-war British politics were sowed that night and it taught me one of the first instincts a historian should acquire, which is to always have in mind "it can't be as simple as that."'

It may seem slightly odd, especially for a sixteen-year-old, but this new fascination comes across as something like falling in love. What was it about the Attlee government that so captured him? 'They were not pessimistic; they had a go at tackling injustice. They thought that Beveridge and Keynes showed that it didn't have to be like this, and that through carefully crafted public policy you could change things. And they did it. They were broader gauge figures. The opposing parties were antagonists of course, but they'd got to know each other working in the coalition during the war. They knew and liked each other.'

Is he a nostalgist? 'There were terrible things about British society and there are so many things we've got better on. But it's nice to go back now and again to time when there was a sense of shared purpose because of the war. Of course there are all sorts of things that one regrets were not done, but it was very productive. I suppose I am a nostalgist, but a nostalgist with a purpose. I want to recapture. I want to be invited back in again, to go back and have a chat with them. And even though I wasn't born until 1947, the early post-war period is familiar enough to do that. I can still smell pre-Clean Air Act London, which was dirty all the time but at its worst during the smogs: all that sulphur from the coal fires in every home, in the power stations, in the ubiquitous steam locomotives. They felt so clingy. The Thames stank of oil and sewage. I can still see the Liverpool Overhead Railway that ran along the docks and remember what it was like to cross the Clyde on the Erskine Ferry. I caught the end of nineteenth-century Britain. It was a scene that was to go, but it would have been recognisable right back to the 1880s. As an evoker of memory, snatches of music or smells do it better than anything. When you catch the smell of coal smoke on a damp November breeze, you're back there. Of course you can only express that side of your curiosity as a historian and author, because you can't really write newspaper articles about coal smoke. And if you're writing books for those who came on that journey as well as those who were never there, you want to give them that coal smoke, the freeze of '63, the sound of the shunting engines.

You want people to have a sniff, have a listen, as they ask, "why was it like that?" We have to remember that people in the past felt as we felt. They wanted food, shelter, warmth, love, security. It helps if you have that instinct, it means you can resist the desire to scold them for their mistakes, like a combination of *Guardian* reader and drill sergeant. Although perhaps you can be too understanding of people.'

Is there something of the curious nine-year-old in the Peter of today? 'It's funny,' he says, 'I've criss-crossed that period since 1945 in so many ways professionally: I've crossed it looking at it as a general historian, looking at the cold war and the nuclear deterrent, looking at the ways politicians behaved and the things that bothered them. I've picked up a bit of social history on the way, even though I'm not a social historian. I'm still trying to catch up with what it all means, this period I've lived through.'

A NOSTALGIST WITH A PURPOSE

Climbing The Napes Needle on Great Gable in the Lake District to celebrate the end of our A levels in 1965. Led by my great friend, Hywel Thomas, who took the picture from the top of the pinnacle.

'You never quite leave your first university': Cambridge, 1966–9

'I'm like a JCB,' Peter says, when asked about his style of scholarship. 'I don't have the width or the cleverness to be a great scholar, but I've got the energy and I'm good at mining the raw materials. I'm quite good at telling a story, and I've got a compulsion for telling it to others, that's all. I know what my limits are.' He says this without any undue modesty or regret. It may be that this lack of intellectual insecurity was one of the reasons that he thrived in the hothouse of an ancient university. He went up to St John's College, Cambridge in 1966, initially to study geography, before changing to economics and then, finally, history ('not enough jokes in the Economics Tripos'). 'St John's used to specialise in plucking the head boys from grammar schools for their undergraduate intake. It didn't have the patina of public-school smoothness that some other colleges had. It's almost unimaginable to think this now, but to be a grammar-school boy in St John's College in the late 1960s felt like being part of the rising wave of meritocracy, we felt we were the cutting edge of social advance. Can you imagine?' He roars with laughter at the thought. 'We all had a sense of public schools. We felt they were places you could buy privilege and that if we could compete on an equal footing, we could show them up. That still lingers in me a bit.' It's clear, however, that he was very aware of his privilege. 'I had the good fortune of being temperamentally suited to an environment that can be overladen with social sensitivities and intellectual insecurities, at an age when one is particularly prone to competition with others. Cambridge was an adventure playground that could have been designed just for me, but I could see that it wasn't for everyone. It was very intense. Whatever mood you're in will be intensified by being in Cambridge. We all knew about the suicide rate. They were planning to rush natural gas – which you couldn't use to kill yourself – into Cambridge first. I think it arrived in my second year. We were well aware of that.'

When Peter talks about his time at Cambridge, however, the overwhelming impression is of someone who couldn't quite believe his luck. 'It was very exciting to be living in a city where quite a high proportion of the historians whose books you were reading also lived. It was full of stunningly good people wherever you looked.' His biggest influence was Harry Hinsley, his director of studies at St John's. 'Harry had been a brilliant figure at Bletchley Park during the war, although of course we didn't know that then. He'd supervise in this huge room with tottering piles of books and bottles of Harveys Bristol Cream everywhere, which he dispensed liberally. He had all the props: the pipe, the old suit, the battered George VI briefcase from the war. And he had this wonderful way of speaking in great grand sweeps. He'd say things like "Remember, my boy, Napoleon III's real problems were not Italy and all that. His two great preoccupations were his wife and his kidney stones." It sounds frivolous but he had a great genius for reminding you to try to get inside people and think about what really bothered them. Once, when I was in the middle of reading him an essay on late-nineteenth-century European diplomacy, he suddenly interrupted, "Stop, my boy, stop. You're making the mistake that all clever boys make of thinking that the people we read about are as intelligent as you and me. They're not, apart from Bismarck and Lord Salisbury. They're usually very dim. Take the Kaiser – the worst kind of perpetual adolescent!" I sometimes wonder if my occasionally gloomy view of people at the top of politics comes from that moment with Harry. His supervisions were always a wonderful performance. The word was that he'd picked up this way of speaking from having to brief Churchill during the war.

'Harry loved teaching and he really looked after his students. For our last supervision with him we took in a bottle of champagne and drank together. I asked him about being in naval intelligence during the war. "Were we good at it?" I asked him. "Oh yes, my boy! There wasn't much we didn't know about in advance." "How come?" I asked him. "Spies in the dockyards, my boy, spies in the dockyards!" Of course it was nonsense, it was Ultra, but we had no idea. It was still secret because we were still practicing signals intelligence on anyone we could. Also – and I discovered this many years later – whenever a British colony got independence, the British government would say, "We've got some coding machines here – quite unbreakable. You can use them for diplomatic traffic." They were repainted Enigma machines – absolutely crackable! So of course, the Brits never wanted the breaking of Enigma to come out.

'Harry left a great mark on me. We weren't particularly close but he was always very kind to me. I'm pretty sure he was the reason that the Secret Intelligence Service never made a pass to recruit me because he knew how talkative I was when I'd had a drink. In my more histrionic moments I like to think I've picked up some of his style, though I could never match his singular glory when in full cry. Without being ludicrous, I've always thought you can turn teaching into a performing art.'

Was he ever intimidated by all these great figures? 'I was anxious sometimes, but not intimidated. One of the great weaknesses of the education I was a beneficiary of was that it was biased towards people like me who could perform on the day, who have a capacity for superior bullshit. You could say that I've spent my entire life playing to that advantage and feeling guilty about it.' He does admit, however, that he did occasionally have academic frustrations, which once boiled over into a spot of light criminal damage. 'I was revising for finals in the University Library with friends and Norman Stone [the historian], who I knew slightly, came to say hello. He asked us how we were all doing. I was a bit glum and made some remark about it all being a bit pointless because nobody who hadn't been taught by Neil McKendrick at Caius was going to shine. It was always thought, rightly or wrongly, that Neil McKendrick got more firsts per square inch than anyone else. It was partly because he was a brilliant teacher, but it was also felt that because he dominated the setting of the papers, the questions reflected his perspectives. "Ah," said Norman, "one of the few stable features in this depressingly volatile world is the sight of McKendrick's well-drilled Prussian hordes marching their way to triumph in the Tripos."

'Well, I was quite taken with this line, as were a couple of my friends. So after the last Bumps supper [a boat club event] we put on our tracksuits and got on our bikes at about two in the morning – we deliberately didn't get too drunk at the dinner. I took a tin of paint I'd bought at Woolies that morning – Prussian Blue – and on the back wall of Caius I painted *SMASH MCKENDRICK'S PRUSSIA* in letters about a foot and a half high. My two friends were at either end of the lane, and if anyone came they were going to whistle 'Beautiful Dreamer' so we could all get on our bikes and dash across the bridge, though of course nobody did. I forget how, but Simon Schama was brought in on this. He was meeting McKendrick for lunch the next day and hatched some convoluted plan to get him to go past this particular wall. Apparently, McKendrick was initially aghast, but then rather flattered that anyone would feel strongly enough to do that. So it totally backfired. I'm told that on rainy, sunny days you can still see a few flecks of that blue paint – my enduring legacy at Cambridge. I've met Neil McKendrick a few times and we got on famously. We talked about it a bit, just a little acknowledgement that he knew it was me, and of course I didn't tell him who the others were. It's a very Cambridge story: self-consciously witty and only comprehensible to the initiated of that strange world.'

Was Peter a radical? 'No. Peter Laslett, the wonderful social historian, later told me that he couldn't believe that an intelligent man like me hadn't been a revolutionary at Cambridge. The 1968 protests all seemed very self-indulgent to me. Here we were, the luckiest generation ever in terms of provision – I was on a full grant – how could I pretend that we were immiserated? That said, several of my friends were involved in the protests, earnestly listening to Joan Robinson lecture them about revolution. But I was friends with the hearties too. It mattered a great deal to some of my radical friends, but I could never take it entirely seriously. What I remember most is the Wodehouseian element of it. Some of my roommate Tony Williams' friends, who were public school reared, left a note saying they were "going to defend the backs" from the radicals occupying the Senate House, as if they were a risk to the realm. One night during the Senate House protests, I remember seeing another one of the St John's students walking down King's Parade stopping people and asking in his plummy voice, "Excuse me sir, are you a damn lefty?" It was pure Drones Club!'

Was he ever tempted to stay and do research at Cambridge? 'You never quite leave your first university. At least I never have. But I was quite clear that I didn't want to stay, because it would have been too easy to be seduced by the river and the drinking. I was quite self-aware about that. I've got a puritan side and I thought I wouldn't work hard enough if I stayed. I didn't want to become a good old boy. Although I probably am a good old boy in some ways.'

Peter returned to academia in 1992, in the rather different environs of the Mile End Road in the heart of London's East End. 'In my last tutorial with him at Cambridge, Peter Stern, my academic tutor, told me that Cambridge had changed the rules about PhDs and that you could now submit published works for consideration. In 1990 I got my PhD by submitting the books *Whitehall* and *Cabinet*. That enabled me to get the Chair at Queen Mary.' What was it like to return to that world after such a long hiatus? 'It was a pleasant surprise in a number of ways. The stimulus history gave me as an undergraduate was unabated, the fires were not banked. Secondly, my colleagues in the history department were, for the most part, very bright and seriously agreeable. All university departments have their tensions, but we seemed to be able to avoid the intellectual civil wars that can exist all too easily when clever people live

Teaching my 'Secret State' special subject at Queen Mary University of London. From left to right: Alban Webb, Matt Grant, Matt Lyus, Justine Rainbow, PH, Samina Malik, and Helen Welch.

cheek by jowl for decades. We by and large avoided the trap that Henry Kissinger described in his great quip: that academic disputes are so vile because the stakes are so low. Thirdly, the mixture of students in our intake was very wide indeed, which pleased me, and stimulated me even more in an extra direction. We also had a leavening of mature students who were pure gold.'

It was a slightly unusual path to a professorship, Peter admits. 'One of my friends told me about a conversation he had with a mutual friend, also a historian, on hearing that I'd been appointed to the Chair at Queen Mary. "Peter's great," this chap apparently said, "but he's really a journalist, not a scholar. He makes telly programmes where he talks to old ladies in Walthamstow!" My friend said, "You're just jealous because you don't know any old ladies in Walthamstow!"' Peter laughs. 'It was the same with journalism. My contemporaries regarded me as a tweedy academic, not a journalist. I suppose it shows what an opportunistic bastard I am that I realised quite early on that this was a very desirable condition. I was a bit odd, but if people have a story to tell themselves to explain your oddity, they find it easier to live with you. I suppose that's why I am a happy amphibian.'

Establishment and meritocracy

Queen Mary valedictory lecture, 7 October 2014

Inaugural and valedictory lectures are bookends best marked, I think, by a few thoughts on some of the running, enduring themes that have fascinated and intrigued the deliverer of said lectures. Valedictories, too, should be shorter than inaugurals. Dotage is bad enough, excessive anecdotage even worse. This evening, I'd like to linger on a pair of themes that have fascinated me since my sixth-form days in the mid-1960s, when I first read one of the great Anthony Sampson's *Anatomies of Britain* – the second one, to be precise, the *Anatomy of Britain Today*, published in 1965.[1] Anthony set out to see if an old British Establishment was, at last, giving way to a rising meritocracy in the command positions of British administration and industry. And it's a historical look at the twin themes of establishment and meritocracy that I'd like to take this evening.

This is an era in which, quite rightly, we are all called upon to declare interests. Do I have to come out, as it were, this evening as either a meritocrat or a member of the British Establishment? I'll have a go.

The first is the easiest. As a classic product of the state grammar-school system in the decades after Rab Butler's 1944 Education Act, if there was a rising meritocracy lifted by the tide of wider educational opportunity unleashed by the 1944 statute, I was one of the grains of sand so raised.

'Establishment' is an altogether trickier notion – more on that

---

1 Anthony Sampson, *Anatomy of Britain Today* (London, 1965).

shortly – but there are a pair of bookends here that may aid my 'coming out' here.

In the mid-1970s, when I was setting out as a young journalist-to-be, *The Times*' Whitehall-watcher, David Butler, introduced me at a seminar in Nuffield College, Oxford as 'the gossip columnist of the British Establishment'. I was faintly piqued by this. We all of us like to think we have a dash of the radical outsider in us. But I soon realised David was absolutely right. In the mid-seventies I even bought my first green tweed suit of highly traditional design, which I wore when taking Whitehall permanent secretaries to lunch in the hope that I might strike them as older and wiser than I was. Though, I fear, none were taken in by the drapery, I literally sweated for my stories.

The other bookend is very recent and relates to the Scottish Question. During the week following the pair of YouGov polls that sent an electromagnetic pulse of anxiety about the outcome south across the border (and, as the Prime Minister's indiscreet words to Michael Bloomberg, the former mayor of New York, revealed, causing what an insider friend of mine called 'near panic' in Whitehall) the *Financial Times* decided to find out what the British Establishment was thinking about the possible fracturing of the Kingdom.[2] And there it was. In an *FT* spread on 12 September, under the headline

Ruling elite aghast as union wobbles

with its subhead 'Establishment', lay a scattering of quotes conveying the aghasting of yours truly. 'For Lord Hennessy', Sarah Neville and Clive Cookson reported,

---

[2] This lecture was delivered three weeks after the referendum on Scottish independence. On 18 September 2014, Scotland voted against becoming an independent country by 55 per cent to 45 per cent. Polls consistently indicated that Scotland would vote No, until the independence campaign gained ground in August and, according to polls, took a narrow lead in early September 2014.

any dismembering of the UK will take Britain into territory for which it remains utterly unready, for all its past experience in colonial handovers. 'This is not the extended family, as the empire used to be called, it is the immediate family', he said. 'This is flesh of our flesh. It is not severance in an "imperial disposal" way; it is rending.'[3]

Somehow I had morphed, in that piece, from being a contemporary British historian passing on what I had picked up of the views of others into almost an incarnation of the Establishment *mentalité* I had been attempting to report on since those early days at *The Times*.

That's the nearest I'm going to get to coming out as a member of the British Establishment this evening. Back to the history of the twin themes.

Over the four decades of which I have been conscious of them, I have carried in my mind a certain idea of the pair. Meritocracy is the clearer of the two – the notion that the gifted and the energetic rise in terms of professions and rewards (salaries and wider status) on the basis of demonstrable merit, whatever the social and financial positions of their families, rather than because of inherited wealth or family connections.

Establishment is fuzzier – a phantom army of the great and good who fill positions in public, cultural, and intellectual life. They can set the tone, influence the direction of public policy and exert considerable sway over future appointments to the professions within which they have risen. Yet plenty of successful people would be appalled to think they were Establishment figures. It is not a label for flaunting. Indeed, many would define themselves against it. Though quite often they quietly slip inside it during their middle and later years while remaining determined not to succumb to its

---

[3] Sarah Neville and Clive Cookson, 'Ruling elite aghast as union wobbles', *Financial Times* (12 September 2014).

state of mind, which is itself the mistiest of concepts. It is also very largely an unmeasurable concept, which does not yield to the social arithmetic that historians, anthropologists, and sociologists normally apply in terms of gender balance, social origins, patterns of education, regional provenance, and so on.

Despite this myriad of ethereal qualities, the Establishment has brought much joy and humour as the perfect tethered goat for satirists. This has been particularly true since the early 1960s, when that genius among satirists, Peter Cook, founded The Establishment Club in Soho for the purposes of nightly lampooning amidst the rich opportunities presented by the Conservative government of Harold Macmillan as it proceeded to decay like a ripe stilton.

Establishments in various forms will always be with us. And here, in my view, one finds the bonding – the twinning – with meritocracy. If we have to have an Establishment, let it be a meritorious one. And yet, as we shall see shortly, there are problems carried aboard that express train marked 'meritocracy' – some undesirable fellow travellers whose *mentalités* can lead to unwanted destinations.

It was in the 1950s that the two themes started to fizz. In the early part of the decade, the historian A. J. P. Taylor and the political commentator Henry Fairlie revived the idea of a shadowy yet potent British Establishment, which exerted an ill-defined and intangible yet real effect in public, political, and cultural life. Writing at much the same time, the historical sociologist Michael Young was working on his *The Rise of the Meritocracy*,[4] which, given the surprising difficulty he encountered in finding a publisher, did not reach the shelves until 1958, and, eventually the pages of the dictionaries as a new social-category-cum-concept.

'Establishment' may be a slippery term but it's everywhere – and has been for decades. When used incontinently, it's easy to wonder if the Establishment exists as more than a notion, a convenient piece

---

4 Michael Young, *The Rise of the Meritocracy: An Essay on Education and Equality* (London, 1958); Pelican edn. (London, 1961).

of linguistic litter to deploy as a weapon of disdain, even denunciation, against individuals or clusters of people who you don't care for, rather resent and wish to annoy.

The Establishment notion does matter because, generation upon generation, so many intelligent and not always so intelligent people have thought it does exist – though the form it takes mutates and is always and everywhere immensely stretching to capture and define. As Jeremy Paxman, who wrote a good book about it in 1991 called *Friends in High Places*, puts it:

> It is a harlot of a word, convenient, pliant, available for a thousand meaningless applications.[5]

Yet there exists a widespread sense of the Establishment as an inner track of people who fix things discreetly, unavowedly, and unaccountably behind carefully painted camouflage, giving it a whiff of genteel conspiracy – perhaps even with a dash of insider trading in the influence market.

Anthony Sampson in his 1960s *Anatomies* drew on that fifties revival of the Establishment notion by the powerful pens of A. J. P. Taylor and Henry Fairlie. Taylor took up the theme in what was then still called *The New Statesman and Nation* in August 1953, in a review of a new life of William Cobbett[6] – agriculturalist, journalist, and great denouncer of the Establishment, which he called 'The Thing'. Taylor's opening paragraph remains, I think, a collector's item:

> Trotsky tells how, when he first visited England, Lenin took him round London and, pointing out the sights, exclaimed: 'That's *their* Westminster Abbey! That's *their* Houses of Parliament!' ...

---

[5] Jeremy Paxman, *Friends in High Places: Who Runs Britain?* (London/New York, 1990), viii.
[6] M. L. Pearl, *William Cobbett: A Biographical Account of his Life and Times* (Oxford, 1953).

By *them* he meant not the English, but the governing classes, the Establishment. And indeed in no other European country is the Establishment so clearly defined and so complacently secure.[7]

Henry Fairlie's assault on the British Establishment in his *The Spectator* column was triggered by the Foreign Office finally admitting in September 1955 that the British diplomats, Guy Burgess and Donald Maclean, who had disappeared in May 1951, were, in fact, Soviet spies and were now living in Moscow.[8] Fairlie convinced himself that the long, if now broken, official silence was an example of 'the "Establishment" at work', and by 'Establishment' he meant not 'only the centres of official power – though they are certainly part of it – but rather the whole matrix of official and social relations within which power is exercised'.[9]

Such matrices, too, are very difficult to trace. In the mid-1980s I tried to pin down at least part of the Establishment matrix when I wrote a pamphlet for the Policy Studies Institute called *The Great and the Good: An Inquiry into the British Establishment*.[10] My cunning plan was to trace the overwhelmingly male tribe that had peopled the royal commissions and committees of inquiry since the Second World War, and to pen mini-biographies of a trio of outstanding princes of greatness and goodness – the civil servant and wartime home secretary John Anderson, the great jurist Cyril Radcliffe, and the philosopher and public administrator Oliver Franks, grand inquirers all.

This was a promising approach at the time but soon became less

---

7 A. J. P. Taylor, 'Books in General', *The New Statesman and Nation* (29 August 1953), 236–7.
8 *Report Concerning the Disappearance of Two Former Foreign Office Officials*, Cmd. 9577 (London, 23 September 1955). See also Christopher Andrew, *The Defence of the Realm: The Authorized History of MI5* (London, 2009), 424–6, 431.
9 Henry Fairlie, 'Political Commentary', *The Spectator* (23 September 1955), 379–80.
10 Peter Hennessy, *The Great and the Good: An Inquiry into the British Establishment* (London, 1986).

so as successive governments rather gave up on royal commissions and committees of inquiry, reaching for task forces, czars, and focus groups and relying on the newer think tanks of varying quality that bloomed in the late seventies and early eighties.

I have a dash of sympathy for anyone who tries to depict the undepictable, to catch the essence or the crewing of the British Establishment at any particular moment in its wraith's progress. Any attempt is likely to look either naive or way off, or both, to those who come later. My own mid-1980s attempt to find them amongst the post-war good-and-great committee people certainly does. And the Establishment concept has been made still more elusive over the past quarter of a century by the rise of a new political economy (the post-Big Bang City of London, hedge funds and all that) plus an electronic media explosion driven by new technologies alongside the grander newspapers, not to mention the new-Britain, young-country-again banalities of 'New Labour', which held the field and tempted the credulous (as did something I could never grasp called the 'Third Way'[11]) for a few years after 1997. We have given up very largely on royal commissions. The 'czars' and 'task forces' that, only in part, have replaced them have not produced *grand corps* comparable to that exhibited by the great inquirers of the past.

Is there a permanent element at the core of the British Establishment – a kind of gyroscope – which embraces the grand old professions like the law and the Civil Service (though the latter is a tad tattered at the moment), the House of Lords (especially sections of the crossbenches where sit the former Cabinet secretaries, law lords, chiefs of the defence staff and Queen's private secretaries), the Royal Society, the British Academy, the learned societies generally, the scientific and engineering institutes, and the great medical colleges? The reach and clout of these institutions and tribes may fluctuate but they never truly fade, let alone disappear. While around this rooted, inner core there swirl the transient elements in the media,

---

11 John Rentoul, *Tony Blair: Prime Minister* (London, 2001), 430–45.

the financial world, and the celebritocracy in constellations that vary from generation to generation. If I were writing that book on the British Establishment, the permanent/temporary divide would govern my approach.

Some, like John le Carré, think there is a British Establishment that really matters and that its core is deep inside the secret services.[12] That is a subject for another lecture, although there may be something in it. I have heard a former chief of the Secret Intelligence Service say on more than one occasion that the secret services and their operations are 'the last redoubt of our national sovereignty' – meaning that in carrying out these special activities we are less constrained, for example, than in the conduct of our diplomacy, which is, of its nature, a multilateral business.

Naturally, those who play – or have played – in the Establishment's equivalent of the Premier League, and very visibly so, have a tendency to resent the very notion more powerfully than anyone else, but for reasons of camouflage or self-image rather than class motivations or social and professional envy. For example, that great lawyer, Cyril Radcliffe, was profoundly irritated by the Establishment idea. Writing in 1961, when the satire boom – *Beyond the Fringe* and all that – was getting going, he said:

> Let a fairy grant me my three wishes, I would gladly use them all in one prayer only, that never again should anyone using pen or typewriter be permitted to employ that inane cliché 'Establishment'.[13]

I fear Lord Radcliffe, up there in the Supreme Court in the sky, is doomed to disappointment. We Brits will never give up on the

---

12 Simon de Bruxelles, 'Le Carré: secret courts will be a stain on our society', *The Times* (1 June 2013).
13 Lord Radcliffe, 'Censors', The Rede Lecture, University of Cambridge (4 May 1961). Reproduced in Lord Radcliffe, *Not in Feather Beds* (London, 1968), 161–82, 175.

ESTABLISHMENT AND MERITOCRACY

Establishment as a notion. It's deep within us. As a theme it's had more comebacks than the Rolling Stones. For all the angry words, the denunciations, the parodies, and the conspiracy theories, we nurture it – almost cherish it. Why? Because quite apart from the fun of trying to determine who is or isn't in it in each generation, it brings fascination to the curious, a target for venting, and, therefore, catharsis to the resentful and stimulus to the conspiracy theorist. The British Establishment, like that great cathedral of a British Constitution which it serves as a kind of flying buttress, is Cobbett's 'Thing'. But it's also a thing of magic, mystery, curiosity, and fantasy.

If I were to attempt a volume of 'Establishment Studies', it would be suffused, too, by the twin theme of meritocracy. I first felt its punch not in Michael Young's pages (that came later) but in Anthony Sampson's second *Anatomy*. There it was, 'meritocracy', with its attendant, fissile formula:

$$IQ + EFFORT = MERIT.$$

As a grammar-school boy, a bit of a swot (though I tried zealously to conceal it), I saw nothing wrong with that equation. For me it was a manifesto and a self-evident truth rather than a warning of what an unbridled pursuit of meritocracy could do.

Not until I finally read Michael Young's classic 1958 fusion of historical sociology, satire, horizon-scanning, and prediction in *The Rise of the Meritocracy*, did I really inhale the fact that this was a warning – that Young was foreseeing another and, once established, irreversible social and economic deprivation that would (my words; not Young's) rank alongside William Beveridge's famous 'five giants on the road to reconstruction' of his eponymous November 1942 report on social insurance: Ignorance, Idleness, Disease, Squalor, and Want.[14]

---

14 *Social Insurance and Allied Services: Report by Sir William Beveridge*, Cmd. 6404 (London, 1942), 6.

For Young saw the possible rise of a society which valued intelligence above all other characteristics as a giant blemish – a society in which the intellectual haves regard the also-rans and the have-nots with disdain and without a trace of the *noblesse oblige* or compassion that had mitigated some of the worst effects of the *ancien régime* of an aristocracy based on blood and inherited wealth rather than the little grey cells. If we could rise – have risen – by our own efforts, hoisted upwards by our synapses, so could they if they put their minds to it now that higher education is increasingly available. That was the meritocrats' cry in Young's portrayal of the breed.

The thought occurs that *The Rise of the Meritocracy* might have been Young's way of projecting his 1950s thinking about family and kinship on to a national, British scale, through the medium of educational opportunity and reward. Could it be that Young, like George Orwell in his great 1941 essay *The Lion and the Unicorn*, saw our country as 'a family with the wrong members in control'?[15] Certainly Young foresaw the wrong mix at the top in the new Establishment that would be created once the meritocracy in his fictional treatment of the post-1958 era had risen: a society lacking a sense of natural familyhood or real kinship between the meritocratic possessors and those they regarded as laggards or dullards.

Young does not draw directly on Orwell in *The Rise of the Meritocracy*. But there is one thinker/writer with a special eye for his country who does suffuse Young's pages. For Young's dystopic vision is partly built on the analysis of his great hero, the saintly economic historian R. H. Tawney in *his* classic work *Equality*, first published in 1931 and updated in 1952. Tawney believed that deep in our collective DNA as a country there was a potent, trumping molecule – a powerful, British impulse towards inequality. Tawney liked to quote Matthew Arnold on the capacity of we Brits to worship a kind of 'Religion of Inequality'.[16] I think this is much diminished

---

15 Peter Davison (ed.), *Orwell's England* (London, 2001), 264.
16 R. H. Tawney, *Equality*, 1952 edn. (London, 1964), 33.

in the twenty-first century, though not for reasons of social solidarity, as Tawney would have wished, but for reasons of anger directed indiscriminately at a variety of targets – for example, bankers post the great crash of 2008 and 'toffs' (Etonian ones especially) in the Cabinet Room following the general election of 2010.

Did the meritocracy rise and increasingly prevail? This question would surely be central to our scholarly cartographer of meritocracy since 1945. What other ingredients might he or she inject? His or her gaze would certainly need to linger on the 'ocracies' that rose which Young did not foresee. For example, 'celebritocracy' – the famous-for-being-famous phenomenon (which sometimes travels under such related 'ti's' as 'glitterati' or 'flasherati'[17]). Related is the rise of the 'media-ocracy' (if such a word is coinable) with its attendant professions of public relations in all its varieties. Another riser is the consulting profession – political as well as managerial – with all the impoverishment it has inflicted upon the language of politics and government, which it would take a George Orwell to map (his 1946 essay on 'Politics and the English Language' remains unsurpassed[18]). How we need an eviscerating pen like his to update that piece as the debased coinage of political exchange is about to be still further tarnished in the run-up to next year's general election, especially if we have another series of leaders' debates dripping with their well-rehearsed spontaneities.

The most difficult task for our scholarly cartographer would be determining where we are today. If one argues that Young was foreseeing the rise of what we would now call the 'knowledge economy' then, in that sense, a meritocracy of the knowledgeable has risen according to figures produced by the Work Foundation[19] covering the past thirty years:

---

17 I am grateful to my friend and former student, Mark Fox, for 'flasherati'.
18 Peter Davison (ed.), *Orwell and Politics* (London, 2001), 397 –410.
19 Ian Brinkley, 'Defining the Knowledge Economy', *The Work Foundation* (2006).

Rise of knowledge workers (as a percentage of the UK workforce)
1984: 31%   2014: 45%

Fall of skilled and semi-skilled workers
1984: 28%   2014: 18%

Fall of unskilled workers
1984: 16%   2014: 9%

The rise of the knowledge worker has gone hand in hand with the rise of inequality. Ferdinand Mount, a former head of Margaret Thatcher's Downing Street Policy Unit, in his *The New Few*, a 2012 study of power and inequality in contemporary Britain, possessed a Michael Young touch in his concern that growing inequality of incomes in the UK had also led to an 'inequality of respect ... It is only in our own time ... that a sharpening inequality of income has been accompanied by a pervading contempt for those who are at the bottom of the ladder and may have less chance of climbing a few rungs than their parents had – and less inclination to try'.[20] Young, in Mount's judgement, in *The Rise of the Meritocracy*, 'was out to show ... that in a society where all the top places are awarded on merit the losers have no hiding place and no excuses'.[21]

The sharp increase of income inequality in the UK was not, I think, foreseeable in 1961, when *The Rise of the Meritocracy* appeared in paperback and Harold Macmillan was in Downing Street. The dramatic opening of such a yawning gap, especially after 1979, has added to the scratchiness of British society and filled the pools of its resentments, particularly since the financial crash of 2008.

My own view is that those of us who absorbed Young's warning when we were about to scale the first rungs of our own professional

---

[20] Ferdinand Mount, *The New Few: Or A Very British Oligarchy* (London, 2012), 257.
[21] Ibid., 256.

ladders were – and remain – riven by the concept of meritocracy. It was a self-evidently worthy impulse but it carried risks of callousness and disdain towards those who did not rise in terms of high status and well-paid jobs. What we were seeking, on reflection, was the best of both worlds – what Young's friend, the great American sociologist Daniel Bell, prophet of the 'post-industrial society' called 'a well-tempered meritocracy' (which has a pleasing ring of J. S. Bach about it).[22]

A 'well-tempered meritocracy' would be one in which its beneficiaries rose to infiltrate the old Establishment in all its forms (except the hereditary monarchy) while never forgetting (a) where they had come from, (b) what it had taken by way of public policy and investment to get them there, (c) the need to keep the ladders they had climbed in ever-greater repair to enable a still-bigger and more accomplished meritocracy to rise after them, and (d) to avoid at all times a creeping inequality of respect falling upon those who did not rise in a similar fashion. As Bell expressed it, 'a well-tempered meritocracy can be a society if not of equals, then of the just'.[23]

For all their inadequacy as tools for social analysis, the idea of Establishment and the aspiration for meritocracy do possess a continuing utility. Certainly the impulse for meritocracy will remain strong, not just as an individual motivator for those wishing to rise but also for collective purposes. As Young caught powerfully in *The Rise of the Meritocracy*, economic survival is the spur and will remain so until that glorious time when British industry, British services, and British finance find themselves on a golden trajectory of ever-waxing innovation, competitiveness, and growth. Until that shining hour, the patron intellect of meritocracy will be the great New Zealand-born physicist, Sir Ernest Rutherford.[24] According to

22 Daniel Bell, *The Coming of Post-Industrial Society: A Venture in Social Forecasting* (London, 1974), 455.
23 Ibid.
24 'Rutherford, Ernest, Baron (1871–1937)', *Oxford Dictionary of Science* (Oxford, 2010), 724.

Cambridge folklore, at a time of funding cuts he called his team together at the renowned Cavendish Laboratory in Cambridge and said: 'We haven't the money, so we've got to think'.

As for the idea of an Establishment, perhaps even in an era when it takes myriad forms and is harder to pin down than ever, we need it as part of the way we imagine the United Kingdom and as a transmitter of tradition – and maybe even a dab of stability. We want it to exist – so exist it does. Meritocracy we need as both a balancer to Establishment and as a bringer of a more efficient and productive society in which the capable and the meritorious receive their rewards. But we don't want meritocracy at the price of creating a detached and self-regarding elite, insensitive towards those who have not soared up meritocratic ladders of their own.

It is possible that any essay on Establishment and meritocracy is a wasted enterprise – an atavistic fascination for mid- to late-twentieth-century notions, no more than residuals in a very different society. Indeed, there are those who think that the Establishment is pretty well reduced to a handful of dining clubs. But I still think there is life in the twin themes yet.

'Do I detect a note of flattery in your voice?': Becoming a journalist, Boston and London, 1971–3

Peter arrived in Boston as a Kennedy Scholar in 1971, into the broiling August heat, which he remembers hit him like a wall as soon as he left the plane. No English heat had been like this; it was the first example of the way in which everything was bigger and just *more so* in the States. Roads, houses, trucks, fridges, ambitions. 'America is not an understated country. Nearly all arrivals, therefore, make for a dramatic experience.'

Newly married, he and Enid moved into a flat in Somerville, a predominantly Italian- and Irish-American suburb to the northeast of Harvard. 'It was a clapboard building, which was typical of the area, painted in creosote brown. The flat was on the first floor just next to a busy intersection and on summer nights the Mack trucks heading to the warehouses and docks of Boston would heave and sigh at the red light, belching fumes from their high side-exhausts into the window, which just added to the humidity.' After cold English childhoods in draughty houses, they couldn't get used to being too hot.

In some ways, it was a more luxurious life than they were used to. They got their first television, 'a huge hand-me-down beast from the 1950s, that was prone to cutting out – you'd have to hit it with a rubber hammer to bring it back to life.' There was an enormous fridge that looked like it was bulging, as if it could barely contain the abundance within. 'The fridge looked like the sort of thing I used to see in adverts for Coke and Pepsi in the *National Geographic*, which was sent to us by a Canadian family we knew. They used to send our family food parcels during the war.' Everything in America was bigger and more plentiful. Peter recalls with great fondness that the portions at the deli, or when they went out to eat, were unimaginably huge compared to back home; even the vegetables in the supermarket seemed to be better fed, enormous and shiny.

They were well provided for with a generous maintenance grant from the Kennedy Trust, and Enid soon found work, but the frugal habits of children of austerity died surprisingly hard. 'We didn't plan to stay long so Enid made us a bed out of plywood. It was quite flimsy, so we had to do a sort of paratrooper roll to get out of bed without snapping the spine.' In the land of plenty, Enid cooked cheap cuts and offal, which she acquired from a butcher the other side of MIT. She cooked kidneys, liver, neck of lamb. American friends were baffled. Peter remembers that one Harvard friend asked why they insisted on eating 'poor people's food', which is a phrase that tells something about liberal Harvard of that time.

Peter liked Somerville. 'I felt at home there. It wasn't desperately poor, people were in work, but it wasn't flash. I'd walk down from our flat to Harvard to go to the library and as I got nearer you could feel the change from the slightly rundown to the cerebral glitter of Cambridge, Mass. J. K. Galbraith would come out from one of the side streets, six foot seven, towering in a huge overcoat in the freezing winter. Sometimes I'd see Daniel Patrick Moynihan. I used to quite like that contrast.'

Peter's Kennedy Scholarship was for research only, and there were no classes to attend, so he spent most of his time in the library or playing squash. He clearly had a sense that he was surrounded by the intellectual aristocracy at Harvard, but on the squash courts at the university's Hemenway Gymnasium, it was this garrulous, slightly scruffy youth that was king. Not, it must be said, as a consequence of any particular sporting prowess, but rather a gift for chat and – almost certainly – his Irish surname.

'Hennessy. You Irish?' asked Frank, the doorman and presiding presence at the gym, the first time they met. 'I told him that my family were, way back. Came to Liverpool after the famine. And that was it.' To Frank, proud scion of the Boston Irish diaspora, Peter was in the club, and could not be treated with too much kindness (or rank favouritism). 'He'd say "I don't want you changing in the usual place – you can use the Harvard locker room." If I turned up and hadn't booked, he'd say, "We're full but leave it to me," and go and bump someone else off the court before I could stop him. It was terribly embarrassing. Apart from Nixon's son-in-law, who was at Harvard Law School that year, I had the most privileged access to those squash courts.' Peter claims he was surprised that the red-carpet treatment became even more pronounced when he bought Frank a bottle of Jameson (what else?) for Christmas. One suspects that he enjoyed it just a little, or perhaps rather enjoyed Frank's relish at exercising a little bit of power for an 'Irish' boy done good, over the more patrician members of the gymnasium.

Very occasionally, Peter would see his supervisor Professor Ernest May, an enormously influential historian of the Cold War. Peter describes him as 'a lovely man: upright, clever, nice,' but they didn't get to know each other well, and it seems they didn't particularly gel intellectually. 'I took him a chapter I was reasonably happy with – a portrait of the atmosphere in Washington in the run-up to the McCarthy era as the Cold War chilled. He said, "Mr Hennessy. I've enjoyed reading this chapter, I really have. It reminds me I think of nothing so much as Murray Kempton's *Part of Our Time*." Well, I was delighted by this and I sort of began to puff up like pastry, thinking, "God this is wonderful! Murray Kempton!" Kempton – a journalist and social commentator who later won a Pulitzer Prize – was something of an inspiration for Peter. 'Then Professor May said, in the very next sentence: "But you have to remember, Mr Hennessy, we would have never given Murray Kempton a PhD at Harvard for that."' With hindsight, it is clear to Peter that the PhD was never going to work. 'It was an exercise in intellectual history, examining different schools of thought. I realised later that I had never been much interested in either. Too much plumbing and not enough poetry.' However, the Kempton comment, and

Peter's reaction to it, were telling. For all his focus on seemingly dry-as-dust institutions, what Peter really likes is people. Not in the abstract, or the realm of the theoretical, but as they really are. He also loves a good story. And although he was there ostensibly to launch an academic career, the most productive part of his year in Boston seems to have been the journalism that he did for *The Times Higher Education Supplement*.

Before he left for the year in the States, Peter was invited to a party for all the Kennedy Scholars at Lancaster House. He had noticed the education correspondent from *The Times*, Brian MacArthur (in those days photos appeared on bylines). The story of their somewhat tipsy exchange is recounted in the Foreword to this book, but the upshot is that Peter arrived in Boston with a loose commission to 'send some interesting pieces from Harvard' to Brian, who had just been made editor of the new *The Times Higher Education Supplement*. Despite a dispute with his wife as to whether this was a serious offer or just a slightly drunk man 'being nice', Peter set about finding things to write about. He wrote articles on local elections, student protests, and occasional academic conferences, along with quite a few profiles, which he particularly loved.

According to Enid, his wife, Peter would ring up and introduce himself as 'Peter Hennessy from *The London Times*', which would have been somewhat stretching the truth. Peter himself claims that he always said '*The London Times Higher Education Supplement*' but concedes that he *may* have placed a little more emphasis on the first three words.

One of his early profiles was of Tom Lehrer, the mathematician and satirical lyricist. 'I'd been a fan of his for years and was word perfect in many of the songs. I particularly liked 'The Vatican Rag' from 1965, which was a send-up of pre- and post-Vatican II Catholicism.' A sample lyric from this goes 'Two, four, six, eight, time to transubstantiate!', which may have been thrillingly close to blasphemy for a Catholic boy from a conservative household. Lehrer hadn't released an album since then, but his songs retained considerable bite in a United States still reeling from the assassination of Martin Luther King Jr and Bobby Kennedy, and from the ongoing trauma of Vietnam. In another song on the same 1965 album, 'National Brotherhood Week', Lehrer sings, 'It's fun to eulogize / The people you despise / As long as you don't let 'em in your school.' Boston's schools were still in a state of de-facto racial segregation in 1971, despite legislation of 1965 which made such segregation illegal.

Peter cold-called him.

'Mr Lehrer?'

'Yeah.'

'I am Peter Hennessy of *The London Times Higher Education Supplement.*'

'Oh yeah?'

'I live close by and I would really like to come and visit you. I want to do a profile on you, portraying you as Harvard's greatest single contribution to Western civilisation this century.'

Slight pause.

'Do I detect a note of flattery in your voice?'

Peter recalls this interview with great fondness. Lehrer, he said, was a wonderful interviewee. 'The piece all but wrote itself. At one point he asked me "Do you have German?" I said I didn't. "Well, let me help you." He held up a newspaper. "This is the *Frankfurter Allgemeine Zeitung*, last year it was. Somebody had spoofed them that I had died and this is their obituary of me. I cherish the opening line and I'll read it to you: 'How fitting that Tom Lehrer who sang all those sick songs should himself have perished from such a loathsome disease.'"

'Lehrer was no longer performing, except for benefits for the radical Jesuit congressman Robert Drinan. He said, "I'm also helping with a programme which might not have reached the UK yet called 'The Electric Company' for young children and I do the songs that help them learn reading. One of my big hits is 'The silent E'." I think it was that interview that convinced Brian MacArthur to give me a permanent job when I got back to Britain. You know, Tom Lehrer's still alive – he is in his nineties now. I've always wondered whether I shouldn't contact him and thank him for being responsible for my career.'

There was also a profile of Noam Chomsky. 'That was tough. I was a bit nervous, although he is a wonderful man, charming and kind, and doesn't throw his formidable grey cells around at all. When I went to see him, the Philosophy/Linguistics Department at MIT was still in these wooden huts left over from the war. We talked about what it was like to be a political activist as well as a scholar.' After he'd written the piece, Peter sent it to Chomsky just in case he'd got anything wrong. 'Then I forgot about it – nobody ever asked to change anything. I remember we had spent the weekend in our flat playing Diplomacy, which we had a thing about, along with drinking copious amounts of beer.' Along with squash, 'Diplomacy Sundays' were a regular feature of their Boston life. Peter's wife, Enid – a non-drinker at that point – particularly excelled at duplicity and enjoyed inflicting ruthless betrayals on players who failed to note her sobriety and her competitiveness. She sensed that some of their friends rather underestimated her skills too – she was a woman working clerical jobs, they were the intellectual elite, the leaders of tomorrow. Peter recalls with some glee explaining to a (very competitive, and somewhat shocked) PhD student that she had just double-crossed: 'But that's what the game is *all about*.' And so it was that with a 'world-beating hangover', Peter found himself crawling out of bed on that Monday morning to answer the telephone, only to find a world-leading intellectual on the other end of the line.

'He said, "Mr Hennessy? This is Noam Chomsky speaking," and I thought, "oh shit, I've got the cleverest man in the world, on whose work the understanding of language is based, on the phone and I've lost the ability to speak!" I was desperate. "It was so kind of you to send the text; it was absolutely fine. It was very good to see you." I managed to croak, "Thank you very much!" That's the only thing I could say. One of these life-shortening moments. It was like talking to Albert Einstein – the ultimate intellectual anxiety dream.'

It was an interesting time to be in the USA, with Vietnam raging and the Watergate scandal breaking. 'One of our Kennedy Scholar mates lived in a commune. When you'd ring up, their standard greeting, instead of saying hello, was "Fuck Nixon". I got quite homesick, even though were really lucky with our host family, John [Bohstedt] and Jinx [Watson], who became wonderful friends for life. It was partly because the winter went on so long. It was the culture too. Cambridge, Massachusetts is a place of genius and great worth, but they compete in the number of hours they work. I couldn't bear that. Work was a clandestine activity in Cambridge, England.'

Peter returned home in September 1972, ostensibly to complete his PhD at the LSE, but his enthusiasm waned. 'I got rather mired in it. Research wasn't firing me but writing the fortnightly column was. I began to read more collected journalism – I. F. Stone, H. L. Mencken, who was a monster but his word power was extraordinary. Brian MacArthur asked me for lunch quite soon after I got back. We got on famously, although it was only the second time we'd met. Towards the end of the lunch, he said, "if you'd like to work with me, come work on the paper." I said: "I'd love to!" I accepted straightaway and then wondered if he had meant it. I went in for an informal interview the next week. They took a chance on me, and I'm not sure the deputy editor thought I was quite right, because I was tremendously viewy and a bit showy. I think they'd had been burned by Christopher Hitchens; when they'd set up *The Times Higher*, they'd hired him. And he was a great writer, but I don't think he was amenable to the grind of that kind of journalism. So they had doubts that I'd be a good fit.

'I started in December '72. And never looked back, really. And it was lovely being on *The Times Higher*, because it was such a small staff. I took over the gossip column from Paul Medlicott. I used to wear my fedora hat and my great Harry Fenton suit, what a tit I looked. I could be such a precocious and rude bugger, but Brian was so forgiving and nice, and very indulgent of me. I was universities reporter and was also encouraged to do lots of features and profiles. It was tremendously good training and dealing with vice-chancellors of universities turned out to be good practice for dealing with permanent secretaries later. Same sort of people.' One of those he got to know was Noel Annan, who was provost of UCL. 'He was fascinating. He'd been a member of the Cambridge Apostles [the secret Cambridge dining club whose members also included John Maynard Keynes, Anthony Blunt, and Guy Burgess] and he'd been in military intelligence during the war. Noel taught me a great lesson in life. I remember saying to him, "To think that every Friday you would leave the War Office and Keynes would leave the Treasury and you'd have lunch at the Athenaeum together. You must have heard Keynes's thinking develop on what became the International Monetary Fund, the Bretton Woods agreement, the post-war settlement and all that. Extraordinary!" Noel said in his fruity voice, "My dear Peter, you don't understand. We never talked about any of that. You see, Maynard loved gossip. He just wanted gossip!" I realised then that you mustn't assume all these great figures were all having mentally footnoted conversations about high policy. I think that's also when I learned that gossip is the lubricant of history as it is the lubricant of everything else.'

Did he regret not finishing the PhD? 'No, but I never look back on it without worrying that I didn't make the most of it, intellectually. Somewhere I've still got all the tapes I recorded with information from archives all over the country. But it was too big a subject for me, and too heavy on intellectual history. It all comes back to the same thing, the journalism, later on the history. I'm of the Max Bygraves school: I wanna tell you a story.'

A Harry Fenton suit and a fedora: first rig of the aspirant journalist. *The Times Higher Education Supplement*, 1972.

Cold War I: Captain Jack Regan, Royal Marines, 'captures' what appears to be a quartet of Russian soldiers in the freezing Arctic landscape of Northern Norway during a 'northern flank' reinforcement NATO exercise in January 1978. Jack, far from being aggressive, was utterly charming in manner and the way he dealt with the journalists. From left to right: Ellis Place (the *Daily Mirror*), PH (*The Times*), Angus Macpherson (the *Daily Mail*) and Bob Hutchinson (the Press Association).

Growing up on *The Times*, 1974–84

In 1978, Peter's great mentor, Louis Heren, published a memoir called *Growing Up On The Times*, about his years as a senior foreign correspondent. Peter's own years on the paper also seem like a formative period for him. He joined in 1974 aged twenty-six and left in 1984. They were eventful years: from covering the Birmingham pub bombings as a reporter on the night desk to carving out a niche as Whitehall correspondent, a process almost derailed by a catastrophic error of judgement. These years also saw, at points, near-constant industrial unrest at the *The Times*, with its owners refusing to print the paper for over a year in order to break the print unions, followed by a journalists' strike. Then came Murdoch and the Wapping disputes. By 1984 it was a very different paper from the one that Peter had joined as a green reporter.

Peter recalls being immediately excited by the atmosphere at *The Times* in the mid-seventies. 'They put me on the night desk to start with. They thought it would knock some of the smooth edges off me. Brian [MacArthur, his former boss at *The Times Higher Education Supplement*] thought I would hate it but I loved the camaraderie.' It was quite a change from working at *The THES*, interviewing vice-chancellors and attending academic conferences. 'It was a terrible time for the country, with the breakdown of the post-war political consensus followed by a growing stridency in politics, endless industrial unrest, and IRA bombs on the mainland. The night editor was Colin Wilson. He'd been around the block and seen a lot. He seemed tough, but I remember appreciating his humanity. One night there was a train crash. They'd sent one of the other junior reporters to the scene. He phoned in and was a bit overcome

– like me he was quite young. Colin said to him, "Calm down lad it's all right, there's a standard drill to these disasters. Try to find a nurse tending to the wounded, she'll be the angel of the scene, then find a priest or a vicar and get a quote. And the final embellishment, if you can find it, is a parrot in a cage squawking for its master." It sounds cynical and hard, but it wasn't, it made the young reporter laugh. It was a kindness. He did something similar for me after the Moorgate crash [another train crash in which forty-three people were killed].'

The night desk had its lighter side. 'We'd play ridiculous games. And you'd get all sorts of calls. There was a man called Philip from Cheltenham who used to ring up quite a lot saying that he was on a parallel dimension with Elvis Presley. We'd say, "How can we be sure? Would you sing for us?"' Peter indicates that he might handle this rather differently now. 'I gave him the number of Christopher Forse, our mate who used to work with us and had moved on to the Press Association night desk. I said, "You must ask for Christopher by name, Philip, he's very interested in parallel dimensions." Christopher then rang up our night desk and said "Is that bastard Hennessy in? I know it was him." When I worked the night desk I'd go and eat in *The Sunday Times* canteen next door in the basement. That was quite a place – all the contraband of London was flowing through it. The printers were having their dinner in there and a lot of them had contacts in that world, if I can put it delicately. I came back from dinner one day and the others were watching the football and said, "Some mad bugger's been on pretending to be Lord Boothby and insisting on only talking to you." He rang back later and it actually was Lord Boothby.

'I loved *The Times*,' Peter says. 'I felt it was my regiment, and it *was* like a regiment in some ways. It had all the hierarchies. And there was the most extraordinary range of character and temperament.' He speaks very fondly of his first editor, William Rees-Mogg. 'William wasn't particularly warm, but he was very good at giving his specialists their head, whatever their nominal position in the hierarchy. I'll never forget the time in '78 he asked me to write my first leading article. *Times* leaders were grand things and you felt you were part of a great tradition. He didn't give me much in the way of instruction. I remember it was about a speech Tony Benn was giving that day calling for a proper adoption of freedom of information by British governments. William said in that slightly strangulated, upper-class voice, "We don't normally approve of Mr Benn on this newspaper, do we?" I agreed we did not. "We rather approve of this speech though, don't we?" I agreed we did. "I need 600 words by half past five," and that was it. If he'd asked me the day before I'd have been terrified, but I just had to get on with it. I tried to think about how Mr Gladstone would have said it in the House of Commons to get the lofty style. I was amazed he trusted me to do it.' Rees-Mogg was an unusual boss. 'William would often give you these elliptical instructions. I remember him saying to me about something or another, "There are two things you should know. I don't find the clerical officer a figure of sympathy and I don't approve of the economics of Sir Douglas Wass, the permanent secretary to the Treasury." With some people you have a sense of what they're going to say, how they're going to think about things. With William, the pieces would fall out in unexpected ways – some of them completely bonkers. Every Tuesday at ten o'clock he'd hold a sort of seminar on a big theme and we'd all think together. He'd sit there in his rocking chair with a cup of coffee, presiding. I'd try to sit next to Owen Hickey, the chief leader-writer, a very austere, very impressive classical scholar. Owen didn't like William and during these meetings he'd draw Doric and Corinthian columns and sometimes write things in Greek, which I couldn't read but I always suspected were faintly abusive about William. It was on one of these Tuesday mornings in 1978 when William said, "I think we should talk about Rhodesia. I have a plan to solve the Rhodesia crisis which I want to try out on you." He went on to suggest giving the problem to Sir Humphrey Trevelyan, who had seen the British out of Aden after a messy civil war. "The Queen's Rolls Royce, carrying

Sir Humphrey, will be put in a Hercules at RAF Lyneham. On a second Hercules will be a little troop of the Brigade of Guards and their horses. They fly to Salisbury unannounced. They drive to Government House and say, 'We are the new government. We represent the Queen. We will stay for two weeks, by which time we will have found a government to succeed this one.' Then Sir Humphrey will go round and talk to people and find the most suitable group of Africans and appoint them the government in the Queen's name. Then the guards, horses and Rolls Royce get back in the Hercules, fly back to Lyneham. What do you think?" There was absolute silence – nobody knew what to say!'

A rather different character that Peter remembers fondly is Clive Borrell, the crime correspondent. 'He was six foot five, very strongly built. Looked, walked, and talked like a copper. Every day at twenty-five past five, just before opening time at the pub across the road, he would come to Rita Marshall, the home news editor, with a new euphemism: "Just off for a libation, Rita", "Just off to tickle the tonsils, Rita". On one occasion in particular she said, "Oh Clive darling, before you go, the last edition of the *Standard* has got something on the Krays, could you phone up the usual person on the Krays? And something's just come over the PA from the Yard. Could you ring up so-and-so, and while you're about it could darling could you ask the Yard the following …". He looked at her with a stony face and said, "Rita, shove a broom up my arse and I'll sweep the floor at the same time." Poor Rita, trembling slightly, reached for her cigarettes and the phrase subsequently became a Hennessy family standard.'

And then there were the printers. 'I remember the first time I met any of the printers, it was when I was at *The Times Higher* and I went to see my gossip column being laid out on the stone. There was a very old printer carrying one of those great metal hemispheres that you fixed to the rolls. He looked a bit shaky and I thought he was having a hernia. I said, "Here, let me help you," and he started shouting, "Don't touch me! Don't touch me!" The others dragged me away from him and said, "If you'd touched him, let alone that bit of metal, they'd all walk out. Demarcation you know, you're not in the union." It was a different world.'

During the seventies and eighties the management of *The Times* was almost constantly at loggerheads with the print unions. Peter recalls a particular moment when he felt this tension very strongly. 'Charlie Douglas-Home, who was then home editor, had written a leader about moving over to the new printing technology that enraged the print unions. He said they were neither morally nor physically justified in claiming a monopoly on the new technology and that it was better done by young women. I went down as the leader writer on duty to make sure everything fitted on the page. There was a very militant printer. I'd spoken to him before – I remember he'd talked to me about how much he admired the writing of Edward Mortimer, he was a real connoisseur of language. But on this occasion he was very cross about Charlie's leader. He had a scalpel that he'd been using to cut pages and so on. He said, "We're clumsy then, are we?", holding the scalpel towards me. He knew I hadn't written the leader – he could tell everyone by their style – but there was an air of menace.'

Talking to Peter, it's clear that these years were formative in all kinds of ways, not least because of the influence of various mentors, most notably Heren. 'I loved Louis. He was a great mixture of toughness and softness. He was a brave, strong man – he'd been in the war in difficult circumstances, but he was a deeply warm-hearted human being and very loyal to his lads and lasses. Louis had an endless fund of stories. He'd done *everything*.' Everything, in this case, included covering the violence of Partition in India, the discovery of the Dead Sea Scrolls, the Korean War, and the deepening of American involvement in Vietnam. Heren accompanied Martin Luther King Jr on his civil rights campaigns in the southern states of the US, and was embedded in the White House of President Johnson, with whom he enjoyed a warm relationship. 'He got on well with LBJ because they were both boys from poor backgrounds. And Louis – because he had this relationship – secured half an hour at the White House for William [Rees-Mogg], as the new editor of *The Times*, in '67. At the end of the meeting LBJ seized William's hand in his enormous paw. Louis recalled it like this. Johnson said, "Mr Mogg, in Lou Heren here you don't just have the finest British correspondent, you have the finest correspondent in Washington, period." And over William's shoulder he gave Louis a great big wink.'

What did Peter learn from him? 'Louis – and this was a gift he shared with Brian MacArthur – was very good at working people in terms of extracting information, and immensely tenacious in pursuit of a story. He was a natural journalist and was also terribly funny. And he had the necessary scepticism of the journalist. He used to say, "Always ask yourself: why is this lying bastard lying to me?"' His operating maxim for writing was similarly direct. 'He'd say "get them by the balls in the intro and their hearts and minds will follow." He would have made a great editor of *The Times*.'

In some ways Heren was an unlikely mentor. 'About once a month, after I'd written a highfalutin introductory paragraph or something, he would say to me, "You are an over-educated, smooth bastard. Only an over-educated bastard like you could fail to see that the point of the story is this ...". And I'd say "only a professional vulgarian would dream of seeing that it that way ...". It was like Centre Court Wimbledon. His face – which was very expressive and strong – would be like thunder, then he would burst out laughing. He used to think that I buried the important stuff in the story. He was invariably right, as I had absolutely no news sense. Probably the only person who had less news sense than me was William Rees-Mogg, who, according to legend, once picked up the previous day's news list at the morning meeting, went through it point by point and completely failed to notice. I never knew whether this was true or someone was trying to see how gullible I was. The point is, it was believable. I remember I took a story to Louis and I'd written "exclusive" on it. He said, "This really is a scoop, not one of the normal ones you just pretend are scoops. Very few things beat

The Prince of Wales comes for lunch at *The Times* in 1977. From left to right: Brian MacArthur (home news editor), Ivan Barnes (foreign editor), PH, Margaret Allen (features editor). The fare was so healthy and frugal (at Prince Charles's request) that we rushed over the road to the pub to fill the gaps with sandwiches as soon as HRH had departed.

a good scoop, perhaps only a fucking good crap or a fucking good screw."'

Despite Heren's frustration at the lack of news sense, he was a huge source of support for Peter. 'He was a great believer in the Whitehall thing I was doing because he believed in digging behind the lines. He was a great news-gatherer; he wasn't one of those who become a grand columnist and an opinion-monger. Even when he was deputy editor he'd still get out his notebook and go and report. Everybody needs a Louis. After he retired he'd write very good book reviews for the *Ham & High*. When he reviewed my books he always found the weaknesses, because he was still my editor, but he was always terribly warm about me. I miss him. And those tough reviews.

'Louis was devoted to *The Times*. His dad – who died when Louis was a young boy – had been a printer and Louis joined as a messenger boy when he was fourteen. But he'd become an officer in the war, so it meant that he could come back and move to being a journalist, given the class structures of all these things at the time.' Was he an anomaly, as a working-class man on *The Times*? 'Pretty well. By the time I got there you could tell the 1944 Education Act was working its way through, but it was still relevant. In some ways though, journalism was meritocratic. Louis once said to me that it's like boxing. If you get something wrong, you can't disguise it and you're knocked out flat on the canvas. He let me know that if he'd been home editor when I named the wrong fourth man he would have stopped me.'

This error of judgement clearly still bothers Peter. Just the mention of it feels like a shadow falling. 'It was June 1977. William came in with a story about a Cambridge don who had known Guy Burgess, Donald Maclean, and Kim Philby at Cambridge. It was suggested that he'd been a recruiter for Russian intelligence and was the so-called fourth man in the Cambridge spy ring. Only a tiny number of us on the paper knew about this story. I was asked to check it out. My big mistake – and it was a deeply unprofessional one – was to concentrate on the early days of the inquiry into Burgess and Maclean's disappearance in the early fifties. This chap's name had fallen swiftly down the list of suspects later on, which I had failed to pick up on because of my over-concentration on those early years. What we needed was someone to say, "Are we really sure about this? Shouldn't we start again from scratch?" It's certainly what I should have said. But we got carried away and ran the story. The very day we published I was summoned by a figure who really *did* know the truth and who told me all about Anthony Blunt [the actual fourth man, whose identity was revealed publicly by Mrs Thatcher in 1979]. William eventually agreed to my request that, without naming Blunt, I should write a letter in our own letters page apologising to the family of the old Cambridge figure who I had wrongly accused. I feel ashamed about it to this day, and probably always will.

'Several years later, when the so-called Hitler Diaries were acquired by Rupert Murdoch, I refused to write the story that was going to appear in *The Times* on the Saturday morning to prepare for the big revelations in *The Sunday Times* the next day. The story stank. I reminded my bosses that I'd gone to the stake a bit over the wrong fourth man and was now, as it were, cashing that in, because it didn't ring true.' Why didn't he believe the diaries were real? 'Well, for example, this alleged diary seemed to fit so wonderfully neatly into the serialisation needs of a national Sunday newspaper. Any historian who's read anybody's diary in the original knows that they are usually untidy things, often obsessed with personal anxieties that wouldn't be of overwhelming interest to subsequent generations. Also, they were all on the same sort of notebook – as if Hitler in early August 1939 had said to himself, "I'm going to be pretty busy for the next five years, I'll just send somebody down to Woolworths to buy me a stack of notebooks for my diary."'

In November 1978 the ongoing dispute between the owners and the print unions about new technology and staffing led to a lockout, and the owners closed the paper until December 1979. Peter used this enforced time off to write a book with his friend, Keith Jeffery, called *States of Emergency*, which was, appropriately enough, about government strike-breaking during industrial unrest. Not long after the paper was back in print, the National Union of Journalists decided to strike over pay. 'I thought it was a terrible idea. I was sure that the Thomsons [the owners of *The Times*] would sell. I told the chapel meeting that I would go and do my own work and not anybody else's, and I would donate the money I earned during the strike to charity. So I crossed the picket line. They were all very nice about it actually, but it was quite a difficult moment.'

The Thomsons did indeed decide to sell. 'William came to address us all in the newsroom. He was quite shy and he'd put his hand into his double-breasted jacket as if he was addressing the Oxford Union. It wasn't his best performance. He said in his precise and fastidious voice, "I'm going to America to try and find a white knight for us." Louis [then deputy editor] called for quiet and barked, "Right, questions?", glaring at me and one or two others; in other words, if you ask awkward questions and embarrass the editor I'm going to have your balls. Louis was very loyal to William. Someone suggested that we had to get the paper in as good a shape as we could, and that we should think about what we didn't do as well as other papers. William said: "Well, I think *The Telegraph* does rather well with its special stories on municipal hanky-panky." *The Daily Telegraph* ran near-verbatim accounts of the sex crimes being tried at the Old Bailey. It was full of terribly graphic details under the guise of plain straightforward reporting; it was known as the "dirt with dignity" tactic. We were very depressed at the idea that we should try to emulate that sort of thing. We regarded ourselves as a very grand outfit.

'We set up a group called The Journalists of *The Times*, which was a cooperative to see if we could buy it, but we couldn't raise the money. The two NUJ chapels [*The Times* and *The Sunday Times*] decided to merge in order to resist Murdoch. I went with the joint chapel to try and sway John Biffen, the secretary of state for trade. We were trying to persuade the government that Murdoch shouldn't have the paper on monopoly grounds because he had so much in the British press already – *The Sun*, the *News of the World*, and so on. I remember waiting in the anteroom to John Biffen's office in Victoria Street with Eric Jacobs, the father of *The Sunday Times* chapel, who was leading our delegation. "We're probably not going to succeed," he said, "but let's try and look on the bright side. Murdoch created *The Australian* and since then he's gone through editors at a rate of about one every fifteen to eighteen months. We can all take turns at being editor. It'll look great on our CVs."

Murdoch bought the paper in 1981. Rees-Mogg was replaced as editor and Heren left when he didn't get the job. 'Louis took us all for lunch in the Garrick Club – his newsroom, his reporters. He said, "I may be leaving but it's your duty to stay. You've got to see the paper through."' What changed under Murdoch? 'Harry Evans was brought in as editor. He was a remarkable man: very brave, full of life. At *The Sunday Times* he more or less invented investigative journalism in its modern form and he picked very important crusades, like thalidomide. But he had his moments. Those who were trying to be detached about him said that his genius was that he'd cause a sort of creative havoc over half the week and everyone would somehow manage to pull the paper together in the second half of the week. But that manic style didn't suit *The Times*. He also brought in a lot of his own people, who told him what he wanted to hear, which meant he didn't realise when resentments were building up. These appointees were all quite young. I referred to them once as "Harry's YTS [Youth Training Scheme]" and then overnight some wag put up a quite convincing sign saying "Harry's YTS" on the door of the features editor. I don't think he ever quite forgave me.'

There was also the looming presence of Rupert Murdoch himself. 'You got the impression from the newsdesk, fairly subtly but not always, about how they wanted the story to come out. Even before you, as the specialist journalist, had done the digging to find out what the position was. I don't know whether they were trying to second-guess the way Murdoch would want to see the story. Murdoch would come to London once a month and with the editors he'd go through all the stories that had appeared since he was last with them. He was a natural news editor, a very gifted man. He'd make it quite plain to them what he didn't like about the headline, the way the story was pitched and so on. And without ordering them to do anything, it just wouldn't happen again. So that's how his influence was exerted, through a combination of his own people on the paper and these retrospectives. He'd undertaken not to interfere in the paper, and he didn't interfere in advance; he did it ex post. We noticed that.

'Of course, he would have seen it as taking over an enterprise and saving it from destruction, because it was too old-fashioned, didn't have any bite, didn't have any style. The sad thing about the whole business was that it sowed distrust amongst the staff. Some people embraced him – he'd saved the paper. But he would also put his people in the key command positions and they would report to him what was going on. So you didn't know what was happening. People wanted to leave in large numbers. We set up what we called the Escape Committee to try and find jobs for other people outside. We'd meet in places like the remotest loos in the building. I was in the gents' way beyond the business news office, plotting with another member of the Escape Committee, and a third person came in, who was thought to be very close to Harry and at that time therefore Murdoch. He said, "I know what this is, it's a meeting of the escape committee." It was quite embarrassing.' Was Peter classed as a troublemaker? 'I hope so.'

In 1982, Peter left *The Times* for *The Economist*. 'It was my last afternoon and a notice goes up on the board from Gerald Long, who'd been brought in from Reuters as a managing editor. He was a strange chap and a ruthless cost-cutter. The notice said something like, "To all staff. No activity that involves expenditure of any kind can be undertaken without prior clearance from me, Gerald Long." And people started writing underneath, "You've lost your touch Peter, this is fucking crude even by your standards". They wouldn't believe it was actually real.'

Peter stayed at *The Economist* for six months before returning to *The Times*, now under the editorship of Charlie Douglas-Home, who had invited him back. He accepted, on the condition laid down by his wife that he didn't come home and moan about it. He wrote a lot of leaders, but his perspective diverged further and further from the paper's line. 'I couldn't conceal my views. Charlie was very pro-Mrs T. in pretty well every way, which I wasn't. He knew I was becoming increasingly uncomfortable writing leaders, and I told him. Charlie and I disagreed strongly about the de-unionisation of GCHQ, which was something I knew quite a lot about. I wrote a leader that I didn't agree with, but I couldn't do it again. I could only parody another man's views up to a certain point. When I got a grant from the Rowntree Trust to go to the Policy Studies Institute and write up my Whitehall investigations into a book, it seemed like a good time to leave. Charlie was very gentlemanly about it. He said, "You do know that as long as I'm editor there's always a job for you to come back to."'

Peter was, he says, 'hugely fortunate. It was sheer luck to have found those patrons, Brian, William, Charlie, Louis. Without them I'd never have been able to work up the Whitehall angle and write the books.' He also says he was lucky to have been a political journalist at that particular time. 'It would be much harder to do that kind of journalism now. The whole ecology in which I would be operating would be very different. Journalism is much more breathless. I've always thought that one of the functions of quality newspapers is to look at slower-moving trends and provide context and early warning. There are some journalists who manage to do this, but it's much harder because politics is much more volatile and the twenty-four-hour news coverage means that the hot story of the afternoon can affect the political weather. The flow of information is faster and freer too. Whitehall was a citadel then, but it isn't now. Bits of Cabinet papers are sent to lobby correspondents on WhatsApp in real time; I used to wait until at least fifteen people had seen something that had been leaked to me before I wrote about it. All of this combined means that everything moves at a manic pace. I had a lot of time for discreet lunches and teas, reading. Laying siege to a story, the thrill of the long-term chase.' He is, despite his reservations about the journalistic trade, clearly a romantic. 'To be operating at today's speed would take away the classical element of the enterprise for me.'

'A bloody nuisance but in the end he's on the side of the Queen': Working the Whitehall beat, 1975–92

There is something curious about Peter's unending fascination with the Civil Service. Whitehall does lack a certain glamour. He laughs at this. 'I took a Whitehall story to the chief sub at *The Times*. He said, "You've got 'exclusive' written on this. It may be exclusive but nobody else would want to write it anyway."' This sentiment is (rather more politely) echoed in the marvellous opening to a review of Peter's 2000 book, *The Prime Minister*, in the *London Review of Books* by R. W. Johnson: 'Peter Hennessy's new book hasn't persuaded me that its central preoccupation, the current dispute over prime ministerial power and its extent, is not sterile and, indeed, rather boring – yet it is a splendid read.'[25]

Why wasn't he drawn instead to the rather flashier charms of party and parliamentary politics, with all the concomitant feuds, gossip, and big characters? He is, he says, fascinated by institutions. 'The interplay between people and institutions expresses how things work: the certain norms that an institution has, where it's come from – the first blob of institutional DNA – where it acquires its folklore, its template of proper behaviour. Its notions of recruitment and survival. And how each generation leaves its mark on it, even the ancient institutions.' He says that this fascination partly comes from his study of British colonial history at Cambridge. 'We would talk about the "official mind of imperialism." The public never knew the names of the specific officials, but they were hugely influential.'

25 R. W. Johnson, 'Bugger everyone', *London Review of Books*, 22/20 (19 October 2000).

Whitehall, he says, was 'heavenly' for a connoisseur of ancient institutions: 'I mean, the lord chancellor's office goes back to the thirteenth century or something, although the Treasury would like to claim it's older because William the Conqueror had a bean-counter called Henry the Treasurer.' How did he approach his Whitehall studies as a journalist? 'You look at the people and how they relate to each other. That idea came from Anthony Sampson's *Anatomy of Britain*, because he showed how it could be done.' Peter said he wanted to cover both the immediate stories and the longer-term perspective: 'Instant, first rough draft of history stuff, but also second rough draft too.'

Perhaps the mundanity of the Civil Service is also part of the attraction. One of Peter's pet hates is when politicians use the phrase 'ordinary people'. ('I wish someone would explain what an "ordinary person" is meant to be because I've never met one.') Detractors of the Civil Service tend to conceive of it as grey men in grey suits doing grey work. Peter sees a great institution of state 'with its own codes and cultures, norms and funny little ways.' He approaches it in the manner a nineteenth-century anthropologist may have approached remote tribes in the hills of Papua New Guinea. Except in this case, the headmen had all been to one of the ancient universities.

Whitehall, published in 1989, was the culmination of this long fascination, the years of legwork, especially on *The Times*, and, according to Peter, 'a series of lucky breaks'. How did he come to work the Whitehall beat? 'Charlie [Douglas-Home, home editor of *The Times*] said to me, "you'll have long periods on the night desk when nothing's happening. I want you to find something the paper doesn't cover much and work it up, write me a few pieces."' Some years before, Anthony Howard of *The Sunday Times*, who Peter much admired, had tried to crack Whitehall but had been frozen out. Peter thought he would have a stab at it.

He had recently written a profile of Ken Berrill, the head of the Central Policy Review Staff. He took Berrill for lunch to check the quotes (there seem to have been a lot of lunches) and broached the subject with him. Peter said he was interested in writing about the dispersal of offices to the regions, devolution, special advisers, and the rules governing political activity by civil servants. By his own admission this was 'fairly boring stuff' and certainly nothing very controversial (though some of those themes would very definitely become so later) and Berrill seemed reasonably amenable. So it was quite a surprise when, a few weeks later while working on the night desk, he received not one, but two, anonymous phone calls. 'The first caller said, "I can't give you my name, but a memo has been circulated in the Prime Minister's name telling us that we mustn't speak to you and have no dealings with you at all."' From the second call he also gleaned that the memo had been circulated very widely. 'I thought, bloody hell, what have I done? I haven't done anything at all!' Peter recalls. 'I was shaken by all this. So I went in to see Charlie and I said, "You know about the Official Secrets Act, what am I supposed to do?" I asked him. He said, "This is magnificent, now you must hit them!"'

As perhaps should have been foreseen by its authors, the memo from Number 10 turned out to be a highly effective calling card. 'It went to all the policy departments,' he says. 'How better to advertise oneself? Most of them had never heard of me before they read that memo.'

Peter would, in his words, 'lay siege' to a particular subject or story with – thanks to Harold Wilson and his memo – the full support of the home editor who was happy to give him the time to put in the groundwork. He would read as much as he could from open sources, then try to fill the gaps with less official ones. From the way he recounts it, it's clear that the 'ban' stoked the fire in him, and he loved the thrill of the chase. 'I was like a poacher hunting on their land.'

Though still on the night desk, he wrote a story on the incomes policy which had come in earlier that year and had cut off the money allocated for positive vetting. 'I alluded to a case – without saying who or where it was, though I knew – about a young man who got a job in a permanent secretary's private office. If he hadn't written "Active member of the Communist Party of Great Britain" on his form, the vetting officers wouldn't have got round to his case for a year.'

It seems that this rattled a few cages. 'Not long afterwards, a fellow strap-hanger on the Tube came up to me and said, "I've just read an interesting file on you from the Cabinet Office. That vetting story you wrote was very close to the bone. In fact, it was in the bone. You've worried them because if you can get that, what else can you get, and who else might you be telling it to? So they've run a check on you."

"What did it say?" I asked.

"Oh, they've been very thorough, got a lot of information on your Cambridge years, pulled your wife's file from the GPO [where she worked]. Yes, they've been very thorough."

"Yes, but what does it *say*?"

"Well, in their language it says that you're a bloody nuisance but in the end you're on the side of the Queen."'

From the outset, he delighted in winding up his quarry. 'I rang up Joe Haines at the Number 10 Press Office and used a form of words which he knew had come from the memo banning anyone from speaking to me. So they knew I knew.' This must have been especially galling as, Peter discovered many years later, it was Haines who was the originator of the memo. Peter came by this information many years later, from Haines himself, by now a good friend.

According to Haines, Ken Berrill spoke to Douglas Allen (then the head of the Home Civil Service) about Peter's intention to write about Whitehall. It seems Berrill recommended Peter as a 'sensible chap' and suggested they provide briefings where they could. 'He thought it might do the Civil Service some good,' Peter recalls. Allen was also amenable to this idea but thought he'd better clear it with the PM. Haines baulked at this, telling Wilson, 'This is going to be another Tony Howard, you want to put a stop to this.' Why did Haines object, when the head of the Home Civil Service had been fairly keen? Peter says: 'Joe told me that he knew that I'd get things out of the permanent secretaries. According to him they'd talk to an Oxbridge smoothie like me in a way he said they would never have done with him or Gordon Greig of the *Mail*, who had both started as copy boys on *The Glasgow Herald*. And it pissed him off. It all came down to class.'

To be fair to Joe Haines, this was almost certainly true and Peter himself was not unaware of it. 'I took some pains to be reassuring, wearing green tweed suits and half brogues and so on.' Why? 'To look older.' And more like them? 'Yes.' In addition to the tweed camouflage, Peter was also patient, taking the time to find common ground and points of connection with potential sources. He took a senior Labour figure to lunch in Odin's in Marylebone. As they left, his companion said, 'That was a lovely lunch, Peter, but I expected you to ask me about the rows in the Parliamentary Labour Party – all we've done is talk about Bernard Donoughue's and George Jones's life of Herbert Morrison.' I strongly suspect that chat about the Parliamentary Labour Party happened at their next meeting.

Following Harold Wilson's fortuitous ban, Douglas Allen struck up an agreement with Haines. 'I didn't know it at the time, but the deal was: we'll keep him [Peter] away from Number 10 and Cabinet committees and all of that sort of stuff. I'd go and see Douglas every six months or so and tell him what I was planning to work on next, and he'd say, "Can't help you with that, too sensitive, might be able to help you with this."[26] My strategy then was that I'd go in and have all these briefings and write stories on them, and they [the civil servants] would get used to me. They'd know I was a serious youth. Then I could recruit them to my network of helpers.'

---

26 This rather cosy arrangement was not universally well received. In a memo of March 1978 relating to relations with the press, Ian Bancroft (Allen's successor as head of the Civil Service) tells Ken Stowe (principal private secretary to the Prime Minister) '[Y]ou should know that Mr Hennessy has asked me to lunch. I understand that he lunched with my predecessor (normally on a strictly background basis) reasonably regularly.' The prime minister, Jim Callaghan, has underlined the last sentence and scribbled 'Oh!' in the margin.

With the help of his 'network of helpers', Peter went on to break the Official Secrets Act a number of times and was subject to at least two leak enquiries. How did he go about it? The kind of stories he wrote were not Watergate-style revelations, and his informants weren't sending him government documents unsolicited, or blowing the gaffe on big government scandals, *a la* Clive Ponting.[27] In tone, Peter's stories were chatty rather than dramatic, featuring colourful *bons mots* from insiders. They also featured a recurring cast of characters, a sort of soap opera for policy nerds. In content too, they now seem quite low key: there would be a revelation about an undisclosed initiative here, a report on an embarrassing and expensive failure of government policy there. Partly this reflects the level of secrecy surrounding government in the 1970s and 1980s, which today can seem positively deranged. For example, the guidelines on proper behaviour for ministers, now known as the Ministerial Code, then as Questions of Procedure for Ministers, was classified until 1992.[28] Even the names of Cabinet committees were withheld from the public domain. 'Anything to do with the Cabinet Office apparatus of decision-making seemed to really upset them. I admired John Hunt, the Cabinet secretary, very

---

27 In 1984, Ponting – an official at the Ministry of Defence – sent two documents to Tam Dalyell MP concerning the sinking of the Argentine cruiser the *General Belgrano* in 1982 during the Falklands War. Ponting felt the public had a right to know that the *Belgrano* (on which more than 300 Argentine sailors perished) had not – as had been claimed in official reports – been sailing towards the British exclusion zone when it was torpedoed by a Royal Navy submarine.
28 'Questions of Procedure for Ministers' was the one Cabinet paper Peter ever received clandestinely. 'I sort of asked for it without asking for it in a column and then the latest version arrived in the post. You can't have a Cabinet paper hanging around the house in case you get searched so I used to hide it with friends who lived round the corner. Nobody was ever going to look there. It turned into a nightmare once, when Nigel Lawson resigned in 1989. Newsnight phoned and said they wanted to talk to me about what the Constitution said about all these resignations. I said I would be ready. I went round to the friend's house to get the key document so I could get up to speed again and everyone was out. They came back just in time.'

greatly. Many years later I met someone who was a young man in the Cabinet secretariat in those days. He said, "We noticed how you would drive John Hunt mad by leaking one Cabinet committee a week." I didn't actually, but he thought that I was drip-feeding them out just to drive John up the wall.

'The Official Secrets Act 1911 Section 2 meant that everything was secret unless you were specifically authorised to make it unsecret, whatever the level of classification,' Peter says. Almost all journalists and many officials thought this was 'bonkers'. Nonetheless, the people who gave him information were contravening the Official Secrets Act – and therefore breaking the law. 'Possibly worse, they were breaking the Establishment Officers' Code, which was the official rule book for Civil Service departments governing how civil servants were supposed to behave.'

The nature of Peter's interactions with his informants was subtle in style and tone. 'We always pretended that we weren't having *that* sort of chat. They would just drop things in: "By the way, I'm sure you know already ...".' He finds it interesting that they always took pains to outwardly pretend that they weren't divulging information, even when it was abundantly clear that they were. Peter recalls getting a call from a Whitehall source 'one afternoon, when all the other senior figures were away. "Peter," he said, "Old X has given me something to read. I can't make head nor tail of it but I'm sure you can understand it." There was a choreography to it that I found very attractive.'

Sometimes he would discuss things 'hypothetically' with sources. He also liked to talk through what he already knew, sometimes deliberately misconstruing a few minor points. 'They had such a passion for accuracy, they couldn't resist putting me right. I played on that ruthlessly. They weren't leakers in the crude sense because I'd also talk to them on the record. I'd go to them when I'd gone as far as I possibly could from open sources and they'd turn the last screw for me. I made it easier for them because they weren't telling me the whole story from beginning to end. They'd just add embellishments.'

He speaks of his Whitehall sources with great affection, and exudes a boyish delight at the secrecy, the adventure of it all. 'I used to love the unplanned snatched conversations at the London Library or on the concourse at Waterloo in the morning. Once you're known for it, people feed you.'

Sometimes Peter felt that his sources were just desperate for a sympathetic listener. 'There was a chap who was authorised to brief me on something. He was very quiet and I liked talking to him. I took him for lunch in June 1979 and I said, "What's it like since the government changed?" and he just unloaded. "You've no idea," he said, "It's dreadful. Do you remember under the Callaghan government when we went round this policy circuit, we went round and round and round and ended up there. Well, they've started again, in a different place, and we're going round and round and round again and we'll end up in exactly the same place. Just dreadful. And that's only the half of it." And on he went, in great detail. He just did it out of weariness. I began to realise that everybody needs to tell *somebody*. The next time I invited him for lunch he sent me a postcard. The *New Statesman* had been running a big series on telephone tapping. Enclosed was a cutting on phone tapping and he wrote "P, I don't think this is the right time to talk" and signed it with just an initial.'

Peter doesn't seem to have been terribly alarmed at the fact his home phone was being tapped. 'I rather expected it, because I knew how leak enquiries worked. It was just a bit inconvenient trying to find a non-vandalised phone box in Walthamstow.' Sometimes he'd pop round to the neighbours' and borrow their phone. Was he open with the neighbours about what he was up to? 'Yes.' Did they mind? 'No, people tended to think it was great fun.'[29]

---

29 Peter feels that the neighbour in question, Ruth Tanner, should have a special mention here. 'Ruth was a kind of Walthamstow Mother-Earth figure, terribly warm hearted, great laugh, tremendously cheerful. She sort of enveloped you into her orbit, and you were terribly pleased to be enveloped.' He recounts turning to Ruth the first time that he was left alone with his elder daughter, Cecily: 'She

Helpful neighbours or not, Peter tried to be careful. He was, he says, 'very sensitive to what John le Carré called "Moscow rules". I didn't want to get anyone into trouble. And if you blow somebody's cover through carelessness, nobody will ever tell you anything again.' One source warned him not to quote directly or put 'rag outs' (pictures of a leaked document) in the paper, as many journalists liked to do 'to show how ballsy they were', in Peter's words. Why? 'Because on sensitive material, the typists would leave a slightly different gap between the words in each copy of the document so you could work out whose copy it was.'

Some of Peter's anti-surveillance techniques had a tinge of the absurd. He knew a common question in government leak enquiries was, 'Have you had lunch or dinner with Peter Hennessy of *The Times*?' (or whoever the subject of the enquiry happened to be). Peter's response was to invite his sources for afternoon tea, meaning that they could answer without having to lie. There is something faintly ridiculous about that question; it evokes a world so certain in its assumptions (of *course*, the only places one could possibly meet a journalist would be over a nice Chateaubriand). Peter is not himself averse to a nice Chateaubriand, but the cuisine of choice for his most secret assignations was kebabs. Later on, as a freelancer, he would take his most sensitive sources to a kebab shop in Somers Town, a run-down area between Euston and Camden Town. It wasn't too far from Whitehall, but they were unlikely to be recognised by any passing servants of the Crown. When an extra level of security was necessary, he would take his contacts to lunch at the Royal Dolphin Greek restaurant on Lea Bridge Road in Leyton (it also had the additional benefit of being approximately four minutes'

---

wouldn't settle, and I couldn't do anything to calm her. She was getting beside herself so I took her down to Ruth and as soon as Ruth held her she just sort of sighed and calmed down. I realised I was transmitting my anxiety to her.' In the early nineties, when Peter recorded a documentary series on early post-war Britain called *What Has Become of Us?*, Ruth and her husband Fred did a star turn recalling VE Day. Peter says, 'every street should have a Ruth.'

walk from his house). 'It was a bit of a scruffy place when we first moved here, but they tarted it up and put a takeaway downstairs with a restaurant upstairs. Velvet chairs, big fishtank, lovely food.'

What merited the 'Royal Dolphin' level of secrecy? He tells me a bit about his involvement in the 'Spycatcher business', which had its origin in an aggrieved MI5 officer, Peter Wright. 'Peter Wright didn't get the pension he felt he deserved. He was one of a relatively small group of intelligence officers who bought the Anatoliy Golitsyn theory that Western intelligence had been very seriously infiltrated by the Soviets. To the very top. They thought that Roger Hollis, the former director general of MI5, had been a Soviet agent. Peter Wright helped Paul Greengrass and John Ware of Granada do a documentary for World in Action on this. I knew Paul and John slightly and they showed me the World in Action programme before it went out. I told them I thought the Independent Broadcasting Authority would pull it because it was so full of official secrets, some of it still operationally relevant. I said, "I can't judge the veracity of what he's saying, but if you're pulled I'll take my notes to Jim Callaghan, as a senior privy counsellor and former PM with a sure touch on intelligence and security matters, and I'll say, 'Jim, I don't know what do with this but I'm giving this to you as you're better placed than me to decide whether you need to go and see people about this.'" But to my surprise the programme was shown. The deal was that on the morning before World in Action went out, I would break the story in *The Times*. I wrote it for the front page.

'As a result, Peter Wright and I got in touch. He would ring me from Tasmania and he took a bit of a shine to me. And he asked me if I would go out to Tasmania for three months with Paul Greengrass to help him write the book on all this.' Was he tempted? 'No! I thought, "I'll go mad if I'm cooped up in a house with Peter Wright for three months." He was obsessional.' The resulting book – *Spycatcher* – was banned in England (though not Scotland) on its publication in 1987 and English newspapers were prevented from reviewing it. Peter won't be drawn on exactly who he was meeting and why in this period, but he says, 'There was one conversation about all of this in the Royal Dolphin. It was bound to be secure. I don't think the KGB for all their might had quite reached the border of E10 and E17. And at the time, for my Whitehall friends – unlike now when Walthamstow is terribly fashionable – it was *terra incognita*.'

Only once did he run into someone in the Royal Dolphin. Peter explains that his clandestine dining companion bristled ever so slightly when a very glamorous lady in her early fifties came to the table to say hello. He says, 'Even by her standards she was looking quite compelling. She had beautifully cut clothes and very high-heeled shoes with little leather ribbons on the back of them. She greeted me terribly warmly and went off to talk to the proprietor. I said to my companion, "Patricia Marino, my daughters' headmistress." and he said, "They didn't have headteachers like that in my time."'

Did his Moscow rules work? Were any of the leak enquiries successful? 'No. I used to get the results of them, quite often over lunch, quite often by the person who'd divulged the information to me in the first place. I took indecent amount of pleasure in leaking the progress of leak enquiries.' This is nicely mirrored in a rather weary 1978 note from Ian Bancroft (then head of the Civil Service) to Ken Stowe (principal private secretary to the Prime Minister) outlining the reasons why, in this case, a formal leak inquiry into something Peter had written in *The Times* might not be desirable. Bancroft writes, 'I think it very doubtful whether we shall in fact find the sources, since the information he discloses is known to a fairly large circle and tends to be embarrassing rather than sensitive. But our efforts to do so may themselves act as a deterrent. Of course, they would probably become known to Mr Hennessy too and might attract his comments. If so, we should have to grin and bear it.'

Clearly, some of his sources were very highly placed. 'It was a late Sunday afternoon, when I wasn't using the home phone. There was a meeting of the permanent secretaries at Sunningdale – they had one or two a year. They broke up at lunch so I rang up a few of them and asked them to be theatre critics about how it went and who performed well. I remember one, of whom I was particularly fond, saying, "Just a thought, Peter, before we say goodbye. Don't be *too* knowing in your piece in the paper tomorrow." It caused outrage because they felt their retreat in Sunningdale had been penetrated.'

It is, therefore, quite interesting to read the comments of (presumably) some of these same permanent secretaries that appear in various Civil Service memos, now declassified in the National Archives. The words that come up most often are 'irritating' and 'mischievous', though clearly at least some of these mandarins felt that a little light shone on the dusty corridors of Whitehall might actually be quite useful. 'I was dancing a sort of stately quadrille with various permanent secretaries and so on. They had their official line, but I got to know them as people because I would see them for a lunch or an authorised briefing, while I also operated twin-track secret operations on the side. It could be the same people who were giving me on-the-record chats with nice photos of them taken by Brian Harris of *The Times*. I came to know them and like them very much. I was working in a kind of symbiosis with them in that my professional pursuit impinged on an – admittedly tiny – part of their professional lives.' Politicians tended to be less keen on the idea. On a 1978 memo regarding special advisers, Jim Callaghan circled the heading 'IN CONFIDENCE' and scribbled 'Hardly. It had already been in *The Times* before I had even heard of it – and my name was wrongly used. Has Sir Ian Bancroft any ideas as to how this came about? Who talked?'.

Peter remains tight-lipped about exactly who did and didn't talk. His admiration for that Civil Service and political generation remains strong. 'I wanted to bring them out of the shadows to give them their place in the scheme of things, which they deserved because they were important. This is where I'm slightly guilty because they were busy people governing in extremely difficult times and they had enough on without having to worry about a rather pushy youth from *The Times*.'

The fraction of the curve: Journalism and contemporary history

> 'In the cycle to which we belong we can only see a fraction of the curve'.
>
> John Buchan, *Memory Hold-the-Door*

Contemporary historians and journalists live on the edge of Buchan's curve – the place where the curve already followed meets the curve to come. The key to the historian's task is making as much sense, as accurately as possible, of the curve we have travelled so far. As someone who has been both a journalist and contemporary historian, looking back at one's life on the page is a sobering experience. It's what isn't there as much as what is that captures one's thoughts. For however hard one tries, journalists observing government and parliament are heavily swayed by pacemaker politics – the interplay of events and people that are making the immediate political weather. It's very difficult, amidst this cataract, to pick up the mutation of old themes and the emergence of new ones, particularly those events that might or might not be going into the making of a new, or seriously altered, collective consciousness. In meteorological terms, it is rather like delineating the difference between the weather and the climate. For political journalists, there is as always a convenient, if only semi-convincing, alibi for all this. It's hard enough to report the week properly in the hours at one's disposal, let alone go wide, deep, and forward. And even if one makes a determined effort to do so, the pacemaking journalism of one's rivals means that you too have to give priority to gripping the hot and the immediate, even if it turns out to be trivial and transient reporting in the wider scheme of things. It is difficult to distinguish 'news that stays news' (to borrow a phrase from Ezra Pound) from the frothily attractive pursuit of who's up and who's down.

During my early professional years from the mid-1970s to the mid-1980s as a young journalist on *The Times*, I used to quote, in my more pompous moments, the owner and publisher of *Newsweek*, Philip Graham, who said on purchasing the magazine in 1961 that he wanted it to provide 'the first rough draft of history'. I thought that's what I should, in a very small way, aspire to do and *The Times* of William Rees-Mogg, Louis Heren, and Charlie Douglas-Home really facilitated such an approach. I tried to imagine how the fragments I was working on might be of use to future historians and how, looking back, my little bits added to the vast cornucopia of material for those seeking to recover that time. I've no idea whether or not I succeeded to any degree at all. But I do think that helping to produce a national daily newspaper towards the top end of the quality market was a memory-creating/memory-shaping business, and all done against the clock in time for the first edition.

The sequence of production flowed something like this: you start off with an existing map in your own mind – a cartography of memory – of history and how institutions and those who people them behave. Against this cumulative backcloth you set a breaking story or judge the novelty of a development or an event. In those days there was a huge cuttings library at *The Times* on which to draw. In the digital age, that now looks puny. But, in its time, it was a fabulous and well-ordered resource. Sometimes there were new bits of paper that flowed as the story broke – a white paper; a green paper; a statement; or a press release.

You swiftly added to this your own rapidly created oral archive. You would get on the phone and chat to contacts. Sometimes you could supplement the fast-growing map in your mind with an interview either à deux or by asking a question at a press conference. If you were wise, you kept your notebooks and stored them carefully as a kind of hidden treasure. I could not have written my big book on Whitehall if I had failed to do my 'squirrel nutkin' act, as my friend Robert Armstrong, the former Cabinet secretary and head of the Home Civil Service, once put it when we were debating in the House of Lords on the subject of freedom of information and archives.

The result of this scramble could often be divided into three parts: a news story; a specialist background piece to supplement it and provide context; and a leading article. All produced within a few hours. It was always incomplete, and ever risky. But, when done well – doing the best with what you had – indispensable as both 'first rough draft of history' and as a contribution to the rolling national conversation. And the bricolage of memory was crucial to its being done as best it could.

When covering Westminster and Whitehall, a feel for history was certainly useful for the present. For example, in the late 1970s, when Jim Callaghan's government, or a tiny fragment of it, was, in intense secrecy, contemplating the replacement of the Polaris strategic nuclear weapons system with Trident, I got a head start from reading Margaret Gowing's wonderful official history of the initial British bomb project after the war. And her depiction of the mix of committees and politico-scientific-diplomatic ingredients turned out, as I'd hoped, to have many similarities to the way Jim Callaghan and his tiny group of ministers were setting about the possible procurement of the new generation of deterrent, almost as if Clem Attlee and Ernie Bevin were at their shoulders.

Similarly, reading about the handling of sterling crises in the late forties and early fifties proved quite a good training ground for my efforts to understand how Whitehall was battling with essentially the same problem in the mid- to late seventies. And my very first book, co-authored with my great friend Keith Jeffery, was about the emergency planning for industrial disputes, which might affect the provision of the essentials of life – directly relevant to the very same question that preoccupied ministers throughout the bulk of the seventies and the eighties.

As both a journalist and historian, I've written quite a lot about institutions. Institutions have their own ways, their own sounds and conversations. They carry the thought patterns of the past into the now and the future. They are not a blank slate. This means that context is especially valuable. Sir Robin Butler, when Cabinet secretary, put it perfectly when I asked him in an interview for one of my 'Whitehall watch' columns in the early 1990s how Whitehall might be preparing for a hung Parliament after the next election. 'We could always go to the cupboards', he replied. Looking back, I've been a cupboards man all my professional life.

Retracing the institutional strand of my journalism, I'm struck by its power to evoke the political flavour and governing culture of the Wilson and Callaghan governments of the seventies and of the early Thatcher years too. It now seems these were the last years of a truly tight and secretive administrative system, held together by an increasingly fading deference about government on the part of the governed. Wilson, Callaghan, and Thatcher all banned civil servants from talking to me. In my more facetious moments, I used to think Mrs Thatcher would classify Hansard if she thought she could get away with it.

Happily, after freedom-of-information legislation, there will be no going back to a walled-in Whitehall. But each age has a way of revealing itself both to the political journalist and the contemporary historian. As we move deeper into the digital age, successive technological transformations now mean that captured in apps are, in effect, real-time conversations, often of the most indiscreet kind, conducted between ministers and other ministers, officials and other officials, about policy and politics as they unfold. This was demonstrated in a hyper-vivid fashion during the COVID inquiry in the autumn of 2023. Gone are the stately minuets of the old paper culture of formalised correspondence, papers, minutes, and memoranda. Although in terms of background and education the cast of characters remains largely the same, Whitehall culture now can feel closer to the Fleet Street gossip columns than the classics departments at the ancient universities. Macmillan's scribbled heckles on the Cabinet papers of, say, his chancellors of the Exchequer, were very vivid, often immensely funny and quite sharp. But they have a wit and a seriousness that is generationally different than the content of the exchanges and the style of their communication sixty years on. The paper culture militated against demotic language and moved the author to a more careful form of expression than in the digital world, whose technologies are – confusingly for the user perhaps – employed both for casual, off-the-cuff chat and serious government business.

Interestingly, this change is probably partly the result of the Freedom of Information Act, which led to practices such as easily disposable Post-it notes being used for the hotter morsels of exchange and later, as the technology developed, quickly deletable WhatsApps. This was a price to be paid for more open government; the contents of the correspondence, policy papers, and notes of discussions of the pre-FOI era provide far richer and more candid seams for historians once the thirty years had elapsed than in the post-FOI world. I remember being very struck, when I sat at a meeting in the Cabinet Secretary's office ahead of the 2010 election with a number of fellow constitutional historians and lawyers to help the Cabinet Office, Number 10, and the Palace think through the byways of a possible hung Parliament, when Sir Gus O'Donnell opened by reminding us that the note of the meeting about to start was 'FOI-able'. I suspect, though one can't be sure, that we were all rather more careful in our conversation than we otherwise might have been. In fact, it became a Whitehall cliche to describe FOI as having 'a chilling effect' on the conduct of central government. Perhaps there was something in that stale old adage, 'be careful what you wish for'.

In my years as a journalist I was already looking back. I regarded digging out stories from the National Archives under the old thirty-year rule as a kind of production line for delayed scoops, which fed neatly and nicely into the 'now it can be told' school of journalism. This was particularly satisfying because in hot-off-the-press daily journalism, you have to go with what you've got, very often on the basis of the skimpiest information. Getting a big, packed, content-rich file is altogether more satisfying, even though both the journalist and historian must always remember that even the most exciting and bulky briefs from the past era are not a surrogate for reality, and are always far from the full story, even if it is a real pleasure to wallow in them. Ours is a cryogenic trade (and unlike the medical equivalent, ours really works). For what else are those minutes and memoranda, Cabinet papers and cost-benefit analyses, intelligence assessments and 'war books' but frozen history? Our job is to warm them up until they twitch a little, their limbs begin to move, their diaphragms to heave until, at last, they begin to talk to us – even if the page carries the cool, deliberately unexciting prose of the Cabinet or Cabinet committee minute-taker. So detached do these officials often seem, whatever the magnitude of the decisions they are recording, you can imagine how they would write up the Second Coming – 'The Cabinet discussed the recent events in the Middle East, which the Foreign Secretary warned may lead to the end of the world. The Cabinet took note and invited the Home Secretary to chair a meeting of COBRA.'

There are pitfalls here. For historians of institutions who rely on archives, there is always the danger that history might go to those who wielded the most fluent pen. For example, Sir Otto Clarke, in the post-war Treasury, could not write a dull word, even though his subject matter might be the very incarnation of tedium. The same applies to the diarists who added the heat and the warmth to their accounts of Cabinet and Cabinet committee life.

Getting the documents to talk is not enough on its own if history is to live and breathe as fully as we can make it with our efforts at revival. Speaking to participants and survivors is indispensable and contemporary historians have a unique ability to do so. A famous example concerns Clem Attlee's Cabinet committee on atomic energy meeting on the afternoon of Friday 25 October 1946 to decide whether or not to authorise the building of a gaseous diffusion plant, without which manufacturing the ingredients of a British Bomb would not be possible. From Sir Denis Rickett's meticulous, classically drafted Cabinet secretariat minutes you would acquire no feel for the drama of the occasion or a particular piece of language that has echoed down four decades of the great UK nuclear weapons debate since we first heard about it from a scientific civil servant present that day in a BBC *Timewatch* interview in 1982.

The great, in every sense, Ernie Bevin, Attlee's foreign secretary, wheezed into the meeting late after a good lunch. By the time he arrived, GEN 75 (to give the committee its Cabinet Office classification) was in the process of being talked out of a British bomb by the economic ministers Hugh Dalton and Stafford Cripps (chancellor of the Exchequer and president of the Board of Trade respectively) on the grounds of opportunity cost – that the country could not afford the diversion of scarce engineering resources from economic recovery and exports. Ernie, as we know from that 1982 testimony of Sir Michael Perrin, one of the Ministry of Supply's team at the meeting (Supply was then the bomb ministry), was having none of this, and he went critical. 'That won't do at all,' he roared, 'we've got to have this ... I don't mind for myself, but I don't want any other foreign secretary of this country to be talked to or at by a secretary of state of the United States as I have just been in my discussion with Mr Byrnes.'

And here comes the passage that has resonated down the years:

We've got to have this thing over here whatever it costs ... We've got to have the bloody Union Jack on top of it.

On the way back to the Ministry of Supply in the Strand from Number 10, Lord Portal, the Second World War chief of the air staff and now controller of production of atomic energy, turned to Perrin and said: 'You know, if Bevin hadn't come in then, we wouldn't have had that bomb, Michael.'

Now here's the frozen-history version in the shape of Denis Rickett's minute:

> In discussion it was urged that we must consider seriously whether we could afford to divert from civilian consumption and the restoration of our balance of payments, the economic resources required for a project on this scale. Unless present trends were reversed we might find ourselves faced with an extremely serious economic and financial situation in two or three years time.
>
> On the other hand it was argued that we could not afford to be left behind in a field which was of such revolutionary importance from an industrial, no less than from a military point of view. Our prestige in the world, as well as our own chances of securing American co-operation would both suffer if we did not exploit to the full a discovery in which we had played a leading part at the outset.

The official note, as always, conveys the essentials; it comes nowhere near to capturing the atmospherics, the Foreign Secretary's *force majeure* or the special Bevinite vocabulary.

There is another risk, too, in the shape of survivors' memories; invaluable and indispensable as they are, they can be a bit of a pain. Shortly before I submitted the manuscript of my study of early post-1945 Britain, *Never Again*, to my publisher, I bumped into Lord Sherfield in Whitehall. As Roger Makins he had been a great figure in the Foreign Office after the war.

Roger was a true friend of contemporary history and historians. 'What have you been finding lately?' he asked.

'A really good story about you and Jean Monnet and the plan for a European Coal and Steel Community, when he outlined it to you and Edwin Plowden that spring day in May 1950 in his room at the Hyde Park Hotel.'

'What story?' said Roger.

'How you ended the meeting with the words, "We are not ready; and you will not succeed".'

'I can't remember saying that,' said Roger.

'Etienne Hirsch, Monnet's assistant, says you did in his memoirs.'

'He's dead. In fact, they're all dead apart from me,' Roger replied.

Ever since I've had to caveat that great story – which perfectly captured the views of the Attlee Cabinet and Whitehall in 1950 towards European integration – by saying 'Lord Sherfield has no recollection of it.'

The historian must also know who the players are; what routes brought them to Cabinet committee table or chiefs of staff suite; the nature of their world, and the world that formed them. Unless we have a sense of this, we'll end up shouting at them – 'Surely you must have known this?', or 'How on earth can you have failed to anticipate that?' – subjecting them to what Edward Thompson famously called 'the enormous condescension of posterity'. Our job, in essence, is to fulfil the duty placed upon us by the French historical sociologist Raymond Aron when he said that the scholar's task is to restore the same level of uncertainty to the past as we feel today about the future. That's why this paper trail, this frozen residue of state activity, is so precious.

There is also the pitfall of excessive emotional involvement. This was vividly illustrated for me during a seminar at the London School of Economics in July 1991 on the writing of contemporary history, with Enoch Powell on the platform and Paul Addison in the chair. Unwittingly I lit Enoch's blue touch-paper when I reckoned in my opening lecture that soon the historical torch would have to pass to a younger generation than mine (I was forty-four at the time) – people, I said, 'who are free of nostalgia; who are not susceptible to the old drumbeat; people who don't get a spasm of one kind or another when the word "Suez" is mentioned.'

Enoch, the first discussant when I'd finished my presentation, turned to Paul Addison, his remarkable voice brimming with emotion, and declared:

> Mr Chairman, I found myself in far-reaching sympathy with the cry from the heart with which Dr Hennessy ended his lecture. I think he is right to put his finger upon a factor which the historian chronically neglects – the emotional factor. One, of course, understands why the historian neglects it. It is unquantifiable. It is rather shameful and it is difficult to handle. But without the emotional factor, I do not think one can understand the turnaround which occurred in this country or some of the most surprising things which this country did in the second half of the twentieth century.

At this point, all but aflame, the seventy-nine-year-old Mr Powell reached into his own past to illustrate his theme. 'When', he said,

> I resigned my chair in Australia in 1939 [he had been appointed professor of classics at Sydney University at the age of twenty-five] in order to come home to enlist, had I been asked 'What is the State whose uniform you wish to wear and in whose service you expect to perish?' I would have said 'The British Empire' ... I also know that, on my deathbed, I shall still be believing with one part of my brain that somewhere on every ocean of the world there is a great, grey ship with three funnels and sixteen-inch guns which can blow out of the water any other navy which is likely to face it.

Then came the peroration, his audience wide-eyed (the young American scholars were mesmerised, having neither seen nor heard anybody like this in their lives):

> I know it is not so. Indeed, I realised at a relatively early age that it is not so. But that factor – the emotional factor – will not die until I, the carrier of it, am dead.

As every reader of history knows, those who practise the historical craft professionally have a compulsion for applying the labels of eras, epochs, and ages to their unfolding stories and analyses. It's not just because it's an intellectual temptation, because it really is a necessity to provide such cartography for one's readers who don't have the time to do the research and writing for themselves. We have yet to see the day where the historical work is entitled 'the age where nothing happened very much'. Journalists are also prone to this compulsion to help their readers make sense of what is happening in the world. Their judgements are more tentative, but just occasionally one did have a definite feeling that one was treading over a contour into a different kind of landscape. For example, it didn't take a reservoir of foresight to realise in the late seventies that the shared norms of the so-called post-war consensus, on the economic and industrial fronts particularly, were crumbling under the battering they were receiving from stagflation and intensifying industrial strife – and that the nature of the party competition was changing in step. A knowledge of the formative years and experience of those in power – or advising power – was indispensable here too. For example, Denis Healey once told me that full-blown Thatcherism was not possible until the political generation that had been young in the 1930s and grown up in the war had passed from the summits of political life.

Sometimes these gradual shifts express themselves particularly vividly and swiftly, such as the Winter of Discontent in 1978 and early 1979, which was the immediate prelude to Mrs Thatcher's first election victory. It was clear at the time that this was news that would 'stay news'. More recently, it was immediately clear that anybody who writes books on the politics and constitutions of the United Kingdom would have to linger for quite a long time on the Johnson experience, because of the threat it posed to the unwritten constitution and the low point it marked in the history of the British premiership. It exposed a weakness, and it's a horror story we can tell ourselves in the future if we get another premier who verges towards the overmighty.

A sense of history, then, can be a huge benefit to a journalist. The danger in this is that occasionally it can give you a feeling of superior but not justified wisdom. There's a risk that one sees British politics, as Alan Watkins put it, as a series of old Movietone newsreels that repeat themselves, changing as time goes by into colour rather than black and white. It can mean as a result that one's not as aware as one should be or could be of developing themes that are different, either because they are a remixing of the old in a substantial way or because they are genuinely new. Context is less useful for the truly novel. And we all have our blank spots. For example, although I'm fascinated by science, I am usually very slow to pick up on the significance of technological advance.

Writing the history of one's own country in one's own time is, of its very nature, a highly individual pursuit and yet it has a collective purpose. It's rather like being a sports journalist reporting on a Saturday afternoon football match. You hope that the supporters packed into the stadium will read your account in the Sunday papers to see where their version of what happened on the pitch accords (or not) with what you think you saw and felt. This holds true for journalism too. Just as no two people will recall the same event in the same way, no two historians or journalists will choose the same examples or prioritise the same factors. Perhaps our best hope is to model ourselves on the old Northern Isles fiddlers, as described by the great Orcadian poet and writer George Mackay Brown, when he said 'each reel and each tale differed in every performance. The tremble of life was in it.'[30]

30 George Mackay Brown, *For the Islands I Sing* (Edinburgh, 1996).

Radio 4 man: Getting ready to join Paddy O'Connell down the line from Kirkwall for *Broadcasting House*, with my grandson Jack Cromby and brilliant BBC Radio Orkney man the late Dave Gray.

PART TWO

CROWN AND CONSTITUTION

Every nation has its own 'rules of the game' (except that government is too serious a matter to be called a game, of course). In the British case, even trying to find out what the basic rules are is a life's work. Our rulers have a genius for camouflage, so even when you think you've found an important bit of the constitution it can turn out to be a fleeting hope. There's a great story about Groucho Marx watching a Test match at Lords. As the lunchtime break approached, he turned to his companion and said, 'When does it start?' Groucho had, I think, also unwittingly caught the essence of the British constitution.

A bit like cricket, for many, the British constitution is as dry as it's impenetrable. It's difficult to explain its attraction for me, but part of it is the very fact that it's uncodified, although much more of it has been written down recently. Everyone loves a mystery, although I concede this might not be a classic type of thriller. The great nineteenth-century journalist and constitutional observer Walter Bagehot wrote about the dignified and efficient parts of the constitution. For me, the joy is finding the dignified and the absurd, the efficient and the not so efficient: high seriousness blended with Ealing comedy. These contradictions are best illuminated in snapshots, and we have an aversion to turning these images into a completed whole.

One can be too flippant, however. We are dealing here with fundamentals – the very configuration of the Kingdom, how the Head of State and Parliament preside over that Kingdom, the superglue provided (we hope) by a deep devotion to the rule of law, including on the part of the mightiest in the land. Most of us may not think of these things much in our daily lives but they do matter, and we notice when they go wrong.

The special value of studying constitutional affairs is that the conventions, even the most elusive of them, capture the decencies on which the entire structure, human and institutional, depends for its proper working. The constitution is a question that lies at the heart of the resilience – or otherwise – of the nation, and not just in terms of our own sense of national worth; it's also critical to how the rest of the world sees us. To be a proper rule-of-law nation is, at the very least, like having an extra armed service in addition to the Army, Navy, and Air Force. It is part of the defence of the realm because it reveals what it is about the realm that is worth saving in every circumstance. Nothing so important can ever truly be boring.

The Queen as a Heineken-lager monarch: The parts of the constitution that only she can reach

Jubilee Lecture Series, Dulwich Picture Gallery, 3 January 2012

1952. It's hard for us to recapture it – even if we were breathing at the time. It is the year of the Great Smog, a cocktail of pollutants which hits London hard. It seeps everywhere. Audiences at the back of the Royal Festival Hall can't see the stage. Mortality rates in the capital rocket up by 120 per cent.

Anthony Eden, our debonair foreign secretary, declares that joining a federated Western Europe 'is something which we know, in our bones, that we cannot do' (some things never change!). The cheese ration is reduced to one ounce per week. The first ever British pop chart is published (Al Martino's 'Here In My Heart' is the first number one). The de Havilland Comet makes the world's first commercial jet flight, carrying thirty-six people from Heathrow to Johannesburg for BOAC.

The Cold War is at near-freezing point. Stalin is still in the Kremlin. We explode our first atomic bomb off the north-west coast of Australia. The Americans test their first hydrogen bomb in the Pacific. The Korean War continues to rage. Eisenhower is elected president of the United States.

But the one thing we all remember is that in early February 1952 King George VI dies and his daughter is proclaimed Queen Elizabeth II on 8 February on her return from Kenya. The first of her twelve prime ministers,[1] Winston Churchill, met her off the plane.

Churchill adored her and began to plan the most splendid

---

1 By the time of her death in 2022, this tally had reached fifteen prime ministers.

coronation austerity Britain could afford. On the night of 3 January 1953, aboard the *Queen Mary* somewhere off Newfoundland and on the way to New York for Churchill's meeting with the soon to be inaugurated General Eisenhower, his private secretary, Jock Colville, sat up late with the Grand Old Man after a good dinner in the huge Cunard's famous Verandah Grill and fired at him questions he might be asked at the press conference.

> COLVILLE: How do you justify such great expenditure on the coronation of your queen, when England is in such financial straits?
> CHURCHILL: Everybody likes to wear a flower when he goes to see his girl.

Churchill was a twenty-four-carat romantic, both about the Monarchy, and the British constitution of which it is the apex. He thought parliamentary government within a monarchical system was nature's last word when it came to ruling free peoples. And he used his great word power and genius for encapsulation to convey its perfection.

Just listen to him at the Commonwealth Parliamentary Association coronation lunch on 27 May 1953 in the presence of the Queen he loved. 'In our island,' rumbled the unmistakable voice,

> by trial and error, and by perseverance across the centuries, we have found out a very good plan. Here it is: the Queen can do no wrong. But advisers can be changed as often as the people like to use their rights for that purpose. A great battle is lost: Parliament turns out the Government. A great battle is won: crowds cheer the Queen. We have found this a very commanding and durable doctrine. What goes wrong passes away with the politicians responsible. What goes right is laid at the altar of our united Commonwealth and Empire.

We'll hear some fine speeches this jubilee year – but we won't get a mixture of Macaulay and Gibbon to match that!

It's the Queen and the constitution upon which I want to concentrate this evening. Churchill made it sound as if the monarch were free of the risk of political peril – of fleeting politicisation – because of our doctrine that ministers advise and carry the can, always keeping the sovereign above the bumping and grinding of party politics and partisanship.

Generally, Churchill's dictum holds. But throughout her reign up to and including the general election of May 2010, the Queen has retained two key personal prerogatives – to paraphrase the old Heineken lager advert, powers that took her to those parts of the constitution that only she can reach:

1. Agreeing to a request from the prime minister to dissolve Parliament, thereby triggering a general election
2. Appointing a prime minister

Her shrewd and affable private secretary, Martin Charteris, explained it in terms of advice with upper-case and lower-case As. Normally, ministers (usually the prime minister) give the Queen Advice with a capital 'A', which she has to take. On the two personal prerogatives of dissolution and prime ministerial appointment, it's lower-case 'a' advice, which she does not have to accept and act upon.

The constitutional patch covered by that pair of prerogatives is the always delicate and sometimes potentially tricky terrain the monarch, from time to time, has to tread. It is all the more precarious because that constitutional turf is so little understood, sometimes even by those who wish to tread it *en route* to the prime minister's chair in the Cabinet Room.

Last year, a chunk of that turf changed. The Fixed-term Parliaments Act did that. 7 May 2015 is the date of the next general election, unless the coalition wishes and is able to activate an interim drill for dissolving Parliament by losing a confidence vote in the House of Commons, or on a motion 'That there shall be an early general election', passed by at least two-thirds of those entitled to vote and after failing to put in place an alternative administration that *can* command the confidence of Parliament over the ensuing fourteen days. As the Fixed-term Parliaments Bill began its passage, the Queen, as she always does, offered up her personal prerogative to Parliament should they wish to take it by statute, which they duly did.[2]

So, Her Majesty is now a modified Heineken-lager monarch. Still only she can prorogue Parliament, and most important of all, only she can appoint a prime minister. And it remains as important, I think, as it ever was at such delicate and fraught moments as an inconclusive result and the prospect of a hung Parliament for the Queen to be kept above the frenzy and neuralgia so that no aggrieved individuals or parties can ever say 'we wuz robbed by the Palace'.

Until very recently, the constitution on the prerogative appointment has remained – in the way we Brits have – unwritten. Until the run-up to the 2010 general election it remained one of what Sir Sidney Low a century and more ago called those 'tacit understandings which go into the making of our procedures and conventions.'

For over forty years we had, as a kind of surrogate for a written constitution on the personal prerogatives, a pseudonymous letter written to *The Times* in May 1950 by King George VI's private secretary, Sir Alan Lascelles (known as 'Tommy'), during a flurry of speculation that Mr Attlee's government might soon crumble having seen its majority tumble from 146 to 6 at the February 1950 general election.

Lascelles, decorum being all, hid behind the pseudonym 'Senex'

---

[2] Post-Brexit chaos put paid to the Fixed-term Parliaments Act. The election of 2017 was called early when Theresa May received the support of two-thirds of the House of Commons to do so. The 2019 election required a new Act of Parliament to allow an early election. The Fixed-term Parliaments Act was repealed in 2022.

– or wise old thing – and his words, *the* prime constitutional artefact on the monarch's personal prerogatives for the bulk of our lifetimes, became known as the 'Senex letter' in constitutional circles.

What did it say? 'It is surely indisputable (and common sense),' Lascelles wrote,

> that a Prime Minister may ask – not demand – that his sovereign will grant him a dissolution of Parliament; and that the Sovereign, if he so chooses [George VI is still king, remember], may refuse to grant his request. The problem of such a choice is entirely personal to the Sovereign, though he is, of course, free to ask informal advice from anybody he thinks fit to consult.

I rather savour the next paragraph – a little treasure from the days of closed government and high deference.

> Insofar as this matter can be publicly discussed, it can be properly assumed that no wise Sovereign – that is, one who has at heart the true interest of the country, the constitution and the Monarch – would deny a dissolution to his Prime Minister unless he was satisfied that (1) the existing Parliament was still vital, viable and capable of doing its job; (2) a General Election would be detrimental to the national economy; (3) he could rely on finding another Prime Minister who could carry out his Government for a reasonable period, with a working majority in the House of Commons.'

The 'Senex' system relied upon a number of things:

1. That all politicians competing for power would do the decent thing, show restraint, act with dignity and, at all costs, avoid any whiff of politicising the monarch. This is an example of what my old Cabinet Office friend Clive Priestley used to call 'the good chaps theory of government'.

2. That the great fixers of state would do their stuff in priming the pitch to enable this to happen. Who were they? They were the men that Philip Ziegler called 'the Golden Triangle' – the Queen's private secretary, the Cabinet secretary and the prime minister's principal private secretary.
3. It would be all right on the night.

A very British way of looking at things – and not without its merits.

However, in 1991, with the polls suggesting a hung Parliament if an election was called, my BBC Radio 4 producer, Simon Coates, and I set out to test Lascelles. Happily, Lord Armstrong of Ilminster, Robert Armstrong, who had sat at two points of the Golden Triangle at the Cabinet Office and Number 10, agreed to speak for the insiders for our programme *The Back of the Envelope*. The transcript of this broadcast, Robin Butler (another Triangle man) later confirmed, thereby became the British constitution on this subject. In essence, Robert confirmed that the Queen's personal prerogatives remained intact. 'In ... the hung parliament situation,' Robert Armstrong said,

> the Sovereign, and the Sovereign's advisers – and, one would hope, the politicians concerned – would have as primary objectives to ensure that the government of the country was carried on, and that everything possible was done to avoid the Sovereign being put into a position where action had to be taken which might bring the Crown into the area of political controversy.

Eloquent and clear though Robert characteristically was, I became convinced that these 'tacit understandings' needed to be written down and said so in my inaugural lecture, which Robin Butler kindly chaired, at Queen Mary in February 1994.

The ever-courteous 1990s Golden Triangle did consider the possibility. But they sided with Jim Callaghan, the former prime minister, who had said on the documentary: 'Well, it works doesn't it? So I think that's the answer, even if it is on the back of an envelope and doesn't have a written constitution with every comma and semicolon in place. Because sometimes they can make for difficulties that common sense can overcome.'[3] By the end of the decade, the Golden Triangle, past and present, had still to be persuaded. And in 2000, I reported their thinking like this:

> First, that flexibility is all-important; precise contingencies cannot be predicted, no two are alike. Published principles would bring rigidity to a part of the constitution which works well partly because of its capacity to adapt successfully to the unforeseen.
>
> Second, why should the Queen be the one person to be tied down? Party leaders might, under the pressure and heat of events, be capable of causing difficulties, but the Monarch could find herself trammelled by principles agreed with a set of departed party leaders, while she remained in post being the one figure in public life who can never retire (privately she has always ruled out the possibility of abdication).
>
> Finally, there is the doctrine of inappropriate time – that a period of trouble for the royal family is the wrong moment to suggest that the Head of State may not be in a position to carry out this part of her job safely and satisfactorily, if required, without change to past practice.[4]

I also made a stab at writing down that which the Triangle then wished to remain unwritten by distilling the essence of the Queen's two remaining personal prerogatives:

---

[3] Peter Hennessy and Simon Coates, *The Back of the Envelope: Hung Parliaments, the Queen and the Constitution*, Analysis Paper No. 5 (Strathclyde, 1991), 18.
[4] Peter Hennessy, *The Prime Minister: The Office and Its Holders since 1945* (London, 2000), 32–3.

- Only she can dissolve Parliament, thereby causing a general election to be held.
- Only she can appoint a prime minister.

After an indecisive general election, she is required to act only if the incumbent prime minister resigns before placing a Queen's Speech before Parliament or after failing to win a majority for that legislative programme in the House of Commons. The overarching principle at such delicate times is that the Queen's government must be carried on and that the monarch is not drawn into political controversy by politicians competing to receive her commission to form a government.

Normally an outgoing prime minister is asked to advise the monarch on the succession, but the monarch has to ask for it, and, if given, it is informal advice which can be rejected, rather than formal advice which can be rejected, rather than formal advice which must be acted upon. After an inconclusive result, if the incumbent prime minister resigns the monarch will normally offer the first chance to form an administration to the party leader commanding the largest single number of seats in the House of Commons.

A prime minister can 'request', but not 'demand', a dissolution of Parliament. The monarch can refuse. The circumstances in which this might happen would be, in Lord Armstrong's words, 'improbable'. But the power to withhold consent could be a check, in Lord Armstrong's words once more, on the 'irresponsible exercise of a prime minister's right to make such a request'. The circumstances in which a royal refusal could be forthcoming are, according to Sir Alan ('Tommy') Lascelles, author of the Senex letter, if 'the existing Parliament was still vital, viable and capable of doing its job' or if the monarch 'could rely on finding another Prime Minister who could carry on [his or her] Government for a reasonable period, with a working majority in the House of Commons'.[5]

5 Ibid., 33–4.

Lascelles's letter, which served as the British constitution on hung parliaments until Lord Armstrong gave his interview to the BBC Radio 4 *Analysis* programme forty-one years later, included a third ground for a monarch refusing a prime minister's request for a dissolution – that it 'would be detrimental to the national economy' – had been, I reported in 2000, quietly dropped in the intervening years.[6] But in 2010, as we shall see shortly, the condition of the economy *did* contribute to the political and constitutional weather system created by the parliamentary arithmetic of the May general election.

What changed? When? Where and why? Come with me now first to Ditchley Park in north Oxfordshire, home of the Ditchley Foundation, impresario since its creation in 1958 by the Wills family (devotees of the Anglo-American membrane) for innumerable off-the-record conferences, which have broadened considerably from the politico-military preoccupations of the Cold War into which it was born. With considerable prescience it hosted a gathering between 5 and 7 November 2009 chaired by the former prime minister, Sir John Major, on 'Managing the Machinery of Government in Periods of Change'.

The theme was transitions and Robert Hazell from the Constitution Unit at University College, London and Peter Riddell and Catherine Haddon of the Institute for Government brought with them impressive primers on the subject produced by their respective institutions.[7] American and Canadian participants came with plentiful comparative experience of their ways of doing it. Among the attendees were the Queen's private secretary, Christopher Geidt, and Alex Allan, chairman of the Joint Intelligence Committee, who, at the time, was deeply involved in helping the secretary of the Cabinet, Sir Gus O'Donnell, with transition planning for the

---

6 Ibid., 34.
7 Robert Hazell, *Elections, Transitions and Government Formation* (London, 2009); Peter Riddell and Catherine Haddon, *Transitions: Preparing for Changes of Government* (London, 2009).

2010 general election (as principal private secretary in Number 10 in May 1997 he had seen John Major out and Tony Blair in).

Ditchley operates on deep 'Chatham House' rules. But its director, Sir Jeremy Greenstock, writes a 'note' after each conference, to which is appended a list of participants. One reads it to the sound of some decorous fixing:

> ... as regards the UK scene, we had a healthy discussion about the procedures that might have to be followed if the election produced a hung parliament. There was no modern precedent for a situation of great uncertainty as to which political leader might be invited to form a government [the 'hung' result of the February 1974 general election being the last]. Moreover the provisions of the 'Caretakers Convention', which covered the arrangements for government in the meantime, were not widely known. Participants regarded it as extremely important to avoid a situation where a government might appear delegitimized, or the sovereign put in an impossible position, by a failure to draw up sensible arrangements in advance.
>
> There were precedents mentioned, particularly from New Zealand, which might have relevance. It was firmly suggested that unwritten rules or gentlemen's understandings were no longer adequate in the modern world. The current expenses scandal in parliament was an indication of that. We also heard an interesting input from recent Canadian experience, where the dual role of the Prime Minister as political leader and constitutional adviser had been seen as awkward [in the autumn of 2008 Stephen Harper had asked the Governor-General of Canada to prorogue Parliament when he found himself in difficulties in the House of Commons in Ottawa. She concurred, but it led to controversy].

'Participants', Sir Jeremy Greenstock's note reported, 'felt that there would be a willingness on all sides to take a very careful approach to this eventuality'. In his concluding list of 'priorities' for the UK, Sir Jeremy included the recommendation that:

> All predictable eventualities surrounding a hung parliament should be studied with some urgency, with clear guidelines written for the principal players, to the extent possible.[8]

What one might call the Ditchley Protocol resonated in Whitehall. The Cabinet secretary, Sir Gus O'Donnell, convened a meeting over a sandwich lunch in the Cabinet Office in mid-February, and at the end of the month he presented its written product to the all-party Justice Select Committee of the House of Commons. In so doing, Sir Gus named the outsiders who had helped draw up the 'Hung Parliament' section of the new draft *Cabinet Manual* (which drew heavily on the existing New Zealand one). And there was a considerable overlap with the Ditchley attendees the previous November, as Sir Gus made plain in his evidence to the Justice Committee on 24 February 2010.[9] Christopher Geidt, Alex Allan, Professors Vernon Bogdanor and Robert Hazell plus Professor Rodney Brazier (who had not been at Ditchley), Peter Riddell (who could not make the Cabinet Office meeting but sent in material), and me. Also there were senior officials from the Cabinet Office and the Ministry of Justice.

Those meetings at Ditchley and in 70 Whitehall marked a significant shift in UK constitutional history. Here are the key paragraphs of the draft *Cabinet Manual* which enjoyed a serious walk-on part in the events of May 2010. The '"Hung" Parliaments' section was captured in five paragraphs:

---

[8] 'Managing the Machinery of Government in Periods of Change', A Note by the Director (Ditchley 09/11, Chipping Norton, November 2009).
[9] House of Commons Justice Committee, *Constitutional processes following a general election*, Fifth Report of Session 2009–10, HC 398 (London, 29 March 2010), Ev 16.

16. Where an election does not result in a clear majority for a single party, the incumbent Government remains in office unless and until the Prime Minister tenders his and the Government's resignation to the Monarch. An incumbent Government is entitled to await the meeting of the new Parliament to see if it can command the confidence of the House of Commons or to resign if it becomes clear that it is unlikely to command that confidence. If a Government is defeated on a motion of confidence in the House of Commons, a Prime Minister is expected to tender the Government's resignation immediately. A motion of confidence may be tabled by the Opposition, or may be a measure which the Government has previously said will be a test of the House's confidence in it. Votes on the Queen's Speech have been traditionally regarded as motions of confidence.

17. If the Prime Minister and Government resign at any stage, the principles in paragraph 14 apply – in particular that the person who appears to be most likely to command the confidence of the House of Commons will be asked by the Monarch to form a government. Where a range of different administrations could potentially be formed, the expectation is that discussions will take place between political parties on who shall form the next Government. The Monarch would not expect to become involved in such discussions, although the political parties and the Cabinet Secretary would have a role in ensuring that the Palace is informed of progress.

18. A Prime Minister may request that the Monarch dissolve Parliament and hold a further election. The Monarch is not bound to accept such a request, especially when such a request is made soon after a previous dissolution. In those circumstances, the Monarch would normally wish the parties to ascertain that there was no potential government that could command the confidence of the House of Commons before granting a dissolution.

19. It is open to the Prime Minister to ask the Cabinet Secretary to support the Government's discussions with Opposition or minority parties on the formation of a government. If Opposition parties request similar support for their discussions with each other or with the Government, this can be provided by the Cabinet Office with the authorisation of the Prime Minister.

20. As long as there is significant doubt whether the Government has the confidence of the House of Commons, it would be prudent for it to observe discretion about taking significant decisions, as per the pre-election period. The normal and essential business of government at all levels, however, will need to be carried out.[10]

This cluster of paragraphs represented a great advance in terms of access to and precision of a particularly sensitive element of a hitherto unwritten part of the British constitution. And yet, there was a problem with it which became apparent once the election campaign was fully underway.

The all-party House of Commons Justice Committee had made public on 29 March that: 'We welcome the evidence of significant thought and effort being put into preparations for the full range of parliamentary election outcomes by the Government, and the Cabinet Secretary in particular'.[11] But Sir Gus had not consulted the Conservative or Liberal Democrat leaders directly[12] and both sounded rather iffy about the newly written 'hung' Parliament conventions when asked about them by journalists.

On 25 April Nick Clegg said:

I read that the civil service has published some book a few weeks ago ... that in an environment like that [Labour third in share

---

10 Ibid.
11 Ibid.
12 Private information.

of votes but in possession of largest number of seats], he would have first call to form a government. Well, I think it's complete nonsense. I mean, how on earth? You can't have Gordon Brown squatting in No.10 just because of the irrational idiosyncrasies of our electoral system.

Mr Clegg added:

Whatever happens after the election has got to be guided by the stated preferences of voters, not some dusty constitutional document which states that convention dictates even losers can stay in No.10.[13]

Quite apart from the means by which 'some book' published 'a few weeks ago' can mutate, in the space of a couple of sentences, to 'some dusty constitutional document', the wider question remained of what the British constitution *is* rather than what a party leader in the heat of an electoral race might *wish it to be*. David Cameron on 3 May, albeit more tersely, appeared to be making a similar point to Nick Clegg when he said: 'There is convention and there is practice and they are not always quite the same thing.'[14]

At the very least, the Clegg/Cameron line on the draft *Cabinet Manual* added to the sense of the British constitution going on heat when the exit poll was released at 10 p.m. on 6 May. From almost that moment on, arguments were made (starting with Theresa May in the first discussion on BBC 1's *Election 2010* programme) that, if the exit poll turned out to be accurate (which it did[15]), that Gordon

---

13 Isabel Oakeshott, 'You can't have Brown squatting in No.10 because of this clapped-out old system', *The Sunday Times* (25 April 2010).
14 Andrew Grice, 'Cameron set to challenge convention over hung parliament', *The Independent* (3 May 2010).
15 The exit poll predicted Conservatives 305; Labour 255; Liberal Democrats 61; other 29. The actual result was Conservatives 306; Labour 258; Liberal Democrats 57; other 28.

Brown had lost and should go. The Cabinet Office's piece of paper, however, turned out to be immensely useful to those who had, as it were, to incarnate the constitution *as it is* across a range of television and radio studios as the 'hung' Parliament unfolded during the small hours of 6–7 May and throughout the Friday morning. If we had only had the Lascelles letter of 1950 and the 1991 transcript of 'The Back of the Envelope' to wave around, our task would have been far tougher.

The Cabinet Office had 'war-gamed' a variety of 'hung' outcomes twice in the weeks before the election.[16] The permanent secretaries devoted much of their annual spring conference at the National School of Government in Sunningdale to related matters.[17] Teams of four civil servants were ready to help with advice and assistance for post-'hung' negotiations from the afternoon of Friday 7 May. A base in the Cabinet Office was established for Christopher Geidt, from which he could report developments to the Queen. Gordon Brown had given the Cabinet Secretary permission for this ahead of the election. He confirmed it on the morning of 7 May when he returned to Downing Street.

The strong advice from the Cabinet Office, the Treasury and the Bank of England was that the clock was ticking, that the bonds and the currency markets might move if deal-making took too long, and that a statement of intent on deficit reduction would be desirable on the Sunday evening before the markets opened on Monday morning. This happened when William Hague for the Conservatives and Danny Alexander for the Liberal Democrats did just that.[18]

In fact, after a flurry of Liberal Democrat/Labour talks on the afternoon of Monday 10 May and the morning of Tuesday 11 May, the Liberal Democrat and Conservative negotiations moved

---

16 Private information.
17 Private information.
18 Roland Watson, Sam Coates, Francis Elliott, 'Britain on hold', *The Times* (10 May 2010).

towards a coalition agreement on the Tuesday evening as Gordon Brown prepared to call upon the Queen with his and his government's resignation. It had taken one day longer to reach the final outcome than in 1974, when Ted Heath drove to the Palace to resign on 4 March.

Sir Martin Charteris, the Queen's private secretary in 1974, later relived the weekend for me when Ted Heath hung on, having lost his majority in the 28 February election, and tried to do a deal with the Liberals. He said, 'it was all very dicey'.[19] The five days that shook the British political system in May 2010 were not entirely dice-free. Neither David Cameron nor Nick Clegg ran against the conventions. And thanks, in considerable part, to the understandings for 'hung' Parliaments having been written down just over three months earlier, the British constitution had shimmered through. It did its stuff. It got us there with the royal prerogatives in place, a government capable of commanding the House of Commons and a monarch unsullied by political taint or the slightest whiff of controversy. The 'great ghost' was no more.

Where are we now?

Ready to have by your side for the early hours of 8 May 2015 – should the next election prove inconclusive – is the relevant section of the final version of the *Cabinet Manual,* published last October.

The wording on the incumbent prime minister's duties in hung circumstances is interesting. Take a look at paragraph 2.10:

> It remains a matter for the Prime Minister, as the Sovereign's principal adviser, to judge the appropriate time at which to resign, either from their individual position as Prime Minister or on behalf of the government.

After the 2010 election, a couple of select committees examined

---

19 Interview with Lord Charteris of Amisfield for the Wide Vision Productions/ Channel 4 television series *What Has Become Of Us?* (6 June 1994).

the question of whether the incumbent Prime Minister had a duty to stay in Number 10 until it was clear what form an alternative government might take. The House of Lords Constitution Committee was plain there was no such duty. From the careful wording of the next bit of paragraph 2.10 it looks as if the Cabinet Office would like there to be such a duty, even if it cannot assert as much. As always, under our historic constitution, the past is prayed in aid.

> Recent examples suggest that previous Prime Ministers have not offered their resignations until there was a situation in which clear advice could be given to the Sovereign on who should be asked to form a government. It remains to be seen whether or not these examples will be regarded in future as having established a constitutional convention.

We have come a long way from the early 1950s and that pseudonymous letter to *The Times* from the Monarch's private secretary.

Suffice it to say that, whatever form her constitution took – that letter, the Radio 4 transcript, the draft *Cabinet Manual*, and now the finished *Cabinet Manual* – the Queen has proved herself to be *the* exemplary monarch on this patch of her constitution, as on all others. Though I suspect that for her, as for us, a large dash of mystery remains.

In October 1992, Her Majesty the Queen visited Queen Mary, whose history department I had joined the month before. The actual occasion was the opening of our new arts building. As part of her programme she dropped into one of my undergraduate seminars, and it was quite plain that she'd been primed that we would be talking about the recently declassified document, 'Questions of Procedure for Ministers' (which later morphed into the Ministerial Code). She has a great gift for indicating when it's time to move on to the next bit of her schedule and, on this occasion, she did so by saying, 'the British constitution has always been puzzling, and always will be.' I thought, but of course did not say, 'Well you're it, ma'am, and if you don't understand it, what chance have we got of fathoming its beautiful intricacies?' Successive generations of my students found themselves baffled by the mysteries of the constitution; I used that quote to cheer them up.

The National Royal Service

Of all the United Kingdom's public services, only one finds its chair and chief executive on the basis of bloodline. Internationally, it is the most famous of all the country's public institutions – even more than the National Health Service. The former chair and CEO held the job for over seventy years. Her successor had been known for four years longer than that, from the moment he was born, in fact.

It was – and is – of course, the Monarchy: the most glamorous public service institution of them all and, the armed services apart (of which the monarch is also commander-in-chief), the only public-service-cum-nationalised industry that could never be privatised.

Interestingly, it was Winston Churchill who first came up with the idea that the British Monarchy was a kind of one-off variation of a nationalised industry. In the late 1940s, he wrote an intriguing short sketch called 'The Dream'. In it, he is painting at his country home, Chartwell in Kent, and his late father, the raffish Randolph Churchill, suddenly manifests himself in his son's studio. Randolph proceeds to interrogate his boy about all the changes to their country since he, Randolph, died in 1895. Naturally, he starts by asking what year it is now. 1947, Winston tells his dad. Part of the exchange runs like this:

'What party is in power now? Liberals or Tories?'
'Neither, Papa. We have a Socialist Government, with a very large majority. They have been in office for two years, and will probably stay for two more. You know we have changed the Septennial Act to five years.'

'Socialist!' he exclaimed. 'But I thought you said we still have a Monarchy.'

'The Socialists are quite in favour of the Monarchy, and make generous provisions for it.'

'You mean in regard to Royal grants, the Civil List, and so forth? How can they get those through the Commons?'

'Of course they have a few rebels, but the old Republicanism of Dilke and Labby is dead as mutton. The Labour men and the trade unions look upon the Monarchy not only as a national but a nationalised institution. They even go to the parties at Buckingham Palace. Those who have very extreme principles wear sweaters.'

Winston always loved teasing Labour.

So far, there has been no real threat to the survival of the British Monarchy since the abdication crisis of 1936. Not even from sweater-wearers on the Left. There have been rises and falls in popularity, however. A YouGov poll in April 2023 found 61 per cent want Britain to continue as a monarchy, and 24 per cent would prefer an elected head of state. Among 18–24-year-olds, 33 per cent wished the Monarchy to survive.[20] After the Diamond Jubilee in 2012, the figures were 75 per cent to 17 per cent, with 64 per cent of the 18–24-year-olds wanting to keep the Monarchy. But generally speaking, from 1994–2021, on average two-thirds of the British people wanted the Monarchy to remain.

Those who would prefer a British republic would, I'm sure, disagree with this notion of a National Royal Service. But I think it fits the recent history of the institution and is embodied in particular in the person of Queen Elizabeth II. Frank Prochaska's notion of a 'welfare monarchy', using its charitable work and its public duties as a way of affirming the institution's place in the affection of the bulk

---

20 YouGov Survey (18–20 March 2023): d3nkl3psvxxpe9.cloudfront.net/documents/Internal_RoyalTrackers_230320.pdf.

of its people, captures the degree to which Elizabeth II was queen of the post-war settlement on which was built not just the NHS but a substantially extended welfare state – all undertaken in a thoroughly non-politicised fashion, though the parties at Westminster were often divided on policy and funding, even at the higher points of the post-war consensus. The Queen's gift was to place herself in the mainstream of national and public life, without the slightest trace of political partisanship.

The Queen's detachment from the political fray, while being richly briefed on its protagonists and its intricacies, was in itself a form of service, made all the more effective because it seemed to come quite easily to Her Majesty, who might, in House of Lords terms, have been characterised as a natural crossbencher.

Her constitutional duties could, at certain moments, such as a hung Parliament resulting from a general election, take her close to the rim of a particularly intense form of politics. But she never crossed the undrawn line. It was made clear by her private secretaries, in their back-channel conversations with politicians competing for power, that the television cameras had to wait at the Westminster end of the Mall and not outside her front gates at Buckingham Palace – in other words, the politicians would have to sort out amongst themselves who should have the chance to become prime minister rather than leaving the choice to her, thereby avoiding any risk of her institution being seen as the determining player in who was invited to form a Cabinet and who was not. Perhaps the most important of our unwritten constitutional rules was that the Queen was not to be embarrassed under any circumstances, a central notion of the 'good chaps theory of government'. An elected president, however distinguished, who had a political past could never be entirely free of suppressed partisanship at such moments of political fluidity.

There was a human element to this, too. People always behaved better in the presence of the Queen than they might otherwise have done, partly because of her natural dignity, but also because of her impeccable observation of the requirements of a limited constitutional monarchy. To argue that she used her plentiful personal charm as a weapon would be a touch crude, but it did help, as one of her private secretaries once suggested to me, that her male prime ministers tended to be a bit in love with her. Perhaps those who were less good chaps than others made the careful calculation (rightly) that if they did appear to embarrass the Queen their political opponents would energetically point this out and the public would not be amused, as happened with the prorogation of Parliament at the request of Boris Johnson in September 2019 (later judged to be illegal by the Supreme Court). Maybe rule number one, even of the most brutal form of British politics, was that you don't mess with the Queen.

In my darker moments, I sometimes think that the only bit of the British constitution since 1952 that's lived up fully to the requirements we have of it has been Queen Elizabeth's conduct of the Monarchy. Her father was a fine exemplar and teacher for her. And her son, Charles III, looks set fair to have an Indian summer kingship of duty, purpose, and distinction without straying into areas of policy where, given his earlier and quite trenchant views on some matters, his well-wishers feared he might tread.

As the National Royal Service's most accomplished CEO ever, Queen Elizabeth II did not put a foot wrong during her seven-decade tenure. She operated without a job description and only once did she make plain her personal manifesto for her kingdom – and that was over tea and cakes with her fellow members of the Sandringham branch of the Women's Institute, not long before she experienced the retirement that, in her case, only death could bring.

She was tiny in stature, funny in private, shrewd rather than intellectual, possessor of the most potent raised eyebrow in the land and loved by the vast bulk of her people. Oh, and lest we forget, she was also supreme governor of a world religion known as the Anglican Church, in whose spiritual boss – Almighty God – she had complete faith.

On the side, through a strange, sometimes impenetrable set of conventions and longstanding procedures and expectations, the Queen presided over the British constitution, which she confessed to find puzzling. I spent a sizeable chunk of my professional life searching for her constitution. I never found it. I was glad I didn't. We all need mysteries we cannot fathom.

She was the number-one customer for the weekly summary of the British intelligence product produced by the Cabinet Office and knew a thing or two about the world and those who led its multiple nations. A head of one of the secret services once told me that the Queen asked him far more penetrating questions than the secretary of state to whom he was nominally responsible. And some of her most secret servants were terribly impressed when, suitably disguised as diplomats, they received an honour from her expressing gratitude for the quality of some of the particular briefings that these secret servants had drafted for her. She was fabulously discreet. World figures relished her company. She was a formidable listener and the globe's mighty told her things. At home and abroad, she believed – as she practiced – all the decencies. Another private secretary spoke of her 'relentless common sense'. She was *the* gold-standard constitutional monarch.

Critics of the Monarchy have always pointed to the huge personal wealth of the Queen and asked how one of the richest people in the world could ever come to understand the lives of those of the poorest or even the middling classes, as they used to be called in the nineteenth century. I think that empathy does not depend on sharing the incomes or the quality of life lived by those less fortunate. It's a human thing, a question of humanity and sensitivity, attributes that Queen Elizabeth had in abundance. Another line of attack from critics of the British Monarchy was that it held in place all the status obsessions which have bedevilled our politics, society, and economics. For me, these blights have far deeper roots than the survival of a constitutional monarchy. For example, the divide between capital and labour – a great rift bequeathed by the industrial revolution – is by far the most potent poisoner and had nothing to do with the occupant of the house at the end of the Mall.

To be candid, I think the real reason I'm such a convinced monarchist is that she showed what her highest of offices could do, not just in terms of soft power influence abroad, but also in making the people she met through the course of her everyday duties feel just that bit better about themselves. Few, if any, politicians have this gift that, for all her shyness, seemed to come naturally to Queen Elizabeth. And as for many of the people who might have been elected president if she and her institution were not there, the laws of libel prevent me from mentioning individuals and their deficiencies.

Her father and mother brought the Monarchy out of the wreckage of the mercifully short reign of King Edward VIII and during the war, as they paced through the hot ruins of many a blitzed town or city, they added mightily to the stock of goodwill their people felt for them and their institution. Their elder daughter added powerfully to that stock of capital.

Unlike other national public services, the stock of esteem in which the institution of monarchy is held relies heavily on the character and personality of the woman or man at the top. Princess Margaret, for all her verve, had perhaps a less acute sense of personal duty. A Queen Margaret Monarchy would undoubtedly have had a different character. Counterfactual history is always perilous, and it is impossible to have any real idea whether or not a Queen Margaret would have enjoyed those approval figures. What is for sure is that a Margaret queenship would have been littered with joyous indiscretions. She would undoubtedly have been a box-office queen in a very different sense than her sister was.

When Queen Elizabeth died, the nation felt a high degree of shock, even though her loss was anticipated. For most of us, she had simply always been there. The sight of mourners, shuffling in zig-zagged lines for twelve hours to see her coffin lying in state in Westminster Hall, was eloquent – even allowing for the peculiar appetite of the Brits for a good queue.

I miss her. I wish her son and her institution well. She did us proud over seventy years in which the UK, and the world – its science, and its economy – changed more, more quickly, than any other comparable period in history.

Queen Elizabeth never gave interviews. One of her courtiers once asked me what question I would ask if she gave me the chance of putting but one. I replied: 'Of all the changes in your Kingdom since 1952, which of them, ma'am, have you found it the hardest to adjust to?'

My friend asked me to guess at her answer. I suggested the loss of civility. My friend thought there might be something in that (as did one of her private secretaries). It was as close as I ever got to what, I suspected, was one of the keys to understanding the inner Queen Elizabeth. A good try, perhaps. Certainly no more than that.

Oh, and that manifesto at the Sandringham Women's Institute, delivered on 24 January 2019 – it's quite short, but it's very her:

> As we look for new answers in the modern age, I for one prefer the tried-and-tested recipes, like speaking well of each other and respecting different points of view, coming together to seek out the common ground, and never losing sight of the bigger picture. To me, these approaches are timeless and I commend them to everyone.

A UK state of mind

When I look back to my shaping impressions of our islands and those who live on them, they are very much influenced by the coronation year, 1953. I was only six years old but boyish impressions undoubtedly were the sediment that later morphed into bedrock of expectations and, indeed, beliefs. I absorbed, partly because of the dazzling new Queen and her handsome consort, that we were a highly favoured nation, which had pulled off a rather spectacular trick. For all the problems afflicting a still war-exhausted nation, we had managed to combine tradition with modernity in a very special way. I became an avid weekly reader, for example, of the *Eagle* comic. The *Eagle* had a marvellous double page on the latest breakthroughs: the plan for a new Gatwick airport, which was going to take care of our air-travel needs for generations (I wish); Calder Hall on the edge of the Lake District, which my Uncle George helped build, was to be the site of the first reactor to put nuclear power into a national grid. We had reached for the sky with the first jet-powered civil airliner, the Comet, though tragically the aircraft began to fall out of the sky because of a design defect which was eventually remedied. Yet, somehow, the coronation, with its ancient language and its near-timeless setting in Westminster Abbey, showed that we had not lost an ounce of our almost instinctive sense of the past. Looking back, it seemed that we showed the world that you could mingle the timeless and the new in a mutually fructifying fashion – in short, that we were a success-story nation. The more I think about it, I have almost unconsciously taken that as my psychological norm when writing the history of post-war Britain, with all its subsequent disappointments, albeit vicissitudes studded with gleaming success stories such as breakthroughs in pharmaceuticals and surgical procedures and, I would argue, the extension of scholarship and learning through vastly expanded access to further and higher education.

My younger grandsons are six and eight – close to the age I was when Queen Elizabeth was crowned. I sometimes wonder what they and their contemporaries might make of their country of birth today. My fear is that it will be much harder for them to acquire the enduring sense of optimism that I've been lucky enough to carry through thick and thin since the early fifties, so pervasive are our current anxieties about society, economy, and politics. The run-up to the world in which my lovely boys are beginning to make their way and acquire their own certain notions of that world and their country are very different from the decades that made me. For example, the first two decades of the twenty-first century were uncomfortable and stretching. A world which we had hoped would stay on a relatively benign trajectory, following the ending of the Cold War without a military confrontation or nuclear exchange, was plunged into what became sustained anxiety after 9/11. It soon became apparent that coping with and containing jihadi terrorism could well be a forty-year task, and one in which our own streets were part of the front lines.

At the end of the decade, the financial crisis – the great crash of our day – showed how instantly vulnerable we were to a serious shock almost anywhere in the global economy. Its ever more sophisticated and sensitive membranes of exchange seemed designed to transmit crisis and instability into nearly every crevice of an increasingly integrated world. In addition to this now perpetual risk was added at least ten years of austerity with a relative starving of funding for public services in nearly all their forms, which inevitably placed immense and constant strain on central and local governments, the National Health Service, and, it sometimes seemed, all the enterprises that went into the making of a society relatively well-provided for by our own particular mixture of liberal capitalism and social democracy.

The cumulative effect of such financial and fiscal austerity was inevitably a society not just less at ease with itself but becoming year-on-year more unequal and resentful. There was even an outbreak of rioting in 2011. It was not on the scale of 1981, but it was still serious enough to shock a country that continued to believe civil unrest was something that happened elsewhere. Sadly, Britain also saw an outbreak of rioting in the summer of 2024.

Some of the destabilising factors were shared with other advanced countries. Globalisation is a cruel geographer. Its disbenefits disproportionately hit those towns, cities, and regions that grew mighty in the First Industrial Revolution. Time and technology were increasingly leaving them behind. The golden triangle of the south-east and the city state of London might glisten ever more brightly, but the once shining areas and the industries that begat them felt the dispiriting pang of relative economic decline. The pain was manifested in dilapidated housing, lack of jobs, the gutting of once proud communities, and a shrivelling of life chances for those who, if more favourably located, would have flourished under more benign and expansive conditions.

There were, naturally, specifically British destabilisers at work, both individually and in tandem, contributing to this age of anxiety. One was the constitution itself – the rules of our own game – which piecemeal and incrementally had seemed to operate so successfully, if incomprehensibly, for so long. There was a time when we almost flaunted our constitution as a badge of eccentricity, like *The Goon Show* or *Hancock's Half Hour*. It brought, so we thought, great flexibility in being unwritten, with very little going wrong that couldn't be put right by a bit of judicious tweaking by Olympian figures in authority deploying restraint, wisdom, and a gift for muddling through. Not so now. The constitution is still baffling but very few think it is working well. It is no longer a shock-absorber, which is its primary function. Looking at my own formative years, I could never have imagined the instability which is now the constant companion of this once deeply settled union. Almost daily, we are beset by capital 'Q' Questions, which, like all big 'Q's, are to a high degree interrelated and interlocked: the Scottish; the European; the Place-in-the-World.

We very nearly lost Scotland in the referendum of 2014. Had a few votes shifted the other way, it would have left us a much-diminished kingdom. I am English. And like many English people, at the grandparent level, I can claim one Scots and one Irish relation, though in instinct, spirit, and identity I feel British. I cannot imagine myself in any other way. This naturally colours how I think about the union of the UK. One of the greater frustrations in recent years has been the fact that I am an observer of the scene, not a participant, having no vote in Scotland. My fear is that the road to Scottish independence – if it happens in the coming decade – will be paved by a degree of English indifference, for all the centuries of lives lived together and the intermingling of families and much, much more. In fact, indifference may be too kind a word in some cases. For one of the three 2022 UK prime ministers thought the solution lay in a single insight – that she should simply ignore the First Minister of Scotland and not talk to her. In the end it turned out to be the only policy of Liz Truss's premiership that was implemented, albeit for only forty-five days.

I am not indifferent. I have been a union man since I was ten years old, when I first went to Scotland in a tiny Ford Prefect full of camping gear and family, driven eccentrically and rather erratically by my father from Finchley to the Isle of Skye (which was a titanic journey in those pre-motorway days). Since then, to adapt the opening lines of General de Gaulle's memoirs, I have always had a certain idea of Scotland – of how we have fought and bled together, taught and read together; invented and manufactured together; politicked and organised together; laughed together and wound each other up, generation upon generation.

For example, Scottish independence would mean no more MPs elected to the House of Commons from Scotland and, after a period of time, very few Scots in the House of Lords. Our political life would be greatly diminished. The spice and wit would go out of many debates. The distinctive tang of Scottish politics, with its different traditions and special instincts, would leave us bereft. Of its very nature, it's hard to predict quite how this would play out and what the characteristics and political culture would be of an overwhelmingly England-dominated and shrunken future Kingdom.

Loyalty to the union for me does not arise as the product of a careful audit of pros and cons, a balance sheet of the two nations. It is above all a state of mind – and a romantic one at that – which takes it far beyond the reach of cost-benefit analysis and the stagnant prose of a management consultant's appraisals. I do wonder if I would feel these factors so powerfully if that Ford Prefect hadn't set forth from North Finchley in 1957 and I'd never visited Scotland or built friendships in its universities and among its politicians and journalists. Mere reading and glancing at an atlas cannot of themselves fire the blood. I like to think that I would be a union man nonetheless, but I can't be sure.

Casting the romance aside, one of the lessons we should have learned from Brexit is how monstrously difficult it is to unscramble an integrated economic market, even though in the case of the EU we had been a reluctant member for no more than forty-seven years. The profoundly deeper integrations that would be seriously altered if not, in many cases, abolished with Scottish independence would make it an immeasurably more difficult operation to carry out than the dreary business of sending European directives back home on the ferry from Dover, always, of course, assuming they're running. Remainer though I was and am, the sound of one solitary Scottish piper, his or her pibroch competing with a howling gale, is far more a summoner of emotion than anything European integration has brought me.

There are multiple Scottish flavours that are the products of place, faith, political conviction, economic experience, and even geology. There are many Scotlands, just as there are many Englands and plentiful Waleses. But I have a special relish every time I'm projected from City Airport, London in the knowledge that I shall soon be landing on the soil of my nation state, yet in a very distinctive country, and that within a couple of hours, as the little plane touches down in Kirkwall, where family live, I shall be in a Norse-touched statelet, itself very different from the central belt where I changed aircraft.

In terms of social instincts, the Scottish characteristic that I cherish most is the powerful pull of egalitarianism. Scotland is in many ways a very class-conscious country, and its political culture is notably more leftward than the English equivalent. Though I have always disliked any trace of class warfare, Scotland does, to me, seem noticeably less burdened by excessive status-consciousness. The northern isles have this in even more abundance. This tempers what, for me, is the worst blight of a certain kind of Englishness. I remember Denis Healey saying to me of my one political hero, Clem Attlee, that as Labour leader he wanted to end the class war rather than to win it. Of course, Clem failed. And it won't happen in my lifetime. Perhaps it's the hardest of our blights to shed, but it's an aspiration we should cling to.

And what of Europe and our relationship with it? No single word is more freighted with political anguish in our recent history. If some clairvoyant had told me in the late 1950s, when I was first reading the newspapers every day, that the political issue which could cause the greatest and most protracted disruption of our national life would be trade, I would have thought they were both wrong and faintly obsessional. Compared to the perils of the Cold War in the thermonuclear age, or even shedding our territorial empire abroad, our trading relationship with Europe would have come a distant and very boring third. I have always been hopeless as a political forecaster.

Historians are discouraged from constructing hypotheticals. But I have long wondered if, had the British economy had grown as dynamically as the French and, above all, the West German in the early post-war years, we would have been tempted down the

European route to industrial and commercial buoyancy. It was as if we flung pretty well everything else at the problem of sputtering economic performance before, reluctantly, turning our eyes south and east to the booming factories and swish new roads of the six members of the original common market. For I think that, apart from a few Euro-enthusiasts, probably most British people have never been fully enthused by the whole idea for a number of reasons. Partly, it lacks romance, but it's also built around a process of continuous negotiations, conducted in impenetrable language by the sort of people you would avoid at parties.

One by one, the alibis for our relative economic failure fell away: after 1965 we were no longer burdened with the running of a large empire; just over ten years later the pound sterling ceased to be the world's second reserve currency after the US dollar – the pound had already ceased to be trammelled by fixed exchange rates in the early 1970s; and following Mrs Thatcher's installation in Downing Street, the back of excessive trade union power was broken. None of them, singly or in combination, turned out to be the elixir we'd hoped, so bit by bit we persuaded ourselves that ours had to be a European future. We developed a lullaby to ease the pain of this reluctant transition. It ran something like this: once we get in, all the high-flown continental rhetoric would give way to the cool, hard realism of the suave professionals in the British Foreign and Commonwealth Office. However, the lustrous self-image we had of our gifts in the statecraft department (and there was much in it) never came anywhere near rupturing the Franco-German axis that made the weather in the Community. We felt we were not built as a people or a country to be also-rans. It hurt – and hurt breeds resentment. Yet the best and brightest we had in politics and diplomacy devoted their peak professional years to getting us in, keeping us in and striving (albeit failing) to get the best exit deal possible. Many of them sit now in the House of Lords and I respect them and feel a high degree of gratitude towards them. But how I wish a growth rate of 4 per cent a year, for this and for so many other reasons, had been ours for the generating, enabling us to be a serious player in the world without the tedium of instructions from Brussels. For, to adapt P. G. Wodehouse, it's always easy to distinguish between a ray of sunshine and a European directive.

This makes me sound, perhaps, like a closet Eurosceptic. I'm not. The greatest single gift that European integration has brought not just to us but to the world is that it ensured that France and Germany would never go to war with each other again (which is why the first industries to be pooled were coal and steel, the sinews of war, in the original Community). Many years later, when the Cold War ended and the former Soviet satellites were freed from the forty-year tyrannies that had crushed them, EU membership was an absolutely crucial element in ensuring they did not return to the dark of a closed and authoritarian society with a grim command economy and a secret police force. Sadly, these geopolitical fruits were not generally appreciated by the British and rarely came up in our endless internal in–out debate. As for the UK now, I am convinced that we would be better in than out, and not just because of the permanent 4 per cent hit to our gross domestic product that the Office for Budget Responsibility has predicted (and indeed is happening already as a consequence of Brexit).

Finally, apart from Ted Heath, the prime minister who presided over our entry, no British premier has sung a convincing song of Europe to our people. Instead, we've had a dispiriting procession of leaders, who have done a perfectly good job of securing British interests at the Council of Ministers, returning home to deliver a protracted whinge about 'how ghastly are some of the partners?' and 'how ruinously tedious are the negotiating sessions?' The only consistently inspiring element in the whole enterprise was the choice of the last movement of Beethoven's choral symphony as the EU's anthem, but not even Beethoven could pep it up in the ears and the imagination of the British people. The hardest audit of all of our European years would be to measure the time and nervous energy we displaced upon this question, time and attention diverted from so many other pressing needs. And why was it so ruinously disrupting of our politics? Because the traditional Left–Right divide could not and still can't handle it. The European question cut like a volcanic fissure through our political landscape and released levels of venom that no other question came close to. At the worst moments of the Brexit debate, its poison saturated our whole political conversation and, unlike so many other political debates, this one reached well beyond the normal limits of political engagement and attention from one end of the Kingdom to the other. Because it became a question about who we are, what we are, and what we're for.

The Master, better known as Noël Coward, had a wonderful line in his 'Mad Dogs and Englishmen':

It seems such a shame
When the English claim
The earth
That they give rise to such hilarity and mirth.

There are a number of things wrong with that sentence. For a start, the Empire was a bit thin on hilarity and jokes for those on the receiving end. But, lurking within it is a recognition of an appetite for expansion, on sea and on land, into places that are not our own. The Empire is long gone and its history is rightly much debated. But the Great Power impulse is not; it is still very present. Europe was a way, we thought, of sustaining our global reach once the realities removed our wholly owned empire.

Have a read of the most recent expression of the British strategic impulse. Its title lacks excitement: *Integrated Review Refresh 2023*.

> In order to pursue our core national interests, and in support of broader international goals, the UK must [note the word 'must'] be able to shape the environment in which it operates. As a permanent member of a Security Council of the United Nations, member of the G7, one of the biggest defence and development

spenders, and one of the largest economies in the world, the UK will always retain a global perspective [note the word 'always'] – and this is becoming more, not less, important in a more contested and multi-polar world.

I have some sympathy with this. The UK has real skills at the mix of diplomacy, defence, secret intelligence, and international development that enable us, with our allies, to do good and necessary things in a nasty world. But I wonder if this is what an old MI6 friend of mine once asked of his service: are we 'the itch after the amputation?' (He was referring to the genuine global reach British intelligence enjoys above all through its special-intelligence relationship with the United States.)

I am too, as I have always been, a believer in retaining a small but significant nuclear weapons capacity against the admittedly highly unlikely day when all that stands between us and ultimate peril is a sheaf of 'don't even think about it' missiles somewhere beneath the North Atlantic.

But what worries me in the *Integrated Review* document, as in all its predecessors since the end of the Second World War, is that the aspiration always outruns the money that the Treasury will cough up for these purposes, leaving the Armed Forces ever stretched in terms of numbers and weapons.

There is another problem whose complexities run through our geopolitical debates like a tarnished thread. We cannot bring ourselves to face up to the possibility that sheer economic stress may at some point require the UK to drop one of the big elements of its place in the world. Instead, we keep up a fistful of core capacities in the belief that global influence more generally requires us to sustain them. The impulse is not ignoble, but perhaps a sense of reality is lacking. Of one thing I am near certain: the successor documents to the *Integrated Review Refresh 2023* will also contain paragraphs deploying such words as 'must' and 'will always' when it makes its case for sustained global influence.

Britain and Europe: The emotional deficit

*Lecture given to the University of Iceland/
British Embassy, Reykjavik, 18 May 2007*

It is 4 June 1944, just two days before D-Day, when the liberation of northern Europe will begin. Charles de Gaulle, the extraordinary leader of the Free French, has just arrived in England from North Africa. He has been rushed from the airport to Winston Churchill's special wartime train, parked in a siding somewhere near Portsmouth, from where a large part of the invading forces were soon to cross the English Channel to Normandy. As so often, the two formidable men have a blazing row, triggered, as it usually is, by de Gaulle's prickliness towards his allies, President Roosevelt particularly. This is how de Gaulle records the scene in his memoirs:

> 'And you!' Churchill cried. 'How do you expect that the British should take a position separate from that of the United States.' Then with a passion which I sensed was destined more for his British colleagues than for myself he said: 'We are going to liberate Europe, but it is because the Americans are in agreement with us that we do so. This is something that you ought to know: each time we have to choose between Europe and the open sea, we shall always choose the open sea. Each time I have to choose between you and Roosevelt, I shall always choose Roosevelt.'[21]

This, to adapt a phrase from the social anthropologist Clifford Geertz, is 'deep play' British politics. Churchill's outburst finds

---

[21] Charles de Gaulle, *War Memoirs Vol. II: Unity, 1942–1944* (London, 1956), 277.

resonance, for example, in the overt words and action of Margaret Thatcher as prime minister and Tony Blair's *actions*, if not his rhetoric. The only post-1945 British premier who was a Europhile both in Brussels and at home and at every other conceivable occasion was Ted Heath – the prime minister (and probably the only leading political figure of the time who could have managed it) who took the UK into the European Economic Community in January 1973.

The EU we know today is very different from the EEC of 1973 and even more so from the original, six-member European Coal and Steel Community of 1951, from which all else has developed. And to understand Britain's relationship with an integrated and ever more integrating Europe it is to the fifteen-plus years after World War II that we must turn, especially as that formative period is now almost entirely forgotten by my fellow countrymen and women – even though we all still live, breathe, and trade in its shadow.

Historians don't normally do theory – we leave that to political scientists and tend to sneer at what they come up with. But I do have a theory about the Brits and international institutions. We are a relatively internationally minded people, but we are only at ease with global institutions if we wholly owned them (like the British Empire) or can convince ourselves that we invented them (like NATO).

General Ismay (universally known as 'Pug') – Churchill's military assistant during the war and the first secretary general of NATO – when asked what the purpose of NATO was, said that it existed for three reasons: to keep the Russians out, the Americans in, and the Germans down.[22] A wholly British way of looking at it. And there's truth in it – as there was in Ernest Bevin's tireless efforts as post-war British foreign secretary to draw the US into a proper alliance with Western Europe.

---

22 I have not seen written evidence of this marvellous one-liner, but it's been Ministry of Defence folklore for generations and was passed on to me by more than one very senior figure.

If the UK *had* made the running on a plan for early post-war European integration and succeeded (and it really was the dominant Western European power for the first ten years after 1945), it would have been a very different animal.

It would not have been a customs union with a tariff wall against the rest of the world, as the European Coal and Steel Community, the EEC, and their mutations had been. It would have been like the European Free Trade Area – a free trade area between seven non-EEC European nations but without external tariff walls against the rest of the world. EFTA was also free of the long-term, Monnet-like vision of an ever-closer political and economic union. This was the 1956–8 UK alternative to the Treaty of Rome. Only when de Gaulle finally wrecked the idea in 1958 was the EFTA set up on the initiative of the British government.

Such an arrangement would have enabled the Brits to sustain their economic relationships with the Commonwealth and the remaining Empire (which had such a dominant place in the 1950s calculations – and emotions – of Whitehall and Westminster). Like all other countries, the UK wanted for itself the best of all worlds.

In fact, in negotiating what became the Treaty of Rome in 1957, the French secured all they needed to sustain their relationships with 'metropolitan France' (their remaining empire). And we all know how brilliantly the early sixties design for a common agricultural policy fitted the needs of French farming (just as the Coal and Steel Community had fitted perfectly the industrial needs of post-war French economic plans).

The Brits really hankered after the loose but effective arrangements of the Organisation for European Economic Co-operation – the instrument for implementing the Marshall Plan. British prime ministers – Heath apart – have, to varying degrees, been uneasy with all the organisations that have followed since.

The philosopher Bernard Williams, in a BBC radio discussion with me some years ago, alerted me to an intriguing idea. Williams's thesis was that the thought patterns of an institution or organisation, and the language in which they were expressed, reflected the minds of the institution's founders and determined the overall organisational DNA for evermore. When you ponder the formation of the Coal and Steel Community (as dreamt up by Monnet during a walk in the Alps over Easter 1950), it was the creation of him and his team of clever, Catholic, left-wing, French bureaucrats. Every one of those words rouses a problem for many Brits.

If a Brit or two had invented the Coal and Steel idea, the language of directives would have been very different; perhaps not quite 'would you mind awfully seeing your way clear to doing this if it's not too inconvenient' but something veering in that direction.

There are many other ingredients to Britain's emotional deficit with the idea of Europe. Prominent amongst the characteristics we believed made us not just a distinctive but a singular nation were our still-recent global imperial experience, our economic, industrial, and technological prowess and our, to us, much-prized gifts in diplomacy and statecraft. Put together, they inclined us to think we were not just any other nation, not one of the world's also-rans. And, to some extent, this self-image of being a highly favoured nation meant that we didn't have to have a written constitution to keep us clean and decent. We knew what proper and proportionate government was when we saw it. Therefore, the idea of an integrated Europe was fine for *them* but quite unnecessary for us. Churchill, on returning to office in 1951, had been critical of Attlee and his ministers for being churlish towards the ECSC. But this is what he told his Cabinet:

> I never contemplated Britain joining in this plan on the same terms as the continental partners. We should, however, have joined in all the discussions and, had we done so, not only a better plan would probably have emerged, but our own interests would have been watched at every stage.
>
> Our attitudes towards further economic developments on the Schuman lines resemble that which we adopt about the

European Army [the French Plan for a European Defence Community]. We help, we dedicate, we play a part but we are not merged and do not forget our insular or Commonwealth-wide character. I should resist any American pressure to treat Britain on the same footing as the European states, none of whom have the advantages of the Channel and who were consequently conquered.[23]

His opposite number, Clem Attlee, put it even more succinctly. His friend Douglas Jay told me that Attlee's very last political speech was made, at Douglas's request in 1967 at a meeting of Labour Euro-doubters, shortly after Douglas had been sacked from the Cabinet by Harold Wilson for his pronounced lack of keenness about Europe. A frail Clem had been helped to the platform and in his characteristically dry, undemonstrative voice said: 'The common market, the so-called common market of six nations. Know them all well. Very recently, this country spent a great deal of blood and treasure rescuing four of them from attack by the other two.' Then he promptly sat down.

The bulk of Churchill's Cabinet thought like him. Anthony Eden, his foreign secretary, famously said in a speech at Columbia, New York, in 1952 of the European Army: 'It is something which we know, in our bones, that we cannot do.'

There are, as John Major's pro-European colleague and later EU commissioner, Chris Patten, put it, real elements of 'psychodrama' in the story of Britain's relationship with Europe from that day to this. It was – and remains, however – psychodrama with a hard geopolitical edge which goes under the name of the US–UK special relationship.

NATO trumped any French attempt at UK–French economic collaboration in 1949. The Korean War loomed far larger in 1951

---

23 Quoted in Peter Hennessy, *Having It So Good: Britain in the Fifties* (London, 2006), 287–8.

Whitehall than the ECSC idea (which Attlee's Cabinet had rejected in the weeks before North Korea invaded the South).

The hard-edged geopolitics of the Coal and Steel Community was not fully appreciated in London except by Oliver Franks, who was ambassador to Washington at the time the Attlee government spurned the idea of Britain joining the ECSC. Franks told me that Robert Schuman, the French foreign minister, explained to him that by pooling the war-making industries, France and Germany would be locked in an embrace so tight that they could not raise their fists against each other ever again. At this, Schuman wrapped his arms around his chest to illustrate the impossibility of raising a fist.

What mattered was what David Reynolds called the 'geometric conceit'. The overlapping circles of the US–UK special relationship, the Empire/Commonwealth and – very much a poor third – Britain and Europe. Still for Tony Blair, the Atlantic relationship will – in tough times – trump the European one. True, I think, of all eleven post-war British PMs except Heath.

The sinews of the 'special relationship' are intelligence and nuclear. There are still those who want the UK to join NAFTA,[24] or, as a second best, to withdraw to an Icelandic position – memberships of the European Economic Area but breaking free in all other aspects (neither is a practical runner). Today most realise that when the guns sound it is special-relationship time, but in everyday, humdrum, sloggy, boring economic and trade affairs, it's the EU.

It took a long time for the Brits – or most of them – to come to this uneasy compromise. And even when the special relationship has been seriously ruptured, as it was over the invasion of Suez in 1956, the restoration of the Anglo-US norm has happened swiftly and as a matter of priority on the British side.

---

24 The North American Free Trade Agreement. A modified United States–Mexico–Canada version of this agreement (USMCA) came into effect in July 2020.

In addition, the concept and importance of Britain in Europe was never so easily explained to the British people. There was no equivalent of Ismay's one-liner about NATO that explained it and made sense to pretty well everybody. The person who came closest to finding a Ismay-type formulation was Nigel Broomfield, the former ambassador to Bonn, who suggested that the idea of the enterprise was to keep democracy in and barriers down.

The *real* value of the European project (beyond the economic) cannot be stated clearly. To my mind, comparable in magnitude to Schuman's notion about pooling the war industries, was the capacity of the EU to become the instrument for absorbing the former Soviet Bloc satellites and Greece, Spain, and Portugal once they had been freed of tyranny – a geopolitical shift of immense and wonderful significance. To my mind, this alone justified the existence of the EU and made the case for our sharing in it, but nobody made the case that way, and even if they had, as time elapses the danger is that, like the Coal and Steel idea of a war preventer, the integration of former tyrannies will be taken more and more for granted and perhaps lose its bite as a persuader.

The emotional deficit so far has never dissipated, and the British have yet to discover how to cherish the EU.

Keeping calm and carrying on: British crises since 1945 and the special case of Brexit

Vice-Chancellor's Lecture, University of Birmingham, 12 June 2017

This lecture was delivered four days after the 2017 general election, in which Prime Minister Theresa May lost her overall majority in the House of Commons.

In offering a taxonomy of crises, I have in mind the remarkable Victor Rothschild, Lord Rothschild, scientist, wartime bomb-disposal expert in MI5, and banker, who became the head of the fabled 'think tank' – the Central Policy Review Staff – which Ted Heath set up shortly after becoming prime minister in 1970.

To describe the nature of government, Victor drew on Aldous Huxley's depiction of life as 'routine punctuated by orgies,' and it's that which I offer as my template for this evening's look at crises. Why? Because they tend to fall into perpetual and, therefore, familiar crises and sudden, unforeseen, and, therefore, often highly destabilising eruptions.

Related to the Rothschild/Huxley approach is Quinlan's Law, so-called in memory of Sir Michael Quinlan, the most outstanding defence intellectual in post-war Whitehall. In December 2008, shortly before his untimely death, Michael placed a note in his private papers which read like this:

A theorem. In matters of military contingency, the expected, precisely because it is expected, is not to be expected. Rationale:

What we expect, we plan and provide for; what we plan and provide for, we thereby deter; what we deter does not happen. What does happen is what we did not deter, because we did not plan and provide for it, because we did not expect it.

Very true – and not just in politico-military matters.

Back to Rothschild. Routine first; by which I mean rolling crises. Some examples first from Quinlan territory. The refreshed National Security Strategy and Strategic Defence and Security Review, on which the Cabinet Office has been working for some weeks in case the government wished to commission one post-general election, will be – if it happens (as I hope it will) – by my calculation the thirteenth since 1945 (they have gone under a variety of labels). The Whitehall analysts' world is one of both routine and orgy. The routine is the constant tension between aspiration and resources and the attempt to reconcile the two. There are no iron laws of British government any more than there are iron laws of history. But there are two near-guaranteed characteristics of defence reviews:

1. The Treasury never fully funds the outcome – hence the rolling crises in defence procurement and spending.
2. They are, in part, always overtaken by unseen events, usually beyond the control of UK governments.

For example, the first of them, the Harwood Review of 1949, was designed to keep defence spending at an average of £700 million a year up to 1952–3 but was blown away by the rearmament triggered by the Korean War, which erupted out of the blue in June 1950. Similarly, the Chiefs of Staff Report on Defence Policy and the Global Strategy of 1952 simply did not anticipate the Anglo-French invasion of Egypt in 1956 – the Suez affair – which had a profound impact on foreign, defence, Empire/Commonwealth, and, eventually, European policy for several years to come.

Other examples of rolling crises are the eternal pressure on health spending, almost constant since 1948–9 when the fledgling National Health Service overspent the Treasury's estimates in the key first year of its life – hence the years since 1948 being punctuated by frequent health reviews and reorganisations. Though interestingly enough, in an intriguing contrast, constant pressure on welfare spending is different. We haven't had what one might call a comprehensive welfare review since the Beveridge Report of 1942 (though Frank Field is working up a paper on the desirability and sizing and scoping of just such an enterprise[25]).

On the economic front, since the time the American Loan ran out in the so-called 'convertibility crisis' of August 1947, we have had a succession of pound-sterling crises thanks to what one seasoned Whitehall figure called our 'thinly lined Exchequer' – a problem which neither the abandonment of fixed exchange rates in 1971 and sterling's role as a world reserve currency after the great IMF crisis of 1976 has remedied. We have, have we not, experienced a huge devaluation of the pound since the early hours of 24 June 2016, when it became clear that the Leave vote was going to prevail, and the pound took another tumble in the early hours of last Friday when the prospect of a hung Parliament loomed.

There was an interesting element of Quinlan's Law at work here. The Prime Minister and Cabinet had expressly forbidden Whitehall departments from doing any contingency planning for a Brexit, just as the Cameron government had earlier done for any planning for a Scottish separation from the UK after the referendum of September 2014. (The same ban, by the way, still applies in the case of Scotland.) I'm beginning to think – in my gloomier moments – that unpreparedness has been elevated to a central principle of British governance. In the case of Brexit, however, the Bank of England, given its independence, could and did plan for a Brexit result last June and was thereby in a better position to help steady the markets.

---

25 This was later published by Frank Field and Andrew Forsey as *Not For Patching: A Strategic Welfare Review* (London, 2018).

By contrast, that other source of constant tension – and occasional eruptions of serious crises – the forty-year Cold War – led to an abundance of contingency planning and transition-to-war exercises every two years (the so-called Wintexes) with our NATO partners – the paper trail of which can now be found in the National Archives at Kew. And a truly chilling read it is, though it does have its lighter touches.

May I briefly tell you the story of Harold Macmillan and the launching of nuclear retaliation in the early 1960s? The background is this. Lord Louis Mountbatten, the chief of the defence staff, was convinced that the British Prime Minister, like the US President, needed to be accompanied at all times by an officer carrying a briefcase containing the launch codes for the country's strategic nuclear weapons capability. Macmillan didn't want any fuss. The Treasury didn't want to spend any money. So a very British solution was created: the Prime Minister's Rolls Royce would be fitted with an AA radio like the ones used by the smartly uniformed Automobile Association men on bikes on Britain's main roads (who would salute you smartly if they saw an AA badge on your bumper). If an unsuspected nuclear assault was picked up by the RAF's radars and aroused the question of retaliation, the AA link would come into play and alert the Prime Minister to get out of the car and into the nearest telephone box.

The file reveals that the new system was ready to go in May 1962 (in good time for the coming but unanticipated Cuban Missile Crisis). Tim Bligh, Macmillan's principal private secretary, was informed of it by Bryan Saunders, his opposite number in the private office of the Minister of Works (then responsible for the Government Car Pool). In an exchange of letters even P. G. Wodehouse could not have dreamt up, Saunders tells Bligh that the 'radios have now been fitted in three cars':

> I understand that these radios are to be maintained by Pye's [then an electronics company based in Cambridge] and it will

presumably be necessary for someone to make a daily or weekly call to the AA Control Stations as a check that they are in working order ...

I understand that if an emergency arose while the Prime Minister was on the road, the proposal is to use the radio to get him to a telephone. Perhaps we should see that our drivers are provided with four pennies [in the early 1960s it was necessary to insert four old pennies and press 'Button A' before a call from a GPO call-box could be connected] – I should hate to think of you trying to get change for a sixpence from a bus conductor while those four minutes are ticking by!

Bligh, it turned out, was on top of the problem. Replying to Saunders, he wrote:

The first sentence of your last paragraph is correct. But a shortage of pennies should not present quite the difficulties which you envisage. Whilst it may be desirable, when motoring, to carry a few pennies in one's pocket, occasions do arise when by some misfortune or miscalculation they have been expended and one is penniless. In such cases, however, it is a simple matter to have the cost of any telephone call transferred by dialling 100 and requesting reversal of the charge, and this does not take any appreciable extra time. This system works both in normal and S.T.D. [Subscriber Trunk Dialling] telephone kiosks, and our drivers are aware of it.

This being Whitehall, there was a fall-back plan forming in Bligh's mind: 'We are considering the possibility of this Office taking up membership of the AA – which would give our drivers keys to AA and RAC boxes throughout the country.'

If I'd been leaked this information (as opposed to finding it in a document) I wouldn't have believed it. Nor would the KGB resident in the Russians' London Embassy in the early 1960s, had it somehow reached him. He would have thought it a spoof – Ealing comedy as applied to the end of the world.

Those AA radios were fitted to the prime ministerial cars in the spring of 1962 in time for the Cuban Missile Crisis the following autumn – the famous thirteen days during which the world came very close to the abyss, far closer than we realised at the time. This wasn't a routine crisis, not like the rolling Berlin crisis which had been running since 1958. This was out of the blue and fast moving, with the danger of escalation haunting every move by each protagonist.

For Macmillan's government – especially the small inner group of ministers he used to run the UK end of it – Cuba was orgy, not routine. Stretching, intense, and highly personal – not just in Macmillan's regular telephone conversations with Kennedy, but in his decision, as prime minister, to place the RAF's V-bomber force on Alert Condition 3 (i.e. fifteen minutes' readiness over the weekend of 27–8 October 1962).

The Cuban experience led to a highly secret review of warbook procedures which fed into revised transition-to-war drills. Near wars, like Cuba, and real wars, such as the three-month Falklands campaign in 1982, are intense absorbers of time, energy, and crisis management far from the routine crisis with which I began. Returning to the contingency planning theme, given Russia's military resurgence – not least its increased and increasing submarine activity in the North Atlantic – it is, in my view, time to revive those 'Wintex' exercises. We are not yet in Cold War II but there are some chilling resonances in play.

To return also to the possible new National Security Strategy and Strategic Defence and Security Review that might be forthcoming in the autumn, it really must include this time, as it did not in either 2010 or 2015, a treatment of the consequences of a Scottish separation, not least because by 2020 the UK's entire submarine strength will be based at Faslane in the Clyde Naval Base. Even though last week's election result has probably caused the next Scottish referendum to move deeper into the 2020s, I think such planning should be done.

The other reason for the Prime Minister to commission a full-blown look at not just UK defence but Britain's place in the world is, of course, Brexit, which, when it happens, will represent the greatest geopolitical shift in our global position since the disposal of the British territorial Empire.

A few initial thoughts on the contrast between those two shifts. Over forty colonies, territories, and dependencies were granted independence between the end of British rule in India in 1947 and the shift from Rhodesia to Zimbabwe in 1980, with a veritable cascade of imperial disposals in the ten years after the Gold Coast became Ghana in 1957. The timing was largely but not wholly in the hands of British ministers and Lancaster House was the scene of many an independence negotiation (the very room, in fact, where Mrs May outlined the UK's Brexit negotiating stance on 17 January in what I hope was an intended piece of symbolism).

Brexit is very different. It all has to be done, if Article 50 is adhered to, by the end of March 2019, and twenty-seven of our soon to be former EU partner nations have to be carried in approving the terms (and/or approving an extension to the negotiating period), as does the European Parliament.

In wider terms, the Prime Minister and the Cabinet have to carry the British Parliament and the public too. Apart from one or two fringe groups, there was some sadness but no great resistance to the shedding of empire. The question did not make the weather in the way the European question does when it transits from the 'routine' (i.e. boring and near-incomprehensible) category to the 'orgy' category, when it catches fire and inflames the British body politic as no other question quite can. In short, Brexit is likely therefore to be both a routine and an orgy experience for the government, Parliament, and country: tedious stretches of negotiation punctuated by great technicolour eruptions.

Now to a few thoughts on the events of the past eight weeks. For

Thursday's vote will be seen by historians as *the* European general election. It would not have taken place if the country had voted to Remain last June. And its nature had a great deal to do with the juxtaposition of the two types of electoral democracy we now operate in this country at the trans-UK level: The so-called plebiscitary democracy, of which referendums are the instrument (still a relative novelty in the UK), and which cut, I think, against the grain of the representative democracy with which we are deeply familiar and which provides the political arithmetic on the benches of the House of Commons.

The essence of the electoral contest of the past eight weeks was the absorbing by our system of representative democracy of the consequences of our burst of plebiscitary democracy in June 2016. And a great deal of tumult and friction it produced – plus a high degree of surprise.

The analysts have barely started work on the deeper significance of the results but there does seem to be a correlation between Remain areas and Labour's unexpected performance, as there does between the surge in voting from the 18–24-year-olds (who in 2015, with but 43 per cent of them turning out, were a byword for lassitude) and the remarkable 72 per cent turnout last week. The surge, in fact, was initially triggered by the European question, because 64 per cent of that age group voted in last year's referendum. So the Euro impact plus the Corbyn effect was one of the serious factors in last week's election result. At last, the great expansion of university education in the UK has changed its electoral geography. Of course, general elections, of their nature, are multiple-issue phenomena, unlike referendums with their binary choices (though many factors feed into those apparently primary-colour options). Mrs May never had a chance of keeping the 2017 election a largely single-issue affair any more than Ted Heath had in the 'Who rules?' election of February 1974 during the miners' strike.

General elections, in terms of policy questions, are promiscuous affairs. They are also what one might call organised crises, with a choreography all their own. The metabolic rate of British politics rises and the political markets run in parallel.

The first political market is the way in which general elections stress-test both political parties and party leaders. The ways both Mrs May and Mr Corbyn conducted their campaigns took pretty well everyone by surprise and powerfully affected the result.

Mrs May, for all her virtues, turned out to be a hopelessly uninspiring campaigner and became embroiled in the intricate matter of funding for social care. Beyond that, she just stuck by her phrase promising strong and stable government, letting the contrast with Corbyn become apparent by inference. What should have been a walkover election victory turned out to be a path to political nightmare. Mr Corbyn produced, by British standards, a hard-Left programme, which most of the British public found unappealing, although he ran a much more successful campaign that anybody had anticipated. A previous Conservative leader, who was actually expected to lose, John Major in 1992, placed his homely, decent characteristics on top of a soap box (literally) and won a smallish overall majority but the biggest vote share ever.

The second political market running in parallel is the internal party one – the power and authority of the party leaders within their own tribe. This ran throughout the election but went into a steep and fast-moving trajectory once the early results began to confirm the exit poll. All day Friday and over the weekend these internal party-political markets played out. They still are and will continue to preoccupy the national conversation when Parliament reassembles next week with the Queen's Speech, originally planned for a week today, coinciding with the first day of Brexit negotiations in Brussels but now due to be postponed for a few days to allow for the Conservatives to attempt to do a deal with the DUP.

The Brussels negotiations will begin in very different circumstances than seemed likely but five days ago. They were meant to be the moment when a prime minister and a government began to unfold their exit-negotiating hand with an enhanced authority and confidence that comes with an overall and increased majority in Parliament. As Disraeli wrote in his 1847 novel, *Tancred*, 'a majority is always the best repartee.'

The opening exchanges next Monday will be polite; the rough stuff will come later. Firstly, I suspect, over the amount of money the UK will have to find for the divorce settlement. Nonetheless, last Thursday's election result will be a weathermaker in that room in the European Commission.

The task for UK negotiators is enormous. And there is no precedent, no road map. The 'exit from Empire' negotiations were very different and there was a high level of consensus in UK politics that the time had come to shift from territorial Empire into a free-association Commonwealth. By contrast, current UK politics is riven both by the Brexit question itself, the nature of the deal beyond it, and even whether such a deal should go ahead without yet another burst of plebiscitary democracy in the shape of a second referendum.

I don't think the magnitude of the task – both the Article 50 process itself and the size of it for years beyond formal exit at the end of March 2019 – has quite sunk in.

The new figures are breathtaking in themselves. Over what will now be forty-six aberrational years spent as part of an integrating European Community, we have put into either statute or statutory instrument 19,000 EU legislative acts. Since 'Brentry' in January 1973, to borrow the neat term coined by *The Economist*, some 900 EU directives have been implemented. And, as the *Financial Times* reported two weeks ago after a special investigation, the UK, thanks to Brexit, will need to renegotiate 759 international agreements with 168 countries.

This will absorb for years to come copious quantities of time and nervous energy in both Westminster and Whitehall. Wherever you stand on the Great European Question, this is going to stretch us with its own special mix of mind-numbing routine punctuated by sporadic political orgies.

Both alongside and wider than Brexit, what I would like to happen once Parliament reassembles is for the Prime Minister to establish a royal commission to take a long hard look at our place in the world as we begin to engineer the extraordinary geopolitical shift of Brexit and afterwards.

The royal commission, were it to be created, could begin with an audit of the assets we possess as a country with a continuing appetite to punch heavier than our weight in the world.

What might such an audit look like? Here's my stab at it:

- We live on top of the world's sixth largest economy (albeit with deep-set problems such as low productivity, which a succession of industrial strategies – the current one is the ninth since 1945 – have failed to remedy).
- We are one of the permanent five members of the UN Security Council and, because of our history, we belong to more international organisations than any other country.
- We have a range of top-flight Armed Forces, containing within them some stunning specialities, such as special forces and the submarine service.
- We possess a top-of-the-range nuclear deterrent that has sustained continuous at-sea deterrence since 14 June 1969.
- We have a fistful of high-quality intelligence and security services.
- Thanks to intelligence-sharing arrangements, we are one of only three countries in the world with global intelligence reach. The key institutions are the so-called 'Five Eyes' and the 'Two Eyes'.[26]
- Closely allied to this, we still possess a first-rate diplomatic service and an uncorrupt civil service.

---

26 The Five Eyes are the UK, the USA, Canada, Australia, and New Zealand. The Two Eyes are the UK and the USA, although this arrangement has never formally been admitted to.

- Now for the trade statistics that always cheer us up: 1.5 per cent of the world's population; 5 per cent of the world's scientific papers; 15 per cent of the world's most cited scientific papers (as everyone in the university world knows, Brexit poses a threat to this prized UK prowess).
- Other elements in our rich barcode of 'soft' power include the BBC World Service, the British Council, publishing, and plenty of other ingredients in what Melvyn Bragg calls our 'cultural world service'.
- Our parliamentary system, which for all its shortcomings – sometimes procedural, sometimes human – remains the indispensable core of our open society.
- Finally – and you may think this is an eccentric entry into our tally of assets – we lead the world in self-irony and understatement (though our understatement is under increasing threat from the rise of the celibritocracy – as opposed to the meritocracy – in our society). As George Steiner once put it, we are an 'oh, come off it!' nation.

That is a formidable list (though I'm sure each of you would wish to add and subtract from it). There are plenty of reasons to be cheerful.

However, even without the political uncertainty and that extra shot of instability provided by last week's election result, we would be contemplating today a particularly vexing rolling crisis across a wide landscape – a range of problems illuminated by the referendum of June 2016. We discovered to what a high degree we have become in the UK an extended family that no longer knows itself. We have become a society of growing individual and locational inequity – a society ill at ease with itself, constantly looking for things to fall out over rather than to fall in about. A country that gives the impression – not least to itself – that we have forgotten the traditions of civility and tolerance on which we can draw. The Brexit debate – which will continue throughout the coming period of negotiation and almost certainly beyond – leaves us on what a Crown-servant friend of mine calls 'permanent grudge-watch.'

As for our Euro grudges, a great book awaits someone on the psychodrama of our relationship with an integrating Europe ever since May 1950, when Jean Monnet turned up in London out of the blue from Paris bearing a plan for a European Coal and Steel Community. We have long, as a country, had both a structural and an emotional problem with Europe. The structural first. Europe is not a Left–Right question and is not, therefore, easily handled by our traditional Left–Right party divide. Europe busts up parties from within. The emotional problem is to do with many factors. It wasn't something we controlled, like the Empire. Nor could we claim we came up with the idea, like NATO. It was almost as it was designed to irritate with its terrible, intrusive directives and its wafty aspiration for 'ever-closer union', to quote the first bit of the Treaty of Rome.

Irritation will be at the high end of the Richter scale on the road to March 2019. Fasten your seatbelts.

Talking of the British Empire, may I finish by telling you of an intriguing moment in its long history – a special benchmark that was crossed on election day. It was 'The Farewell Event' of the Overseas Service Pensioners' Association – the members of the old Her Majesty's Overseas Civil Service. They gathered in the Grand Connaught Rooms in Holborn – the district officers, the agricultural advisors, the engineers, members of the colonial governors' secretariats, and their families – for a drinks reception with the Prince of Wales, followed by a farewell lunch, as there are but a few of them left.

As we waited for Prince Charles to arrive, Richard Luce – Lord Luce – who began his professional life as a district officer in Kenya before becoming a politician and, later, a government minister, turned to me and said, 'the Empire dies today.'

So it did. On 8 June 2017. It went out quite unnoticed, thanks to the cacophony of an election day brought about by the vicissitudes of the great post-imperial adventure which was supposed to be our place in Europe in the 1960s, when nearly all the remaining colonies and crown dependencies were, quite rightly, granted their independence. Fifty years on from Brexit, will old Euro hands gather in the Grand Connaught Rooms for a final farewell lunch? I suspect not.

On the Shelf: Peter Hennessy on Walter Bagehot's *The English Constitution*

The Sunday Times, *3 December 1995*

Each time I try to make sense of the foibles of our politicians and the rules of the game they pretend to live by, there it sits above my desk staring at me through the modest rust covers in which Fontana enclosed its 1963 edition – Walter Bagehot's *The English Constitution*. It has followed me around, literally and intellectually, ever since the autumn of 1966 when as a newly arrived undergraduate at Cambridge I began turning its pages late one night in that bit of the Library which St John's College kept open for the sleepless and the hyper-conscientious.

Bagehot was at my shoulder in the 1970s when I attempted to portray the secret workings of government as *The Times*'s Whitehall correspondent. He stayed there in the 1980s as I sought to calibrate just how much collective responsibility had suffered from Mrs Thatcher's fabled handbag. And he sat right beside me in the 1990s when, quite deliberately, I revisited his chapters and wondered in my book *The Hidden Wiring* what he would now make of the once-golden pentangle of monarchy, prime minister, Cabinet, Parliament, and the Civil Service were he still among us.

Every monarch since Edward VII has learnt what being a constitutional sovereign means from Bagehot's pages – which began as columns dashed off for *The Fortnightly Review* in the 1860s. And ironically, his zest-laden paragraphs on the monarchy reflect the part of this bafflingly unwritten phenomenon that Bagehot understood least. He was wonderfully well-connected in Whitehall and

Parliament, but the palace never yielded to this extraordinarily energetic man.

As every undergraduate knows, *The English Constitution*, published in 1867 (the same year in which the Second Reform Act extended the vote to a chunk of the urban working class, thereby changing the nature of British politics profoundly as its effects seeped through the pores of the body politic) was in the process of obsolescence almost before Bagehot checked the proofs. His approach, however, is timeless.

For Bagehot sought the 'living reality' behind the persiflage and, with a few exceptions, found it, by observing acutely and talking widely. He is – or should be – the patron saint of every political journalist who veers towards the analytical and the thoughtful rather than the trivial or the transient.

He hated the notion of a fully enfranchised nation and feared the coarseness and the small 'c' conservatism that the uneducated might inflict on the rational Liberalism he embodied. His heroes were Peel and Gladstone. He cared not for Disraeli and loathed the 'mob'. Had he not died at 51 in 1877 he would, I suspect, have found that the future was another country and regretted it.

In other ways Bagehot was far ahead of the pack in his prescience. As early as 1871 he sensed politics moving away from Westminster to 'out of doors', as Gladstone put it, when he witnessed that self-same Mr G working a crowd of out-of-work dockers from sullenness to enthusiasm in his Greenwich constituency. It was acuteness of observation plus sheer wordpower flowing through a turbo-charged pen that made (and has kept) Bagehot so special. As a result *The English Constitution* has gone through edition after edition. It's very rare for anybody's words to cascade so powerfully down the generations, stimulating yet more cataracts as they roar by.

Bagehot might even have his uses within the Leader of the Opposition's office as Tony Blair prepares for the real thing. For, two years before he died, he wrote a sparkling essay on the premiership which ought, even now, to be absorbed whole by any aspirant to the top job.

The prime minister, Bagehot wrote, 'is at the head of our business, and, like every head of a business, he ought to have a mind in reserve. He must be able to take a fresh view of the contingencies and keep an animated curiosity as to coming events. If he suffers himself to be involved in minutiae, some great change in the world ... may break out like a thief in the night, and if he had not elastic thought and no spare energy he may make the worst errors.'

'Mind in reserve', 'animated curiosity', 'elastic thought', 'spare energy' – these are as crucial to an effective premiership in 1995 as they were in 1875. How's that for enduring utility?

Speech on the Rwanda Bill

House of Lords, 29 January 2024

This extraordinarily controversial bill to send failed asylum seekers to Rwanda was eventually passed by the Sunak government, but one of the first acts of the Starmer government was to stop the planned flights to Kigali.

My Lords, to understand a nation and its people, you need a feel for the inner bundle of practices, characteristics, and states of mind that create the image a country carries of itself, which, in turn, shapes the way that others see it.

For those of us fortunate enough to have been nurtured within the bounds of our cherished archipelago in the cold northern seas, the rule of law has a fair claim to be the most lustrous of our values – almost talismanic in its properties. So anything that threatens, weakens, or tarnishes our crucial, defining value – the inspirational principle for governing and living well together – is a first-order matter.

I regret to say, My Lords, that the Bill before us today falls into that category. For this is a moment of immense significance for Parliament, the Judiciary, our people, and the very quality of our democracy.

In no way do I diminish the electric charge the question of uncontrolled immigration generates. But I fear that the Government has become fixated on its talisman – the Rwanda policy – which, ministers claim, will break the economic model of the cruel, evil, heartless people who put the boats and their desperate passengers to sea off the beaches of Northern France.

For what it's worth, my own view is that it cannot be beyond the capability of Whitehall to work up a scheme for the swift despatch of asylum claims with safe and humane shelter provided in the UK for claimants while they wait for the results of their applications.

By rushing this emergency legislation through Parliament with the intention of getting the deportation flights to Kigali underway by late spring, the Government has already secured for itself a special place in British political history.

The day may not be far off when the Rwanda Bill, having cleared all its parliamentary stages, will be forwarded from the Cabinet Office to Buckingham Palace to receive the royal assent. In the few minutes it takes to pass down The Mall and across the tip of St James's Park on its return journey to Whitehall, our country will change.

For the Government will have removed us from the list of rule-of-law nations. We shall be living in a different land, breathing a different air in a significantly diminished Kingdom.

My Lords, is that what any of us *really* want?

Selling my book *The Prime Minister* with a little help from my friends. London, 2021.

PART THREE

PRIME MINISTERS, PARLIAMENT, AND POLITICIANS

Often the most interesting places to be as a student, a writer, or a journalist are the borderlands. I've been drawn for decades to the often-baffling frontier where Parliament and government meet in functional and human overlaps. It's partly that politicians change when they become ministers – I don't just mean in the crude sense that they acquire airs and graces, though some do. It's wider and usually more honourable than that. Clem Attlee, customarily pithy in his summing ups, caught it perfectly when appointing Jim Callaghan to his first junior ministerial post in 1947. As Jim recalled for me, Clem said, 'Remember Callaghan, you are playing for the first eleven now, not the second eleven. And if you are going to negotiate with someone tomorrow, don't insult him today.'

I have a genuine appetite for institutional history, something which is not widely shared even perhaps by most of my fellow historians. As a writer, I've often found that mini-biography is the best way to kindle interest in a wider period. After all, the human factor is a more appealing place to start than, say, the public expenditure cycle. And prime ministers, are, by definition, quite unusual – and therefore interesting – people. For example, nearly all of them have a highly developed appetite for power and, therefore, an equally elevated self-belief in their specialness and utility to the country fortunate enough to have acquired their services. On the other hand, they almost all have a high and genuine public-service impulse as part of their wider motive power. These two elements can seem paradoxical and even in conflict with one another. But their interplay is one of the fascinations of the craft of political biography.

I've met ten of the seventeen post-war prime ministers, some just briefly, but others I've spoken to in some depth, almost invariably after they've left office and are willing, as it were, to fall into the arms of political historians. On such occasions, I've usually warmed to them more than I expected. This may, of course, partly derive from their no longer being in command of all the trappings of office. All of the prime ministers I have met have been genuinely interesting people. Quite often their character in person is distinctly at odds with the public perception. For example, John Major is a deeply engaging man: self-ironic, rueful, and straightforwardly good fun, quite unlike the grey figure of media portrayal. Alec Douglas-Home, similarly, could be terribly funny about himself and was not the stiff, remote aristocrat of the caricaturists' imagination.

Of course, of all the post-war prime ministers, I would have loved to have met Attlee, although the interview would have been rather short. Looking back, I envy the Queen having had a chat with all of the prime ministers since 1952 once a week. Her first encounter with each as prime minister would have been at a moment of relative euphoria on their part, as they arrived at Buckingham Palace to metaphorically kiss hands and accept her invitation to form her government. She would also have seen them in the pits of despair, when this often-cruel profession cast them low. The Queen was well-known for being a sharp and witty observer of character. Just imagine what a stunning book she could have written on her prime ministers.

Of course, it's not just the man or woman at the top that matters. Parliament made them, and Parliament can break them. Even when a prime minister is not facing a profound crisis, his or her reputation is in play every week when Parliament is sitting in Prime Minister's Questions. The thirty-minute weekly torment of PMQs amounts to a barometer of reputation, and a leader's performance at the despatch box, faced by a sometimes howling opposition, is a crucial element in their party's morale. Equally a run of good PMQs is no protection against a sudden fall.

Nearly all prime ministers are obsessed by how history will judge them. What follows is not as lofty as that. It's a series of overflights of the living, some in real time, and reprises of the dead. In the case of Tony Blair, his reputation has been so overshadowed by the invasion of Iraq it may seem rather quaint to revisit a piece from the time before that searing event. However, as a historian it's useful to remember that it's not just the great weather-maker events that are deeply revealing of a premiership.

There are also two pieces that focus on the arrivals and departures of prime ministers. I'm not given to grand historical theories, and you will find none here. Rather these are offerings that may show some interesting commonalities, if not grand historical patterns.

Never did so many talk such drivel: On the quality of political language today

The Independent, *25 September 1989*

Am I alone in finding the party conference season the most depressing phase in the political year? It gets to me every time. If I think about it, there are three reasons for my revulsion.

First, the spectacle of the politically inflamed, dropping prejudice after banality into a hall packed with people similarly afflicted by a high political charge, is deeply unpleasant. Almost anything goes, the cruder and more partisan the better – and it's on television hour after hour.

Fear amounting to terror is piled on disgust when I remind myself that these are the people who pick the candidates for general elections. As a group they are the selectorate for the Cabinet ministers of the future. Just think what evasions and half-truths any half-way decent person would have to perpetrate to prosper before them.

The third reason possesses a resonance which vibrates far beyond the conference halls. It has to do with the quality of political language in general. It reminds me of what Matthew Arnold once said of TB Macaulay – it's impossible to tell the truth in a style of language like that (I paraphrase). Arnold, for my money, was too hard on Macaulay, who had a genius for bringing the past so much alive that it rises from his pages and grips you by the throat.

Arnold's Law applies to most politicians most of the time. They are also guilty as charged by George Orwell 40 years ago when he said that 'as soon as certain topics are raised, the concrete melts into the abstract and no one seems to be able to think of turns of speech that are not hackneyed: prose consists less and less of words chosen for the sake of their meaning, and more and more of phrases tacked together like the sections of a prefabricated hen-house'.

Doesn't this accord with our current experience, a few exceptions, such as Tony Benn, John Biffen and Enoch Powell, apart? Isn't the 'hen-house' phenomenon even more pronounced in the age of the 'sincerity machine', the 'sound bite', the PR man and the speech writer? Its blight reaches beyond the prepared text. It disfigures *Question Time* on BBC Television too. Don't you, like me, often feel able to predict the rest of an answer once the first pair of sentences has appeared, like chunks of pre-stored paragraphs rising up the screen of a visual display unit?

Mind you, the party conference floor sees all types of political language at their worst. Even the nicest and most fastidious of politicians succumb. I remember hearing Sir Keith Joseph as Secretary of State for Social Services in 1972 or 1973 at the party conference in Blackpool engaged in the worst kind of exchange with the delegates. He was asking them rhetorical questions about the Welfare State, the answers to which were as predictable as the standing ovation that awaited the Party's Leader (Edward Heath in those distant times). Listening to Sir Keith I couldn't help remembering JP Stern's brilliant description of Hitler's skill in doing just that – the 'Tinkerbell ploy', he called it in his *Hitler: The Fuhrer and the People*.

A few years later, during a brief, discontented spell as a Westminster lobby correspondent, the seriousness and wider importance of the inadequacy of our political language struck me with a vengeance. One night on the late shift, I sat waiting for the first edition reading Ian Robinson's *The Survival of English*.

Robinson, a teacher of English language at Swansea University and an astringent campaigner against linguistic litter, places in that book a chapter on 'English and the Art of the Possible' which encapsulated nearly all I had come to feel about the verbal conduct of politics as witnessed from my place in the press gallery. He was especially good on the early Seventies' habit (which has endured) by which 'both parties talk a good deal about "packages" and their conception of style as a way of delivering the goods is very contemporary with the packaging revolution in the grocery trade'. Chancellors of the Exchequer ever since have been unwrapping 'packages' of economic measures whenever crisis has struck.

It was another paragraph of Robinson's, however, that has stayed with me, it's this: 'If a government is responsible to an electorate, it has to communicate with the electorate, whether by deceiving it, debauching it, pandering to it, or striving to make political sense with it. Public opinion is essential to a society with representative government, for that is where communication can take place in the other direction, where criticism can enter the language of politics, and where a change in political language may redirect political events by making different sense of them ... so the way in which governments explain themselves and are criticized matters, absolutely, because that is the existence of the politics of any community.'

Now I have a suspicion that the professionalisation of contemporary political life – politicians plotting their careers early and reaching Parliament young before they have cracked another job first – means that the familiar and the clichéd are all that they bring to political life. They have no past, in which learning and non-partisan experience have flourished, to decline from once they have slipped past the selection committees and into their safe seats. Ian Robinson's strictures are all the more justified in such circumstances.

What can be done about it? It would be encouraging if an older fashion were to return in which a familiarity with books, with the past, with life outside the political circle was a standard part of a tyro-politician's equipment. In an era of polarised politics, that is probably beyond reach.

There is another tack that might be tried: appealing to their self-interest. Reaching the foot of what Nye Bevan called 'the staircase of preferment' is one thing. Scaling it is another. Crawling, as Bevan said, is one propellant for the upwardly mobile. Another is to be singular, to be so special that only an insecure or an ideologically rigid prime minister could keep you down and out indefinitely. Intellect, knowledge, temperament, and personal values have everything to do with a politician's specialness. So do words and the power to express them.

And here who Harold Macmillan called 'the past masters' have much to teach. Macmillan himself learned a great deal from Lloyd George. LG heard one of Macmillan's early speeches in the Commons, approached him afterwards, told him he liked it but said it could have been better. The old man explained why. 'First of all you are a new member, you always speak in a thin house ... Never say more than one thing. Yours was an essay ... Just say one thing; when you are prime minister winding up a debate, perhaps three ... Of course you wrap it up in different ways. You say it over and over again with different emphasis, and different illustrations. You say it forcefully, regretfully, even threateningly, but it is a single clear point. That begins to make your reputation.'

Macmillan learned well. As prime minister, he was a mixture of Lord Acton and Max Wall – great sweeps of history intermingled with music hall. Lloyd George's speeches depended a great deal on delivery and timing. On paper his performances do not match Winston Churchill's. But their vitality and spontaneity led many to rate him the greater orator.

No young politician should seek to imitate Churchill for three reasons: it always sounds like a parody; nobody these days could genuinely compose in such a style; radio and television mean you couldn't get away with it. Why? Because the great man used the same word patterns time after time and he got away with it because his audience was always different.

Take his famous eulogy to the Royal Air Force in 1940: 'Never in the field of human conflict was so much owed by so many to so few.' It had a very long antecedence. The first time it saw the light of a public meeting was during the Oldham by-election in 1899: 'Never before were there so many people in England and never before have they had so much to eat.' It went through several refinements in the next four decades, the most bizarre being Churchill's reflection, as a junior minister at the Colonial Office in 1908, while gazing over a dam across the Nile, that 'nowhere else in the world could so enormous a mass of water be held up by so little masonry.'

To the hypercritical, this reworking of old material might qualify for Orwell's 'prefabricated hen-house' jibe. But in the case of Winston in 1940 we could – and should – forgive him everything.

Researching the deep Cold War with former student and *Silent Deep* co-author Dr James Jinks on board the Royal Navy Trafalgar-class submarine, HMS *Talent*, having just surfaced off the Isle of Arran.

What are prime ministers for?

Lecture at the Cheltenham Literature Festival, 6 October 2017

I owe my question to a young boy in the late nineteenth century – who may well have not existed beyond what one might call plausible and useful legend – who was present the day Queen Victoria opened Blackfriars Bridge across the River Thames.

As the little old lady in black passed in her carriage between her loyal and cheering subjects on either side of said bridge, the lad turned to his papa and inquired: 'Dad. What is that lady for?' Unless Dad by chance was an avid reader of 'The Monarchy' chapter in Walter Bagehot's *The English Constitution*, he would have been a bit pushed to provide the precocious child with a pithy answer. I know this evening how that late nineteenth-century parent felt. I shall have a go; but 'pithy' I fear, will not be the word to describe my efforts.

One way of approaching the question is to think a bit about what a prime minister inherits once he or she has kissed hands with the Queen, delivered his or her carefully rehearsed lines on the step of Number 10 and marched down the corridor to the prime ministerial office past the same applauding principal private secretary and Downing Street staff who had clapped the predecessor out about an hour earlier as he or she set off for the Palace to resign.

Here my top twenty of the bounty which falls into the lap of the new PM:

1. An £800 billion pot of public expenditure a year.
2. Twenty-two seats around the Cabinet table for those ministers who will fight it out in front of you as to who will spend how much of the money pot and on what.

3. A direct labour force of about 400,000 people called the Civil Service.
4. Forty government departments.
5. Three secret agencies and some high-class security and intelligence co-ordination and analytical machinery in the Cabinet Office.
6. Some 160,000 personnel in the Armed Forces.
7. A bomb of thermonuclear proportions and four very sophisticated submarines to carry it.
8. An interesting and usually leak-proof chat with the Queen each week if you are both in town or if you pop up to Balmoral to see her in September. More on that later.
9. A nice place in town plus a decent house in the Buckinghamshire countryside.
10. Round-the-clock protection from some highly trained and agreeable policemen noted for their sharpshooting.
11. A dominant share of parliamentary time.
12. The weekly torment of Prime Minister's Questions when the House of Commons is sitting.
13. Heaps of patronage in Whitehall and quangoland.
14. A press pack watching – or imagining – your every move on a twenty-four-hour basis.
15. A seat – through your New York diplomatic representative – on the United Nations Security Council as one of its five permanent members.
16. A seat on the European Council as one of its twenty-eight members until the end of March 2019; ditto the NATO Council (indefinitely, we hope).
17. Certain special operational functions such as the shooting down (or not) of a civilian airliner that might be in the process of carrying out a 9/11-style attack on the United Kingdom.
18. A slew of intractable problems at home and abroad, some of them centuries in the making, and a hand of history that

falls upon you straightaway which is, for most premiers, both awesome and covered in calluses.
19. Very few direct levers of power.
20. And, finally, perhaps the most daunting responsibility of all, the writing and signing four 'last resort letters' – for placing inside the inner safe of the four Trident submarines – containing your wishes: to retaliate, or not to retaliate, if you and much of your country are wiped out by a nuclear bolt from the blue.

My first reaction to any list of this kind is 'why on earth would anybody wish to do the job of prime minister of the UK?' More on that later. My second thought is to be intrigued by the absence of any job description for those who become the Queen's first minister. There is no statute which lays out the parameters either for the premiership or for Cabinet government. (I'll come back to that, too, in a moment). You just have to get on with it.

Most of the prime ministers who have taken office during the past century had sat in Cabinets before and seen other PMs in action. Some had not: Ramsey MacDonald in 1924; Tony Blair in 1997; David Cameron in 2010. Mr Cameron, however, did possess an unusual characteristic in May 2010. He had been schooled as an undergraduate in Oxford by the ace Professor Vernon Bogdanor at Brasenose and, as part of the PPE formation, familiarised himself with the great rolling debates about Cabinet government and prime ministerial government – a gratifying thing for those of us who labour our way through The National Archives and slog our way through the lecture halls and seminar rooms. And, in an interview he kindly gave me four years ago, he was intriguing on the themes which have turned into a thousand exam questions since John Mackintosh and Dick Crossman revived the old creeping prime ministerialism debate fifty years ago.

'Vernon had trained me', said Mr Cameron. 'Dare I say I'd even read your book on the prime minister.' ('Dare away', I thought

– albeit silently. Those of us in universities who live under the curse of the Research Excellence Framework have to find 'impact' where we can). I asked the PM what else, apart from the Bogdanor training, had helped him form his view of what the job of prime minister involved before he found out for himself after May 2010. Our conversation ran like this:

CAMERON: The picture of the job I had was formed by watching John Major a bit because I'd helped him with Prime Minister's Questions. So I'd seen inside the black box of Number 10. I'd worked in the Conservative Research Department when Mrs Thatcher was prime minister ... trying to understand how much a chairman and how much a chief executive – that was something I'd thought about quite a bit having worked in business. Having studied the whole debate about how much Cabinet and Cabinet committees ... informed decision-making structures, I'd thought about that a bit. I think I was determined to try and make it a little bit more formal and structured than it had been under my two immediate predecessors. Not necessarily because I had some sort of deep view that there was ever a perfect kind of Cabinet government, not that, just that I'm a fairly structured person. I like meetings to start on time, finish on time. I like process ... and making decisions ...

HENNESSY: So it's for temperamental reasons rather than constitutional propriety?

CAMERON: A bit of both. I think things had gone too far towards the sofa and it needed to come back a bit.

Mr Cameron added that much 'depends on circumstance, it depends on what's happening politically, it depends on the characters.'

I asked him if he had talked to previous prime ministers before he came into office.

CAMERON: I talked to John Major. I did talk a bit to Margaret Thatcher. John Major I talked to quite a bit.
HENNESSY: What did John Major tell you in terms of dos and don'ts?
CAMERON: He gave me quite a lot of don'ts, of things he'd done, as it were. He said that he didn't manage his time as well as he should have. He wished he had made more time to think.

The Prime Minister's answer made me think that I'd missed an important twenty-first item in that list with which I began of what a premier inherits: finite time, thinking time especially. Mr Cameron has plainly pondered that a good deal. Later in the interview I put a follow-up question to him on the time/thought theme.

HENNESSY: Walter Bagehot writing on Peel ... said that a prime minister needs a 'mind in reserve' for those things that come out of the blue and really stretch. Do you think you're good at the mind in reserve?
CAMERON: Oh, that's a very good one. I think there's enough flexibility ... in the job so that when something does come up, you can extract yourself from some of the things you're doing. So when, for instance, a Libya happens or a hostage crisis happens ... you can step outside some of the day to day ... I try to make sure that my life is not too cluttered. You do need to have time to read, to think, to not get exhausted, so then when something does come up that means you are really burning the candle at both ends, you've got the energy and the time to do it.

David Cameron, in a way, did a Bagehot on himself – a bit of self-placement in the great rolling debate about prime minister and Cabinet. His prior thinking had led him to see the job as an executive chairman of the Cabinet and he reckons that is what he has been.

CAMERON: ... you're the executive chairman; you're chairing the Cabinet; you're driving progress ...
HENNESSY: Before the election you said that you wanted to be more collective, in the way you described earlier. But would I be right in thinking that the coalition made sure you were virtuous?
CAMERON: I think there's probably some truth in that. I think that I am quite a collegiate person ... I think it will be true that coalition adds an extra sort of buckle to prevent too much sofa government.

The tone, pitch, and style of a government a prime minister can shape – has to shape. And it's possible – as David Cameron had plainly done – to think a good deal about it before you reach Number 10. But, after that – there's no road map, war book, useful set of instructions for what you do and how you do it. You are, to borrow a phrase Winston Churchill liked, the 'spear-point' – everybody knows it and expects you to be spear-carrier-in-chief. But what are you really for?

I had hoped to put the question to Theresa May as I had to David Cameron four years ago. I'd planned to request an interview in the early autumn of 2017, by which time – so I thought – she would be well settled into Number 10 and in a reflective mood. 'Settled' as it turns out, is hardly the word and I doubt that she has much time for reflecting on her style of government – so I didn't put the request in to Number 10. Nor given the harsh, relentless scouring of 'events' will she have much of that 'mind in reserve' that Bagehot detected in Peel. So what I shall briefly say about the May premiership so far is without the benefit of a chat with her. But here goes.

Prime ministers always have to live with the political equivalent of a floating exchange rate in the currency markets. But when the political market is – as it is this autumn and for the immediate future at least – volatile, vexing, and stretching in both policy and personal terms, it is very testing indeed for a prime minister.

In my judgement, the ecology which is playing into Theresa

May's exchange rate in the political market is powered by three things:

- The result of the June general election and the sudden – and unexpected – loss of authority and relative power this engineered, not just in the Cabinet Room but across the country. It was, to extend the metaphor, a serious devaluation in her political currency, which cannot be restored to where it was before 8 June.
- The question of Europe: always a great disturber of the British political system, which has not been able to handle it for sixty-seven years, and now especially fissile and disruptive for the foreseeable future.
- The admixture of personal rivalries and resentments among some of her immediate Cabinet colleagues, which feeds still more destabilisation into the mix. And not the so-called plot of those one might call 'the Removers'.

In fact, our entire political system is being tested on the anvil of Brexit.

The election result changed Mrs May's style of government – made it much more collegiate, as did the departure of her two special advisers who guarded access to her and, by all accounts, operated on her behalf with a ferocity and sometimes a coarseness that did neither them, their boss, nor good government any favours.

When they fell the day after the election, you could feel the *schadenfreude* surging through Whitehall. Her Number 10, headed by the admirable and consensual Gavin Barwell, is a very different operation now. We are in a really fascinating phase for watching the operation of Cabinet and premiership.

Back to my theme of what prime ministers are for.

The question may seem a touch luxurious for those who have held the office of prime minister because you're never short of things people are asking you to do, on top of that most terrible of special-delivery parcels labelled 'events' that turns up on the doorstep of Number 10 with wearing frequency. Henry Kissinger once said that in the US system the prize is 'to rescue an element of choice from the pressure of circumstance'. And the sheer rapidity and variety of decisions you need to make is very sapping on the energy levels and the grey cells. As the neuroscientist, Daniel Levitin, expresses it: 'Each time we shift attention, there is a metabolic cost we pay in glucose. We don't actually do two, or three or ten things at once, we just switch from one to another to another. Some brain activities are more expensive than others, and switching attention is among the most expensive'. This applies to prime ministers in buckets.

One way I have tried to get a bit of purchase on 'what prime ministers are for' is to attempt a functional analysis – to look at the mix of three things:

1. The functions that only a PM can carry out.
2. The things they have to do when certain events dump themselves on the prime ministerial desk.
3. The new functions the job has acquired over the decades that tend to stay in Number 10 once they have arrived and are rarely shed or passed to somebody else thereafter.

The idea of trying such a functional analysis came to me in the late 1980s and early 1990s after just such an attempt – an internal secret one conducted within Whitehall in 1947 – had finally reached The National Archives. It had been prepared by a young Treasury official, William Armstrong, in response to a request from the Institute of Public Administration for help in preparing a paper on the functions of the British prime minister, to be presented at an international conference on government chief executives in Western democracies.

William Armstrong, who went on later to head the Treasury and the Civil Service, sought the help of the senior and the wise in the

ON THE BACK OF AN ENVELOPE

Cabinet Office and Buckingham Palace before sending off a brief to the public administrators and placing the result, for the purposes of the Whitehall collective memory, in what was then a new artefact of the constitution called the *Precedent Book*. In 1947, the collective wisdom of Whitehall and the Palace came up with twelve functions:

1. Managing the relationship between the monarch and the government as a whole.
2. Hiring and firing ministers.
3. Chairing the Cabinet and its most important committees.
4. Arranging other 'Cabinet business', i.e. the chairmanships of other committees and their memberships and agendas.
5. Overall control of the Civil Service as first lord of the Treasury.
6. The allocation of functions between departments, their creation and abolition.
7. Relationships with other heads of government.
8. An especially close involvement in foreign policy and defence matters.
9. Top civil-service appointments.
10. Top appointments to many institutions of 'a national character'.
11. 'Certain scholastic and ecclesiastical appointments'.
12. The handling of 'precedent and procedure'.

Had I been at William Armstrong's side (I was but a few months old at the time) I would have added to that core dozen. But its contents intrigued me. I made a few inquiries and, as far as I could establish, there had been no such audit before and none since. What's more, no prime minister had seen this job description.

So, a plan formed in my mind. Why not pretend to be the William Armstrong of the early 1990s, draw up a modern list along 1947 lines, send it to the discreet and the wise on the inside for a bit of tweaking, and then 'contrast and compare', as we like to say in exam questions. This I did in the mid-1990s and placed the result in a book I was then preparing on the constitution called *The Hidden Wiring*. I had another crack at it a few years ago with my friend and former student, Dr Andrew Blick, and placed it in a study of the writing of contemporary history entitled *Distilling the Frenzy*.

I shan't go into the details this afternoon but some interesting things emerged from the exercises to update the 1947 taxonomy of prime ministerial tasks.

First, the 1995 audit produced thirty-three functions compared to William Armstrong's twelve in 1947. Even allowing for those that should have been there originally – such as dealing with opposition on a privy counsellor basis, overseeing the preparation of 'war books', the distribution of honours, contingency planning for industrial disputes that might jeopardise the essentials of life, and a few more – this represented quite an accumulation of functions and, it might be argued, an accretion of prime ministerial power that altered the balance within what we like to think of as a collective Cabinet executive.

The biggest change in terms of the quantum of personal prime ministerial responsibility was the question of authorising the release of nuclear weapons, which had fallen to successive premiers since the first UK atomic bomb was delivered to the RAF in November 1953. More on that in a moment.

A particular function that one does not associate with the diminuendo qualities of Mr Attlee was an increasing preoccupation with the media, either in terms of attempting to massage and manipulate it or to fend it off. The Attlee years, too, were almost entirely free of the counter-terrorism work that fell to prime ministers after the Troubles recrudesced in Northern Ireland from the late 1960s and during today's domestic and international terrorism, which absorbs so much ministerial time.

When Andrew Blick and I set to work on our 2011 audit we wrote down forty-seven functions, nearly four times William Armstrong's.

A swathe of them were specific to the coalitionist requirements of the job after May 2010 and disappeared after the May 2015 general election. Examples include managing intra-coalition relationship within the so-called 'quad' of PM, deputy PM, chancellor, and chief secretary meetings, plus a more complicated process for some ministerial appointments such as agreeing with Nick Clegg who shall be the law officers.

Other accretions since the mid-1990s are not coalition-specific, such as deciding with the relevant minister whether or not to use the ministerial override on disclosing information as allowed by clause 53 of the Freedom of Information Act 2000. An area where, unusually, a PM has shed individual power is, in effect, choosing the moment to trigger a general election by asking the monarch for a dissolution of Parliament, which is now a matter of statute under the Fixed-term Parliaments Act 2011 and for the House of Commons to determine short of the five years stipulated.[1]

The wider national security responsibilities of the prime minister have also increased and Mr Cameron's most important innovation within the machinery of government – the creation of the National Security Council – reflects this. Indeed, when I asked him in our conversation of autumn 2013, 'What surprised you most about the job when you started?', the Prime Minister said: 'I knew that the national security, terrorism, intelligence services role of the job was very big, but it still surprises you how big it is.'

It's a very sombre and sobering aspect of a premier's national security responsibilities that most intrigues audiences at literary festivals when one gives talks on the secret state or related themes – the preparation of the 'last resort letters' for the inner safes of the Royal Navy's Trident submarines, answering the question of 'retaliate or don't retaliate' after a nuclear attack which has wiped out the prime minister and his two or three alternate nuclear deputies drawn from the Cabinet on a personal basis.

---

1 The Fixed-term Parliaments Act was repealed in 2022.

In an interview this summer for the BBC Radio 4 *Reflections* series, I asked Sir John Major how he had felt in the early days of his premiership when he had been briefed on this intensely prime ministerial duty. 'It is a shock', he replied:

> The first time I realised that I was going to have to write post-Armageddon instructions to our four Trident submarines [they were, in fact, Polaris boats still doing the patrolling in 1990] was when the Cabinet Secretary told me. And it is quite an extraordinary introduction to the premiership. I remember I went away over the weekend and I thought about it a lot, and it was one of the most difficult things I ever had to do, to write those instructions – the essence of them being that, if the UK is wiped out but its Trident submarines are at sea with their weaponry, what should they then do with their weaponry? And eventually I reached a conclusion and I set it out.

I'd heard that David Cameron had called him in before he, Mr Cameron, wrote his letters for the submarines:

> I talked to David about that. I'm not going to say what I said, but we discussed the parameters of it, and I left him to make his own decision, as he did.

Later I asked Mr Cameron about his nuclear session with John Major when we talked in his office at Number 10. 'Yes', said the PM,

> I asked John Major in and asked for his advice, and I talked to him about it. I also talked to the Chiefs of Staff, I talked to [the] CDS [Chief of the Defence Staff] I think. But then, in the end, it is you know, it is you in the office on your own. I sat at that chair and there's a great big shredder that was placed right here and you write ... you choose which basic letter you want, make any amendments to it you want, and then you seal it up and you

shred all the rest. And so nobody, hopefully, will ever see these letters. It goes into the safe of the Trident submarine and then hopefully when you stop being prime minister they take it out and burn it and no one will have ever opened it.

As with John Major, I suggested that this 'must be when you realise what being prime minister really is all about because no one else ever does that'. It is, Mr Cameron replied, one of the 'big moments' –

going to see the Queen, walking through the door of Number 10, chairing your first Cabinet. It's probably, yes, because it's the oddest in a way. You've seen prime ministers drive up to Buckingham Palace. You've seen them walking through the door of Number 10. You can't really believe you are doing it yourself. But that bit in the office, writing out the letters, with the shredder ... is such an extraordinary thing to have to do, you can't really imagine it until you do it.

If Parliament ever manages to create a system, either through a House of Commons resolution or a war-powers statute, to regulate the capacity of a prime minister and Cabinet to take military action, this 'last resort' prime ministerial function will obviously remain prerogative pure, by which I mean that, heaven forbid, those letters are ever opened and they say 'retaliate', it will be under the ancient prerogative powers of the Crown that the Trident missiles will fly.

Is it possible – or desirable – for Parliament to acquire a say in the powers and reach of a British prime minister and Cabinet in the carrying out of their normal functions far away from the contingency planning for nuclear war? There's a little-noticed section in Jack Straw's memoir, *Last Man Standing*, published in 2012, which takes a look at this very question.

In the book, Jack is critical of some of the style of decision-taking on the road to the Iraq War of 2003, in which he was closely involved as Tony Blair's foreign secretary. 'Tony's reputation', wrote Jack,

> has suffered because he used informal 'sofa government' methods of decision-making rather than ensuring that Cabinet (and its committees) were proper, formal bodies where collective decisions were made. The criticism is justified. Look at Iraq.

Jack went on to say,

> I was fully involved in the decisions over Iraq, made informally and formally. Because Tony had agreed that any decision to take military action would have to go through the Commons, there had to be a high degree of involvement by Cabinet (and the Parliamentary Labour Party) in the final decision. The end point of this discussion chain was very formal indeed – a resolution of the House of Commons. But it would have been better – for Tony and his reputation, as well as for good government – if he, and I, and the Defence Secretary, had had to discuss progress with, and seek decisions from, a National Security Council, in turn reporting to Cabinet – and on paper, not by way of oral briefing.

Jack reached the conclusion that 'The days of self-regulation of Cabinet Government should be over' and recommended the framing of a Cabinet Government and Executive Powers Act.

Of course any such act, were Parliament to pass it, would create a collective framework for the conduct of central government – which is meant in the UK to be the norm as enshrined in the Cabinet Manual, the Ministerial Code and the code's predecessor, Questions of Procedure for Ministers, which ran as the core constitutional document (though it was secret until John Major declassified it in 1992) from 1945 until 1997. But such a statute would not – could not – ensure that a collective spirit prevailed always and everywhere in the Cabinet Room.

For the style of a particular government would, as David Cameron suggested, continue to be shaped by the circumstances of the day and the temperament of the occupant of Number 10. And prime ministers, after all, set out their own stalls. Some set out to be transformers – Harold Wilson in 1964 to substantially raise the rate of economic growth (which he failed to do) and Margaret Thatcher in 1979 to, as she put it to a Cabinet Office official, 'change the facts' of the UK's political economy (which to a large extent she did, by injecting successive tranches of economic liberalism and curbing trade union power). Ted Heath, though rarely seen as a transforming premier, also qualifies by steering the UK into membership of the European Economic Community in 1973; and Harold Macmillan did so between 1957–63 by engineering the UK out of great tracts of its remaining territorial empire. A side thought – will the PM who sees us out of the European Union qualify in that sense? I think so. As would perhaps a PM who presided over a Scottish separation.

Others, because of circumstances or temperament, do not set such high bars for themselves. Jim Callaghan was obliged to be a survivor/get-us-through premier during the protracted economic and industrial crises of his three years in Number 10 between 1976–9. John Major, in his *Reflections* interview with me, was eloquent about what he wished he could have done for health and education had he possessed the funds and a further governing spell after 1997 (which he made plain he never expected) that enabled him to do so.

Historical memory can be – usually is – hard on the incumbents of Number 10. By seeking the highest office they set themselves up to be brought down in a variety of ways. Remember Enoch Powell's famous law, as he wrote in his study of Joe Chamberlain, that: 'All political lives, unless they are cut off in midstream at a happy juncture, end in failure, because that is the nature of politics and human affairs'.

For me, it is Quintin Hogg, Lord Hailsham, who put it best. Hailsham, who for a few days came close to succeeding Harold Macmillan as PM in October 1963, was interviewed in 1989 by Anthony

Clare for BBC Radio 4's *In the Psychiatrist's Chair*. Hailsham was asked, did he regret not making it to the premiership? He replied:

> I've known every prime minister to a greater or lesser extent since Balfour, including Balfour, and most of them have died unhappy ... It doesn't lead to happiness.

It's as if in their often-lengthy post-premier life, reflecting in tranquillity is not their lot – to have had that position and power and yet to have left substantial things undone that might have been done.

The nature of prime-ministerial memory, too, can linger on what might have happened but did not in terms of catastrophe avoided. Harold Macmillan told his grandson, Alexander (now the Earl of Stockton), 'that as an old man he only had nightmares about two things: the trenches in the Great War and what would have happened if the Cuban Missile Crisis had gone wrong'.

As I mentioned earlier, who on earth would want the job of prime minister – especially in the era of directional microphones and twenty-four-hour rolling news – however much they cherish the UK and its wellbeing?

Yet the British prime ministership remains the 'glittering prize', as F. E. Smith put it nearly ninety years ago, 'to those who have stout hearts and sharp swords' and relish political power. Gaining it, however, is invariably an exhilarator but rarely a joy-bringer in the longer run.

It's not a job one would wish on anybody – and perhaps you have to be a little odd to want to do beyond a certain level of appetite. But I have, I confess, a sneaking regard for those who have walked through that famous door, felt that inheritance and taken that range of tasks on. And, we can't do without a prime minister. We may be – and I hope will be – a collective-executive nation; but we need a man or woman to take the flak that assaults those at the point of the spear.

How to build a prime minister

I've always thought that your notion of the job of prime minister is shaped by the first holder of it with whom you're familiar. Naturally this is true of many people one encounters, but in the case of prime ministers you almost get a crash course in their rolling biographies once you start getting interested in politics. For me, the prime minister whose character and style was deeply and swiftly engraved on my young mind was 'Uncle' Harold Macmillan. I read about Macmillan in the newspapers every day from start to end of his premiership and as a result I, subconsciously, came to expect all prime ministers to be steeped in the classics and prone to ham acting of the highest order, with the whole confection suffused, like a drizzle cake, with slivers of self-mocking. I've been very largely disappointed ever since. When I first arrived at Queen Mary in the early 1990s, my students seemed to take Mrs Thatcher as the norm, even though she was aberrational in so many ways. The news media's expectations of a premier remain heavily influenced by the imprint Mrs T. left on the politics and governing institutions of her country. It would take a pretty dominant prime minister to dislodge her from that eminence.

Mrs Thatcher also arguably created the expectation of longevity. Tony Blair certainly and David Cameron possibly were in office long enough to reinforce an expectation that tenures could be and indeed tended to be quite lengthy. But, as so often in human life, when you think a new norm has been established, largely unforeseeable developments can throw the particles of perception into the breeze once more. Recently a combination of events (in particular Brexit and its aftermath) and ineptitude has eaten three prime ministers – May, Johnson, and Truss – as if in a swift gulp. Before then, Gordon Brown lasted only three years and afterwards Rishi Sunak only managed two. The only people to have done well out of this brutal turnover are the political commentators and the political undertakers in the historical profession, who wait for them with open coffins.

The Brexit-related maelstrom illustrates one of the primary, though not only, reasons why attempts to compile league tables of 'good and bad' prime ministers are doomed to fail. The circumstances surrounding each incumbency are so very different. All one can judge, probably, is the fist each prime minister made of a job given the circumstances in which they operated. Often there is no equity in this process. It was Jim Callaghan's tragedy as a prime minister that his great gifts as a party manager and a seasoned politician were largely absorbed by holding the financial and economic line during his time in office. The particular European virus absorbed a high proportion of John Major's energies. However, his handling of the European question, given the performance of his successors, makes him almost look like a British Bismarck. Like Major, Gordon Brown suffered from following a dazzling star. And in some ways, he may have been ill-suited to the demands of the premiership. When he was about to take office, I took part in a private seminar in Whitehall about the new PM. I suggested that his greatest problem might be his appetite, ever the scholar, for concentrating on the one big question in hand. Later, the best Brown watchers in Whitehall told me how difficult he found it to handle the multiplicity of problems that inevitably arise in Number 10 even compared to the Treasury, a department which has an interest in every policy matter where money flows. Indeed, this tendency did seem to make life very difficult for him when he first became prime minister. But when the global financial crisis struck, these same characteristics turned out to be a true bonus as Brown sought, with considerable success, to be the Franklin Roosevelt of his day on both the domestic and international stages. That he had read a cornucopia of literature on Roosevelt and the Great Depression added mightily to his sureness of touch in 2008. And when the crisis hit, he applied his considerable focus and intellectual gifts exactly where it mattered. In the longer sweep of history he will be held in high esteem for the way he marshalled the advanced economies to cope with the consequences of the financial crash of 2008.

The office of prime minister is so multifaceted – almost mercurial in its ebbs and flows and in the casework it places on a prime minister's desk – that generalisations about the job are probably best approached with caution. As the experience of Gordon Brown shows, there is no such a thing as prime minister for all circumstances.

But what would a portmanteau of desirable attributes and approaches for a new prime minister look like? There are some basics: a high degree of physical stamina would always be in the top flight of needs. Even in the quieter times, the job is relentless. Problems tend to reach you only if they cannot be settled lower down the decision-making structures and by definition, therefore, they are tough ones. There are always breaking events, some anticipated, most not, that you have to find time for. Premiership is not a steady-state job. A capacity for hard and consistent work is indispensable. You can't rely on 'essay crisis' gifts; you cannot busk being prime minister. A flashing phrase always helps but it is no substitute for hours reading and thinking in the study. And then there is possibly the hardest line to tread, that which wriggles between decisiveness (which is desirable) and over-assertion (which is not).

There is also the deeper question of the personal baggage that prime ministers bring with them into Number 10. What is it, and how does it influence their conduct of the job for good or ill?

Quite often, collective political memory coalesces around a single word – often a location – when encapsulating a prime ministerial formation. Harold Macmillan, famously, would lace his Cabinet meeting performances with reference to the trenches in which he had fought during the Great War, and Stockton, which he had represented in the twenties, thirties, and forties. John Major, in a good way, never ceased to be a Brixton boy from a not very well-off family. And for Mrs Thatcher, it is the word 'Grantham' that evokes the true influence of her political philosophy, far more than Friedman or Hayek. On the Labour benches, Gordon Brown was the very incarnation of the manse – the Church of Scotland at the despatch box.

Macmillan, for example, detested the mass unemployment of the 1930s and avoiding a rerun was a perpetual motivator in every aspect of his economic and industrial thinking. This allied itself naturally with the intense shared comradeship of the trenches into a conservatism that was patrician on the surface but much, much more than that in terms of lived experience and ambition for his country. This was also true of Jim Callaghan and Ted Heath. War and slump were the key, I've always thought, to their inner as well as their outer selves. In Macmillan's case, his speech as a very old man in the House of Lords during the miners' strike of 1984 reflected perhaps almost his grief that the antagonisms of the age had reached this level and drew from him an unforgettable paean of respect for the pitmen whose fathers and grandfathers had fought the Kaiser and Hitler, and the communities that lived atop the coal seams.

It's a good question to ask of any prime minister: who or what are the shadows in the room when they are attempting to steer their Cabinet from the PM's chair? Margaret Thatcher's values of hard work, thrift, and meritocracy, and the ever-present and always inspiring legacy of her father's approach to life and work were what really mattered to her, I suspect. She called them her 'stars to steer by'. This sense of compelling mission in her premiership – and her tendency to win elections, much helped by Labour's special talent for civil war – explains why, Churchill apart, she left the deepest mark on the collective memory of the occupants of Number 10 since 1940. There were intriguing manifestations of this mixture of formations. She could be almost Marxist in her detestation of Tory grandees who she thought patronised her while living off their unearned privilege and inherited status, which eventually proved to be part of her dramatic undoing. Her temperament also got in the way. By the late 1980s she really did seem to think that she could do the jobs of all her secretaries of state better than they could. That usually proves to be the moment of maximum vulnerability. For example, Geoffrey Howe was interesting and well primed on pretty well everything he spoke on, but his very being and quiet persistent voice seemed to drive Mrs Thatcher to near distraction. It was finally pushing him too far that triggered her downfall; the nation's leading carnivore was slain by one of its mildest herbivores.

As much as early formation, experience matters. As preparation for the premiership and political life more generally, the gold-standard experience was being in the coalition during the Second World War. It wasn't just a case of running big executive outfits; that generation had to learn how to get on with people of a different party while handling a whole range of events that, had they gone wrong, would have irrevocably damaged the country. The stakes were at their very highest in 1940. If huge errors had been made in that critical year there could well have been a Britain that was not recognisable by the end of 1941. However, interestingly, this wartime experience gave that political generation huge self-confidence and a sense that anything was possible. For example, one of the most striking characteristics of the politics of Second World War Britain was the mind applied to the post-war period that was to come. As early as November 1942, the Beveridge Report laid out what was, in effect, a British New Deal (though nobody called it that) embracing full employment, the National Health Service (free at the point of delivery), a comprehensive approach to welfare benefits, and the reorganisation of state education, which was overseen by the coalition. The report was the very bedrock of the post-war consensus, as it came to be called. The blueprints were detailed and – extraordinarily – they were almost ready to go by the time the war ended.

The war also forced those on the battlefield to grow up very fast and most thoroughly before political life could be contemplated.

As Willie Whitelaw said when he left office in 1988, the big difference in politics of the 1980s was not between Left or Right, wet or dry, but between those politicians who grew up in the slump and fought in the war and those who did not. Denis Healey felt the same way. Whitelaw, who led his men in their tanks across the minefields of Normandy, was powerfully shaped by the experience of calling upon the families in the North of England of those who didn't come home. He felt a duty to those bereaved families and the communities in which they lived, and devoted his professional life to it. Those who fought not only forged a bond within their own generation, but carried an understanding of a wide range of people whose formations were very different from theirs into the peace, which made it quite inconceivable that they could swathe their political opponents in ignorant caricature. They might have argued about public ownership and free enterprise, but they understood each other and the values which trumped all others. They were grown-ups. Ted Heath, as a progressive conservative student at Oxford, toured the Spanish Civil War battlefields and met Jack Jones, the trade union leader who dominated the Labour movement when Heath was prime minister. This encounter meant that each spoke very highly of the other, even at the height of their disagreement. On one occasion, during a tense meeting in Number 10, the ever-witty Vic Feather of the Trade Union Congress (TUC) asked Ted to play 'The Red Flag' for Jack on his celebrated piano, which Ted duly did. It is easy to romanticise these flashes of solidarity amid strife, but they do matter and, one suspects, pretty well ceased to happen once the generation who had been formed in the thirties and forties had passed from political life.

Of course, one can't rely on world wars and economic crises to make good politicians. However, it does help to have cracked a job where evidence is the main determinant of what is done or decided. One of the perils of living in the age of special advisers is that you can slither from student activism, through time in a highly politicised think tank or service in a minister's private office, to ministerial positions and eventually the premiership without being required to be anything approaching evidence driven. As David Marquand observed, success in politics depends on the competitive mobilisation of prejudice. It has become a cliché that if a politician was your airline pilot, your doctor, or even your lawyer, you would look elsewhere for professional services. If a politician does climb the modern-style ladder of preferment it also tends to mean that they have only mixed with people who think as they do, which contributes to what is known as 'confirmation bias'. I've never really understood this. Talking only to people who think as you do can be highly comforting, but it is also intensely boring. Allied to this deformation can be an ignorance of the past – of being what the philosopher and politician Bryan Magee once described as 'provincial in time'. At its worst it can lead to a year-zero approach – the unwillingness to learn from one's predecessors and the dangerous tendency to see everyone who came before as failures, as Liz Truss (her worship of Mrs Thatcher apart) seemed to do.

There are other kinds of baggage that the new man or woman carries into Number 10 with them, and this can be critical to the shaping of their premiership. One – which Jim Callaghan emphasised the importance of – is prior reading. Unless you are an obsessional bibliophile like Macmillan, you get very little time to pick up a book in the Number 10 flat of an evening. Interestingly, future prime ministers tend to have done quite a lot of reading about the lives of those they hope to emulate. Prime ministers are, the monarch apart, the most biographised figures in the land. Their would-be successors have every opportunity, therefore, to study their minds and their practices. It's probably fair to say that prime ministers have a surer feel of their predecessors than any CEO or permanent secretary or military chief of staff. As prime minister, unlike most other jobs, there is nobody else on your level to chat to and learn from; you are the fairy on the Christmas tree. Most prime ministers will tell you how lonely the life is. It's almost as if only previous prime ministers can understand how tough and isolated it can feel. New premiers tend to call in their surviving predecessors quite early on for a cup of tea and a bit of homely advice. This is especially important if you haven't been lucky enough to have served in Cabinet to give you an outline in your head about how the job might be conducted.

I have a bias towards respecting and trying to think the best of British prime ministers, of whatever party. Even though they have volunteered for the position, one must always remember that it is of its very nature relentlessly demanding. And it matters. The job being well done is crucial to all sixty-seven million people living and working on these islands. Their daily performance and appearance are the chief front window that we offer to the rest of the world. And yet there is always a nagging worry about those who seek the office. You plainly have to think you're quite special if you try to become prime minister. And the perpetual danger is of what one might call a lurking messiah complex on their part – that their gifts and insights are touching on the indispensable in their generation. This can, on occasion, crowd out the crucial antidotes of humility and self-irony. As a consequence, I've always been especially fond of those prime ministers who didn't really want the job, the truly humble ones like Clem Attlee and Alec Douglas-Home (who, incidentally, were good friends). Quite a high level of toughness and conviction is required from prime ministers so perhaps it is inevitable that they strike more normal people as obsessional and self-absorbed. The problems arise when the country finds itself led by someone who has swallowed their personal legend whole. It almost always ends in tears – ours and theirs alike.

Temperament will always trump most other factors. Every prime minister, like all of us, has to carry their temperament around with them all day. I've always thought it must be sheer hell to work for the sort of prime minister who appears to wake up by asking themselves, 'to what can I apply my sense of personal destiny today?' Such characteristics affect the tone and priorities of an administration. At the other end of the spectrum, indecisive prime ministers can also afflict a large measure of wear and tear upon their colleagues. There is also the question of whether they are what Noel Annan used to call 'life enhancers' or 'life diminishers'. His ministers used to describe Macmillan's Cabinets as fun. Nobody so depicted Margaret Thatcher's, and Ted Heath's, to put it mildly, did not exude warmth. Harold Wilson, wreathed in pipe smoke, could almost never shut up at the optimum point. Clem Attlee sucked grandiloquence out of the air and famously said to students at Oxford University during his retirement that 'Cabinet government depends on government by discussion, but it only works if you can stop people talking.' I often wonder if he anticipated that history would come to see his humility as legendary. Though it was humility with an edge. Certainly people told stories about him based on his ability to use silence as a weapon. He once upbraided, albeit in private, the occupant of the other pole, Winston Churchill, by telling him tartly, 'a monologue is not a decision'.

All else aside, there is an absolutely critical characteristic which occupants of Number 10 need to display, either naturally or by careful acquisition. The decencies and probities of public life, what King Charles calls the 'precious principles of our constitution', have to be observed in every instance, for they are conventions for all seasons. If they are neglected or, worse still, disdained, a cruel and damaging distemper afflicts the body politic from the first to the last days of their tenure. Perhaps the most singular trace Boris Johnson will have left of British political history is that in modern times he was the most complete disdainer to have held the highest office. The informal system of conventions and codes saw us through eventually in July 2022, but it was a truly close-run thing.

All prime ministers come into office wanting to change things, be it institutions or the country as a whole. But you've really got to love and understand a country or an institution before you can reform it. To do this, you have to understand people you admire and trust who've come to a different conclusion about what their political allegiance should be. You have to have an empathy for the formation of people who think differently than you do. Post-Brexit, the first reaction we have in political conversation is very often to shout at each other and parody our opponents, to recriminate rather than respond with empathy, a bit of humour, a bit of forbearance. If you operate like that you haven't got the slightest chance of understanding the other side or the wider society.

It's also important to have a feel for people's everyday experience. As Ralf Dahrendorf suggested, much of politics is about promising people a better yesterday. One way of empathising with people whose background is not like yours is to understand what it is about their yesterdays that they want to put right. For example, if you've come from a run-down area and there wasn't quite enough money even in the good years, and you know how easy it is for households with no margin to fall into really quite serious economic difficulties. And this is not a problem only of yesterday. Now the sixth largest economy in the world has to think about putting a warm room next to a food bank. Yet there are too many in politics who can't empathise and seem to truly believe that if they 'made it', anyone can, even if all the dials are set against them.

Finally, there is the knowledge of when it is time to go. Harold Wilson confessed to his press secretary in 1975 that 'the trouble is, when the old problems reappear I reach for the old solutions.' Knowing when to depart the scene is quite rare. There is always so much more that you want to do and so many doubts about the likelihood of your successor being able to do them. Naturally, the more destiny-minded prime ministers also fear the slowing to a trickle of the adrenaline rush that being prime minister gives you pretty well every day. How prosaic the prospect of life after Number 10 can seem. Even the comfortable consolations of the red benches in the House of Lords cannot really compensate.

Casting one's mind back over the extraordinary range of humanity that has filled Number 10, even in my own lifetime. It's interesting that even successful prime ministers don't always set an example that ambitious would-be successors follow. Nobody, I suspect, would have built Attlee-levels of terseness into their ideal make-up. And of course there are some whose service to historical memory will above all be an example of how not to do it. There is one bonus brought by the British fascination with their prime ministers and the biographical approach to their stewardships. For students of politics and the public more generally, it's a very good way of initiating an interest in wider politics as it cuts through the outer crust of the enormously complicated factors that go into governing. This was certainly my experience on first encountering the public style and, as I later discovered, hidden depths of Harold Macmillan. And for this I thank our prime ministers too.

The incomparable Clem

Lecture to mark the unveiling of the statue of Clement Attlee at Queen Mary, University of London by the Rt. Hon. Lord Mandelson of Hartlepool, 4 April 2011

Clement Attlee has been much on my mind of late and not just in anticipation of this evening's splendid unveiling, for which I thank Peter [Mandelson] warmly. For example, watching *The King's Speech* left me regretting that the story stopped in 1940. I dearly wish it had stretched to Mr Attlee's post-war premiership. Just think what the film's scriptwriter and director could have squeezed out of the weekly audiences when the Prime Minister called on King George VI for a chat and a fag – the occasions formally known as the Head of State receiving his Head of Government?

Let the incomparable Clem tell the story in his own words:

> Reading the lives of my predecessors I have often thought how fortunate I was to have to deal with a George VI and not with a George IV or even Queen Victoria. I am struck by the difference between the stiffness and formality of the past and the ease of the present ... I gather that Queen Victoria expected her prime minister to stand during an audience, whereas now he comes in and is invited to sit down and have a cigarette.
>
> The conversation, too, was I think, very formal. Queen Victoria may have unbent a bit to Dizzie, but not to Gladstone. I cannot imagine her saying to Lord Salisbury, for instance, 'How is Joe getting on with the colonies?' but it would have been quite natural for George VI to say to me, 'How is Mannie [that's

Shinwell] hitting it off with the French generals?' or 'Well, Nye [that's Bevan] seems to be getting the doctors into line.' I, on the other hand, might have said to the King, 'The old man [that's Churchill] was really rather naughty in the House yesterday about India'.

This was positively grade-one-listed banter compared to their initial encounter as sovereign and prime minister on the evening of 26 July 1945, just a few hours after Mr Attlee, at his Limehouse constituency count in our very own People's Palace, first realised he was on the way to Number 10. Mrs Attlee drove her husband to Buckingham Palace shortly after seven that evening, once Churchill had tendered his resignation to the Monarch.

According to Number 10 legend, the King and Mr Attlee, who had come to know each other well during the war, were temporarily overcome by the natural shyness they shared. Attlee finally broke the silence by saying: 'I've won the general election'. To which his sovereign replied: 'I know. I heard it on the Six O'Clock News'.[2]

British constitutional practice changed that evening. Ever since then the Downing Street and Palace private offices have prepared 'Audience Notes' lest monarch and premier require a prompt.

Brevity was an Attlee hallmark. As Douglas Jay, who was his economic assistant in Number 10 in 1945–6, said of his boss: 'He would never use one syllable where none would do.' Yet in terseness there lay wisdom. Attlee could make a very few words go a long way.

Another reason he has been on my mind is a recent conversation I had with Tom McNally, deputy leader of the House of Lords, about the occasion in 1963 when he, as a student at University College London, invited Lord Attlee to speak to the students. Over dinner the conversation went like this:

MCNALLY: Lord Attlee, what made you a socialist?

2 Peter Hennessy, *Never Again: Britain 1945–51* (London, 1992), 56.

ATTLEE: Limehouse [where he had served as a youth worker as a young man].
MCNALLY: Lord Attlee, what's the greatest gift the British political tradition has given the world?
ATTLEE: Tolerance.

As for the Attlee character sketches, he turned miniscule – not just mini – biography into an art form.
Here he is on Lord Halifax:

Queer bird, Halifax. Very humorous, all hunting and Holy Communion.

And on Winston Churchill:

it was poetry coupled with energy that did the trick ... History set him the job that he was the ideal man to do.

And as for autobiography, listen to Attlee's reply to his official biographer, Kenneth Harris, when Ken asked him if he was a Christian:

Believe in the ethics ... can't believe the mumbo-jumbo.

Nobody distilled character, conviction, and politics better.
I thought of Clem a good deal last year too, especially during those, for us, novel Leaders' Debates in the run-up to the May 2010 general election. I tried to imagine such a thing in 1945, 1950, or 1951. Both Attlee and Churchill, in their different ways, were hopeless on television. Can you visualise them head-to-head? Churchill would have addressed the camera as if it were a vast public meeting with a global sweep and a grandiloquence that would have sounded hugely overdone. Attlee would have been so terse that the questions would have run out (as they tended to do in his occasional

and totally unrevealing meetings with the Westminster political correspondents).

I can give you an idea of Attlee under questioning with the transcript of a newsreel interview shortly after the 1951 general election had been announced:

> INTERVIEWER: Tell us something on how you view the election prospects.
> ATTLEE: Oh, we shall go in with a good fight. Very good. Very good chance of winning if we go in competently. We always do.
> INTERVIEWER: On what will Labour take its stand?
> ATTLEE: Well, that is what we shall be announcing shortly.
> INTERVIEWER: What are your immediate plans, Mr Attlee?
> ATTLEE: My immediate plans are to go down to a committee to decide on just that thing as soon as I can get away from here.
> INTERVIEWER: Is there anything else you'd like to say about the coming election?
> ATTLEE: No.

Unforgettable – and utterly unimaginable today.

Propagandist Clem was not. He was a stranger to the soundbite and, therefore, entirely unsuited to televised hustings of any kind.

Part of me was very much in favour of those pre-election debates last year as they seemed to quicken the curiosity of the 18–35 age group, which is the cohort least likely to vote. Another part of me was anxious. Because, henceforth, when parties choose their leaders, high among the considerations will be how the candidates will perform in those pre-election debates. And the primary skills needed to shine on those rostrums are those of the glib and the fluent, not the characteristics required for the long hard slog of premiership in stretching times. The Leaders' Debates will, I fear, prevent some very substantial people from acquiring a party leadership, and hence, a crack at Number 10.

In fact, even by the standards of a long-past political age, Attlee was an accidental party leader. When Ernie Bevin demolished the saintly George Lansbury's pacifistic leadership during the 1935 Labour Party Conference, Attlee was chosen as an interim leader to get the party through the imminent general election, from a tiny Parliamentary Labour Party of a mere forty-five MPs after the 1931 wipe-out. And big figures, such as Herbert Morrison, were expected to return to the House of Commons at the coming election and duly did. A decade later Morrison, famously, tried to get the leadership question reopened on 26 July 1945 before Attlee called on the King, but Bevin, who couldn't abide Morrison, was having none of it. (In one of the great alleged one-liners of twentieth-century British politics, Ernie, hearing a Labour colleague opine that, 'The trouble with Herbert is that he's his own worst enemy', replied, quick as a flash, 'Not while I'm alive he ain't'. I say 'alleged' because sometimes it's claimed Bevin directed that barb at Nye Bevan.)

Attlee was the stopgap who stayed serving as deputy prime minister in the wartime coalition, prime minister for six and a quarter years, and Labour leader for twenty. In doing so he set, I think, the gold standard for the conduct of the premiership and for standards of duty and decency at the very top for all subsequent prime ministers. In personal terms, he was far too modest to allude to this during the Downing Street years or afterwards. Amongst the fascinating collection of Clem's journalism gathered by Frank Field in his *Attlee's Great Contemporaries*, however, one finds a clue. It lurks in the article Lord Attlee penned for the *The Observer* in early 1960 on the theme of 'What Sort of Man Gets to the Top?'

'I have often been asked', he wrote, 'what it is that makes a Member [of Parliament] respected. I would say it is very simple: a man has to know his stuff; he mustn't talk too much; he must be good-tempered, not conceited; and be known to be a decent chap'. Later in the same piece he suggested:

> Just as a man cannot be a leader for long if he is not trusted, he cannot be a leader for long if he cannot trust. The only kind of

authority worth having is what is given without being sought for.

Men who lobby their way forward into leadership are the most likely to be lobbied back out of it. The man who has most control of his followers is the man who shows no fear. And a man cannot be a leader if he is afraid of losing his job.

That, I suspect, was about as close as Clem Attlee came to describing the stars of behaviour he steered by as leader of the Labour Party and prime minister. To our eyes, attuned as they are to the age of the professional politician, the lifers who have pursued no other trade; who have, in the saddest and most tragic case of Gordon Brown, converted every particle of energy since late boyhood into asphalt that would pave the road to Number 10 – to our eyes and ears that passage of Attlee's might sound thoroughly honourable but way out on the rim of political naivety.

More's the pity for us and the political generations to come if a high sense of duty, a strong charge of self-effacement and an instinct for near silence are wreckers of the potential to rise in our parliamentary and governing systems. Yet I must admit it's hard to see a Clem Attlee being selected to fight a losable seat today, let alone a winnable one. But, as I wrote in an 'Afterword' to Frank Field's *Attlee's Great Contemporaries*: 'I remain convinced that if, by some benign fluke, a decent, modest, understated figure did reach the top of a party today, great political advantage would accrue to him or her'.

However, whenever I'm canvassed to contribute a vote to those league tables of who were the best/worst prime ministers of the twentieth century, I'm reluctant to take part. Why? Because the conditions the men and one woman faced were so different when they entered Number 10; the fluctuations of the political, economic, and global weather so capriciously variable while they were there.

What was Clem Attlee's inheritance; the hand that history, to his great surprise, dealt him in the People's Palace alongside the Mile End Road on 26 July 1945?

- The country had lost a third of its wealth in, with its allies, licking Hitler and the Axis powers. As Keynes said of the British Empire standing alone in 1940–1: 'We threw good housekeeping to the winds. But we saved ourselves and helped save the world'.
- The tasks of demobilising ten million men and women from the Armed Forces and related Civil Defence forces and finding a high proportion of them employment and homes with so many houses and factories rubbled, which were enormously stretching;
- Handling an eye-watering range of international responsibilities as one of the victorious powers while sustaining a huge territorial global empire of what are now forty independent countries while steering the biggest – India – into India and Pakistan with the inevitable, bloodstained wrenching involved;
- Finding the money for, by the standards of the past, an ambitious and generous universal welfare system based on the wartime Beveridge Report;
- Providing both the funds and the systems for shifting 2.3 million members of the workforce from the private sector into the new, nationalised public corporations (the task led by Herbert Morrison, who was a natural and formidable organiser);
- Creating in the National Health Service the most trusted piece of our public services and public sector, with a workforce (still today) the third in the world in size after China's Red Army and Indian State Railways (and here Clem Attlee backed Nye Bevan rather than Herbert Morrison in the great Cabinet debate on the configuration of the NHS in 1946; on vesting day, 5 July 1948, NHS hospitals were combined in a single hospital service rather than a patchwork in which the local authorities, dear to Morrison's heart, continued to run a sizeable proportion of them).

- On top of all these demands on the depleted financial and physical capacity of the UK, Attlee had to eventually rearm against the Soviet Union and its allies as the Cold War chilled and to oversee the construction of a considerable Cold War 'secret state' here at home.
- All of this produced a continuous economic and financial overstretch, the ebbs and flows of which sometimes baffled Attlee who, as his young president of the Board of Trade, Harold Wilson, later said, was 'tone deaf' on economics. In fact, the whole, hugely ambitious programme – both the anticipated and unanticipated bits – would have been impossible to sustain without the dollar lifeline provided by the United States, first by the so-called American Loan and later through Marshall Aid.

We see the current Conservative–Liberal Democrat coalition governing in tough financial times while reforming public provision ambitiously and trying to build a 'Big Society'. How instructive it is to compare what Attlee called 'this tremendous social experiment' of 1945–51.

May I now turn to the human side of his 1945 inheritance? The British people were exhausted; relieved and proud to have come through the war; attuned both to the collective provision the war had made necessary; and optimistic, for the most part, about what collective provision could deliver in the peace. The state, unusually for the UK, was, albeit grudgingly, held in some regard as a provider in hard times and a fashioner of 'blueprints from above' in planning for post-war reconstruction.

What of the emotional geography inside his Cabinet Room? Attlee kept apart the two big figures and the two chief dislikers of each other, Ernie Bevin and Herbert Morrison, in portfolio terms (Bevin at the Foreign Office and Morrison as overlord of the home front as lord president of the Council). In Cabinet meetings Attlee adopted a similar ruse. He, Clem, would open very briefly and unlike, say, Mrs Thatcher he would not declare what he wished the outcome of the discussion to be by summing up before the debate had started. Morrison would speak next. Only after everyone else had finished would Bevin be invited to weigh in.

Giles Radice is right in his fine study of that government, *The Tortoise and the Hares*, to argue that only Clem Attlee could have handled those tremendous competing egos, temperaments, and personal insecurities that swirled among the likes of Bevin, Morrison, Dalton, Bevan, and Cripps. The tensions were real and ever-present but there was no truly damaging eruption until the spring of 1951 when, with Attlee in hospital, Gaitskell's Korean War-shaped rearmament budget (which involved prescription charges for teeth and spectacles) led to the resignations of Bevan, Wilson, and John Freeman and carved the Bevanite split which divided Labour for much of the fifties.

Denis Healey was interesting on this theme here at the Mile End Group in January when he repeated his view that by 1951, Labour had finished the business that all sections of the party were agreed upon – the implementation of Beveridge – and were vulnerable to splits thereafter. This centrifugal tendency in his party caused Attlee considerable trouble in his last four years as Labour leader. Jim Callaghan once said: 'The secret of Attlee's success is that he never pretended to be anything other than himself ... so he won the confidence of them all without ever becoming a faction fighter'. But this understated magic ceased to work after the 1951 defeat.

Attlee's conduct in the Cabinet Room generally was fascinating. He couldn't bear command or overmighty premierships and spent a good deal of his retirement warning against them. A prime minister, he said in 1961,

> must remember he's only the first among equals ... His voice will carry the greatest weight but you can't ride roughshod over a Cabinet unless you're something very extraordinary.

He was, too, the reverse of a destiny prime minister. Destiny premierships nearly always end in tears. In 1965, asked if he felt he was, like Churchill in May 1940, walking with destiny in July 1945, Clem famously replied: 'No. I had not much idea about destiny ... No, you see I didn't regard myself as a potential hero'. He believed in government by discussion. But, as he put it in one of his all-time classic Attlee-isms to an undergraduate society in Oxford in 1957, 'it is only effective if you can stop people talking'.

So, finally, how can we sum up – tersely, naturally – the legacy of Clem Attlee? Distilled to its essence, it has two chief ingredients: policy and style.

As Nigel Lawson recognised in a 1988 lecture to the Centre for Policy Studies, the post-war period has been shaped by two exceptional book-end premierships – Clem Attlee's and Margaret Thatcher's. The Thatcher governments, he claimed,

> transformed the politics of Britain – indeed Britain itself – to an extent no other government has achieved since the Attlee government of 1945 to 1951 ... [which] set the political agenda for the next quarter of a century. The two key principles which informed its actions and for which it stood, big government and the drive towards equality, remained effectively unchallenged for more than a generation, the very heart of the post-war consensus'.

Not all of us would nowadays reach for the bundle of policies put in place either by Mr Attlee or Mrs Thatcher. But Nigel Lawson was right. Those two administrations were the twin weathermakers of the post-war era, which for me begins with the Labour victory of 1945 and finishes with the political demise of the Thatcher government in 1990 and the ending of the Cold War.

As for style, that sparse yet collegiate governing approach of Mr Attlee's, the lack of show or any of the more absurd displacement activities that so often mar premierships – the insecurities, the vendettas, the occasional tantrums, and the illusions aroused by an excessive sense of personal insight and destiny – these, in personal and process terms, make Clem Attlee's conduct of government such an enduring gold standard.

When the wartime coalition broke up at the end of May 1945 against the wishes of the great warrior, Churchill threw a farewell party in the Cabinet Room. With tears streaming down his face, he declared that 'the light [of history] will shine on every helmet'. The light of history, for me, will always shine on Clem Attlee's helmet as long as I'm writing and breathing. How honoured we are to have our gold-standard prime minister in bronze on our Queen Mary campus in his beloved East End.

Harold Macmillan: Healer of the nation's scars

The Listener, *8 January 1987*

For Lord Hailsham 'there was an element of the dining club, the country house party about his conduct of Cabinets'. For Lord Home 'he was marvellously entertaining always – you did your business but it was great fun at the same time'. Harold Macmillan *was* a very funny man on occasions, both formal and informal. Picture first the scene in Wellington, New Zealand, on Macmillan's 1958 Commonwealth tour. Macmillan had been trapped by Walter Nash, the Kiwi premier, in a leaden conversation on Project Zeta, the latest British wheeze for producing cheap and abundant energy.

> NASH: How does it work?
> MACMILLAN (looking vaguely about him): Well, you just take sea water and turn it into power ... (pause) ... We're pretty good at sea water.

Move on some 17 years to an informal occasion at Birch Grove, Macmillan's country house in Sussex. Present are the Thatchers, Margaret and Denis, and a pair of Macmillans, the old statesman and his grandson, Alexander, who inherited the Earldom of Stockton last week. Alexander takes up the story:

> She had been leader for about six months and she came to have lunch at Birch Grove. She was getting to grips with her foreign policy brief and she talked at great length and at great speed about all matters to do with foreign policy, and my grandfather just nodded sagely. After almost a monologue for over an hour,

they drove away and he turned to me and said, 'Do you ever get the feeling you've just failed geography?'

In preparing his radio obituary last year, it was stories like that which boosted my already substantial affection for Macmillan. In the last hours of his life last week, I was in the Public Record Office sifting Treasury files dealing with his efforts to protect sterling from the Suez crisis. Every few pages one would come across his rather illegible scrawl in the traditional red ink used by the Chancellor of the Exchequer when writing comments on minutes. Reopening that file the morning after his death was strangely poignant.

If, like me, you are a sucker for the Macmillan style, conscious effort is required to prevent his six-and-three-quarter-year premiership from becoming bathed in a golden Edwardian afterglow. And never before has a British prime minister been so well placed to condition the first rough draft of his own personal history. Churchill had his books for autobiography and his epic war memoirs. Macmillan had a shelf full of volumes and, crucially, a series of gala performances on television, first with the late Robert McKenzie, more recently with Ludovic Kennedy and, to cap it all, a miniature series of televised speeches in the House of Lords, each one a collector's item, since he accepted the Earldom of Stockton on his ninetieth birthday.

After his second Lords speech, he appeared for a few days to be the de facto leader of the Opposition. Nigel Lawson felt the need to publicly rebut this unrepentant expansionist nonagenarian. Great care had gone into that performance, according to Alexander:

> He had taken about two months to prepare it. The system was that he would dictate a first draft, which would be typed out and then read back to him. He would then dictate a second draft and quite often a third and, if there were difficult bits, he would ask me or somebody else to record it so he could play it on a machine and he would learn, almost verbatim, great chunks. But the thing

that impressed me very much was, having been involved with the draft, he would move the chunks round in his brain, even while he was on his feet, rather like a word processor, and produce them according to how the audience was greeting him.

His fellow peer, Lord Olivier, appreciated the histrionic arts packed into a Stockton performance. He noticed that when his great anti-monetarist declamation began, Macmillan was standing resolutely parallel with the Conservative front bench, facing the Opposition, but as he became more critical he turned and finished up parallel to the cross benches.

Now he has gone, and never again can the irony, the analogy and the parody be forged into an elegant, gleaming weapon, the revisionists of the hard Right will chip away with greater determination at the Macmillan legacy. From the Right he will be portrayed as the deliberate inflationist, soft on the unions, who added layers of flab to the British body politic. The Right would argue that a tough successor, Mrs Thatcher, was needed to strip away that flab, along with that patrician tradition of *noblesse oblige* which produced many a memorable Macmillan monologue in the Cabinet Room about that stature of the ordinary man in the trenches and the ravages of interwar unemployment. For him, the scars of war, if not of deprivation, were ever-present and real. As Alexander Macmillan put it: 'He was a mass of scar tissue from the neck to the knees – and to his dying day great chunks of Krupp steel were still in his body.'

The Left, particularly its old English deeply patriotic wing, will always cherish the Macmillan of the Somme and Stockton. But they, and their less romantic colleagues, are likely to criticise him for his great conjuring tricks on foreign and defence policy, sustaining the great power illusion well into the Sixties when, as those fraught Treasury files from October and November 1956 show, he knew more than anyone else just how decayed were the economic sinews of British power.

Finally, why did he accept that Earldom? I had admired him for

20 years for not becoming the Earl of Bromley (for some reason I thought he would take his title from his last constituency not his first). As Prime Minister he had made great use of honours. He once told an audience in his beloved Oxford University: 'I rather enjoy patronage. I take a lot of trouble over it. At least it makes all those years of reading Trollope seem worthwhile.' Yet Macmillan himself seemed above all that. According to the new Lord Stockton [Alexander, Harold's grandson], three things changed his mind:

> He was by then very blind; he couldn't read any more and he was getting very frustrated, and he felt he didn't have any method of playing a part even in the background. The second thing was that my father (Maurice Macmillan) had already announced privately that he wasn't going to stand in the forthcoming election and so there was no question of inhibiting my father's career, which had been quite a consideration back in 1963 because he had, after all, retired through ill health and was told by his doctors that he was unlikely to survive that year ... And the third reason I think was a sort of romantic one, which was that here was his ninetieth birthday and two women whom he admired enormously, in the shape of the Monarch and the Prime Minister, put it to him that it would, in a sense, be a birthday present from the nation.

Given his use of that birthday present, even the most ardent opponent of the hereditary principle must be glad he accepted it.

Whitehall brief: Shades of a Home Counties Boudicca

The Times, *17 May 1983*

There is a school of thought that sees Mrs Margaret Thatcher as a Home Counties Boudicca riding roughshod over traditions, institutions and Ministers. It has branches in the universities and the lobby correspondents' room at Westminster.

It is easy to appreciate how it has coalesced. Her style exudes prime ministerial will. The nouns 'consensus' and 'compromise' and the adjective 'collective' are part of her glossary of 'boo' words.

At first sight the evidence for Mrs Thatcher as the destroyer of Cabinet government is fairly convincing. She leads from the front both publicly and privately in Cabinet and Cabinet committee. She denies full Cabinet any real opportunity to discuss economic strategy.

Those early stories of her not wanting any Cabinet committees (though she now has 25 standing and about 95 ad hoc groups), of wishing to get rid of the Central Policy Review Staff and the Oversea and Defence Secretariat of the Cabinet Office and treating the Cabinet as a rubber stamp, all are true.

Press coverage over four years has tended to solidify first impressions. The first draft of political history flows from the barrel of a lobby correspondent's pen. The journalists glean their impressions from Mr Bernard Ingham who, even more than most Downing Street press secretaries, is a classic example of the HMV (His Master's/Mistress's voice) effect.

There is a danger that the compost of accumulated press cuttings will soon flower into learned articles in political science journals, turning the Boudicca thesis into a new orthodoxy.

But is it true? Not if you talk to the people in the front row in Whitehall who, as civil servants, have seen administrations come and go and are connoisseurs of prime ministerial substance as well as style. Front-stall Ministers agree as well, though some are worried what might happen if Mrs Thatcher triumphs on June 9.

Those who insist that Cabinet government is intact point to big and small issues. She did not get her way on public expenditure. During the Falklands crisis she ran the war from her tiny Oversea and Defence (South Atlantic) Cabinet committee. Yet according to one Cabinet minister not on it: 'She had to carry us on every major decision. That task force would never have sailed without Cabinet approval.'

As little examples of the power of departmental ministers go, her session last year in a Number 10 dining room, for Mr Michael Heseltine to explain his managerial efficiency system to colleagues, was a classic:

> Ministers gave Michael the two fingers. The PM stood up and pleaded with them for 25 minutes. That showed the power of Cabinet.

The most convincing evidence, however, is negative rather than positive. One seasoned Whitehall figure said: 'Ask yourself why there is no Cabinet committee of just her and her sympathizers on trade union reform? Answer: Because what they produced would not have got past Cabinet, let alone to be sure of a majority in the House of Commons.'

Another exponent of negative evidence picked Northern Ireland. Mrs Thatcher shared the view of her late confidant, Mr Airey Neave, that what is needed is not a restoration of Stormont but of good local government.

A Cabinet committee which pushed that line would not have included Mr William Whitelaw, the Home Secretary and former Northern Ireland Secretary. She knew that he would have stopped it dead in Cabinet by reminding colleagues that it was bad local government in Londonderry that started the Troubles in the first place. So a special Northern Ireland committee did not materialize. Officials in the front stalls are not surprised by the recent debate about a possible Prime Minister's department.

> Heath, Wilson and Callaghan by the end of their time were all terribly frustrated by the system. They felt they could not get things done. The issue of some kind of departmental change arose with all of them, including Mrs Thatcher.

Britain has experienced prime ministerial government before. It operated under Lloyd George, who ignored Parliament and was called an imperial Caesar. Professor George Jones of the London School of Economics believes that if, in 1922, his personal secretariat, the so-called 'Garden suburb', had survived, and the Cabinet Office perished, prime ministerial government would have become the norm.

If she wins a second term Mrs Thatcher will import more personal advisers into Number 10, packing possibly up to 20 in basements and garrets, with a Chief-of-Staff in charge of this new attic breed. But a beefed-up Prime Minister's Office will live alongside, but not supersede the Cabinet Office, the stronghold of collective government. In appearance she may be more Boudicca-like than ever, but in reality the constitutional balance will be intact.

Exit the Tigress

The Tablet, *13 April 2013*

Undeniably, Margaret Thatcher was a phenomenon, a primary-colours politician who gave her country an 11-year Technicolor premiership which dazzles to this day. She was not just a politician who made the political weather, as Winston Churchill famously described Joseph Chamberlain, she was even rarer – a climate-changer, too. She lived and governed in an atmosphere of drama up to the very moment she fell, slain by her own Cabinet, in November 1990. She thought she was 'a tigress surrounded by hamsters', wrote her disenchanted former Cabinet colleague John Biffen. But they had had enough of being biffed about in Cabinet. Several thought she was going off the rails in her growing hostility to the European Community. Even more were concerned about the impact of her 'flagship' poll tax on the Conservative Party's electoral prospects. So the hamsters sank their teeth into her when her deputy, Sir Geoffrey Howe, could take no more and resigned. Michael Heseltine challenged her leadership and did sufficiently well in the first ballot of the Parliamentary Conservative Party to topple her, though the crown fell to John Major, not him.

Yet even now, nearly 23 years on, when we detect shifts in politics, economy, society or world affairs, Margaret Thatcher and her 'ism' are among the prisms through which we refract events in our attempts to make sense of them. She knew from the beginning of her party leadership that if she could only get into Number 10, expectations and ways of working would never be the same again. What she saw as a wretched post-war consensus, based on a mixed public-private economy and a welfare state, she believed was a recipe for stagnation and national decline – that such post-1945 accretions would have to be dynamited away to reveal the old granitic nineteenth-century virtues of free enterprise, free trade and individual self-reliance.

In February 1979, with the majority-less Callaghan Government caught in the coils of a winter of discontent, she told Kenneth Harris of *The Observer*, 'It must be a conviction government. As Prime Minister I could not waste time having any internal arguments.'

This self-labelling stuck, although I think it is partially misleading. True, her Cabinet Room style was to announce at the beginning of the discussion what she wished the outcome to be. But she was not happy unless she had a good argument on the way to getting what she wanted. In this sense she was a much more collective Prime Minister than Tony Blair, who didn't like argument and was surrounded by much more supine Cabinets than hers. And at moments of greatest crisis such as the Falklands War of 1982, she was genuinely collective in her approach.

Those who worked closely with Lady Thatcher attest to a caution, a sensitivity, a lack of complete certainty in private that was out of kilter with the Boudicca-like qualities of her public face and pronouncements. There were hints, for example, that she refrained from visiting certain parts of the country hardest hit by the collapse – in some cases, the disappearance – of once jobs-rich heavy industries whose demise was speeded up by her Government's monetarist politics and spending cuts, lest sentiment divert her from what she saw as the first-order problem of halting, then reversing, Britain's deep-seated relative economic decline.

In pursuing these policies, she was running as much against the policies of the Conservative premierships of Harold Macmillan 1957–63 as those of the Attlee Governments of 1945–51. She ran against Heath's interventionist policies as much as she did the policies of the Labour Governments of Harold Wilson and Jim Callaghan of 1974–79. The early Heath had wanted a dose of relatively free-market economics to revive British industry to enable it to better fund the welfare element of the post-war consensus.

On taking office in May 1979, she went for the public sector as bloated and inefficient. Later she privatised the nationalised industries with a vengeance. Although critical of the Civil Service as risk-averse, she rated most of the officials she worked with closely and adored the Queen's most secret servants. From the beginning she read the intelligence reports avidly and sent them back covered with scribbled comments and questions. If a Royal Navy submarine had brought back some particularly rich intelligence from the highly sensitive Barents Sea as part of the deep Cold War, she would have the commanding officer into Number 10 on his return for a debrief and to thank him. On their part, the armed services relished her decisiveness when war came with Argentina in 1982.

Prime ministers, a touch crudely, can be divided into copers, scene-shifters, transformers or disasters (like Sir Anthony Eden and Suez in 1956). Her predecessor, Jim Callaghan, was forced to be a coper, heading a minority Government, a divided party and presiding over a shaky economy poisoned by fraught industrial relations. Macmillan was a scene-shifter, disposing of the vast remaining bulk of the British Empire. So was Heath – only he at that time could have levered the UK into membership of the EEC. Wilson in 1964 brimmed with technocratic flair plus substantial parliamentary and media gifts, yet he came nowhere near to transforming the British economy through his planned-for 'white heat' of a technological revolution. Mrs Thatcher did transform. She broke excessive trade union power, ended exchange control and let markets rip as much as she dared.

There were trade union showdowns with successive bursts of industrial relations legislation, and a specific fight with the National Union of Mineworkers and Arthur Scargill in 1984–85. She also sought to handbag Europe by relentlessly demanding 'our money' back in the form of a budget rebate from the commission, which she eventually won. She had still more tussles with her own people – her Defence Secretary, Michael Heseltine, resigned over the Westland helicopter affair in 1986; her Chancellor, Nigel Lawson, went in 1988 over Number 10 interference with his economic policy; finally, her deputy, Geoffrey Howe, lit the last fuse beneath her in 1990 when he went over European policy.

Her successor, John Major, found it near impossibly difficult to govern in her constantly shimmering shadow even after he won an election in his own right with a small majority in the spring of 1992. By that autumn, battered by a huge currency crisis and wounded by civil war inside the Conservative Party over Europe, the long, slow decline to electoral catastrophe in 1997 had begun. Major was emollient where she was abrasive, [and] sought consensus, an approach she loathed. His was rightly described as a suffix premiership (as Alec Douglas-Home's had been between Macmillan and Wilson).

Tony Blair used Thatcher as an alibi, wrongly, for his eschewing the collective processes on which UK Cabinet Government is built. Though the Blair and Brown Governments invested hugely in public services and spending after the lean Thatcher and Major years, they neither reversed the privatisations nor did they restore trade union powers and legal privileges. They, too, governed in her shadow. David Cameron and George Osborne are the generation politically of Mrs Thatcher's children. But Cameron's governing style is more Macmillan's than Thatcher's and would still be, I suspect, even if he were free of Coalition.

Her sole rival for the palm of top weathermaker PM since 1945 is the diminuendo Clement Attlee, who was different in every way from Thatcher: understated, terse, lacking charisma, he nonetheless presided over a government that built the post-war settlement to whose dismantlement Mrs Thatcher had tasked herself, though she never succeeded in doing so on health and welfare.

The day in 1990 when John Major became Prime Minister, I was delivering a lecture at Georgetown University in Washington DC on 'Mrs Thatcher as History'. Among the significant and enduring transformations she had wrought, I listed the breaking of trade union power; the end of big nationalisations and focusing the argument instead on regulation, not ownership; the move, with nine million shareholders, to a 'property-owning democracy', and a million council houses sold into private ownership on very favourable terms.

Today I would also add her key part in helping end the Cold War by turning Ronald Reagan away from his 'Evil Empire' rhetoric (and by developing a special personal relationship with Mikhail Gorbachev from 1984).

In accumulated achievements, she is eclipsed only by the wartime premierships of David Lloyd George and Winston Churchill. Yet she never turned the UK into the kind of full-blooded free-market economy she believed in. As for that feared handbag and her fabled Cabinet Room style, she said in retirement, 'There's not much point in being a weak and floppy thing in the chair, is there?' That, she never was. Margaret Thatcher was an earth-mover among politicians.

The rise of Napoleon Blair

The Times, *25 September 2000*

Even before he formed his Government on May 2, 1997, there were signs aplenty to suggest that command and control would be the Tony Blair style in government. He and his inner group of advisers seemed determined to operate inside No 10 as they had within the Labour Party – driving policy and presentation from the centre, later defined by Blair, as 'my own office, the Cabinet Office and the Treasury'.

The one great exception to this was the Chancellor-in-waiting, Gordon Brown. For the deal at the heart of Blair's style was that a command premier would operate alongside a command Chancellor licensed to dominate across a wide range of economic and domestic policy. As one of Blair's closest associates told me two months before the election: 'You may see a change from a feudal system of barons to a more Napoleonic one.'

I was sufficiently alarmed by this to throw a fit of constitutionalism-in-advance. 'Command premierships of a highly personalised and driven kind, usually end in tears,' I declared. Getting your own way simply by stamping the prime ministerial foot is conducive neither to good government nor to personal survival, nor to a contented retirement.

From the beginning it was plain that the Blair–Brown axis would dominate economic policy, that the full Cabinet would be nowhere and that its main economic committee (which Brown would chair, the first time a Prime Minister had vacated this slot since 1966) would be scarcely better placed. One of the most significant economic decisions of the Blair administration was also taken during the first week of its life: the shifting of responsibility for setting interest rates to the Monetary Policy Committee of the Bank of England. Only two other Cabinet ministers had prior knowledge: the Deputy Prime Minister, John Prescott, and the Foreign Secretary, Robin Cook. Not only was the full Cabinet unconsulted, it had not even met for the first time when the decision was announced.

As a well-placed official put it quite starkly: 'This is not a collective government. We must accept that the old model of Cabinet government is as dead as a doornail.' Early observations did indeed suggest that the Blair Cabinets were extraordinary affairs, and not just because of their brevity. A 30-minute one just before the 1997 summer recess may well have been a postwar record for a full-dress, as opposed to an emergency, Cabinet. They rarely lasted more than an hour. There was (and remains) no proper agenda, merely regular items: 'parliamentary affairs', 'economic and domestic affairs', 'foreign affairs'. The three regular headings are supplemented by a very new Labourish addendum – 'The Grid' – a plan for the forthcoming week linking the timing and presentation of ministerial and departmental announcements and initiatives with political, cultural and even sporting events generally.

From the preparations for the first full Cabinet of May 8, 1997, it became clear that Blair would not use a formal agenda as had been the norm since the Cabinet Secretariat was introduced in 1916. Nor did he necessarily keep to the order in which the regular business items appeared. Cabinet Office note-takers wrote up the discourse as best they could. Non-Cabinet ministers found the Cabinet minutes among the least important parts of their weekly reading. One particular longstanding customer of the Cabinet minutes noted that they 'are different under this Government. There is much more in them about presentation and how to do down the Opposition.'

Blair's reputation as a centralist was confirmed beyond question by the notorious paragraph 88 of the Ministerial Code, which became swiftly treated as the classic statement of 'control freakery'.

All major interviews and media appearances had to be agreed with the No 10 Press Office and the content of all major speeches and press releases cleared in good time with the No 10 Private Office.

An intriguing interpretation from a well-placed insider argued that No 10's assertiveness over policy and presentation stemmed from a sense of weakness rather than potency. There is much in this. Whenever you talk to those who live at the 'Blair Centre', they all give the impression of how powerful everybody else in Whitehall seems to them. They tend to go on to make the case for an even more forceful centre, as Philip Gould, the Prime Minister's pollster and political strategist, has done publicly. Gould believes that without a greater capacity 'to integrate and reform' at the centre through a Prime Minister 'supported by his own department that is powerful, talented and fast enough to cope with the speed of changing circumstances ... good government will become increasingly elusive'.

Hence the transition from Prime Minister's Office to an unavowed Prime Minister's Department, with a doubling of the number of special advisers to 74 in Whitehall as a whole between May 1997 and early 2000 and the trebling to 24 of the No 10 quotient over the same period. The concentration of power was also evident in Blair's version of that Thatcherian phenomenon, government by unit. There was a difference, though, which was evident almost from the moment the Social Exclusion Unit and the Performance and Innovation Unit were created by the Prime Minister in late 1997 and the summer of 1998. They were housed in the Cabinet Office but they belonged to Blair, who laid down the tasks and to whom they reported. They were not constructed as a shared resource for the Cabinet. The innovation has led one seasoned Whitehall figure to worry that 'this is the way into the American system by the back door'.

There were several worrying features about excessive prime ministerialism in the conduct of British central government. It cuts against the collective grain, which runs that way for a purpose – as just about the only barrier against undesirable accumulation of power that can all too easily accrue around a single figure. An excessive focus on the premier can both overburden the Prime Minister (Blair acknowledged publicly that he found the job 'remorseless' just before the Balkan war began) and, in the words of an American journalist, 'threaten to drain the political oxygen available for other projects' if the head of government faces too many huge sappers of time and energy. Blair had no shortage of these in the spring of 1999. Kosovo and Northern Ireland alone were enough to induce the oxygen starvation effect. Blair was in danger of wearing himself out.

There is a paradox at the heart of the Blair style, however. How can he be a control freak running a command premiership? Hasn't he presided over a Government that has dispersed more power in its first three years than any in history? To which I think the answer is 'True – but'.

Senior civil servants and the judiciary had an acute sense of the combined effect of Blair's constitutional reforms, but the political class (including a high proportion of the membership of the Blair government and even Blair himself) failed to appreciate what was happening. Why was this? As another well-placed Whitehall insider put it: 'Most of the senior ministers involved in constitutional reform don't believe in it, aren't interested in it or don't understand it.' Ministers and the political class generally were treating the Government's constitutional reform programme as a restructuring of an existing political culture rather than seeing it as the cultural transformer it was almost certainly going to be.

Take the creation of a Scottish Parliament: it marked only the beginning of a protracted negotiation and a series of adjustments between Westminster/Whitehall and Edinburgh. From the outset one had a sense of this from the 'Concordats' drawn up by the Cabinet Office to map out the procedural side of the relationship between Westminster/Whitehall and the devolved assemblies. But the Concordats will succeed only if relationships are relatively harmonious. The edifice of devolution is very largely constructed on the harmony model. But that desirable state of affairs cannot be guaranteed. Far from it. And, if it does go wrong, the Prime Minister will be central to the resulting conflict management.

Already, in the late summer of 1998, the Prime Minister's spokesman, Alastair Campbell, was reflecting his boss's sense of 'constitutional overload'. A year later the avoidance of 'gridlock' was the great phrase one heard in No 10, which boded ill for the prospects of electoral reform for Westminster. (Blair was very irritated by those coalition governments among the NATO allies who had to broker deals back home before deciding on the line to take on Kosovo.) The 'gridlock' aversion was powerfully fed in late 1999 and early 2000 by disagreements with the Scottish Executive about student fees and beef and with the Welsh administration over both beef and the travails of its first Chief Minister, Alun Michael. And 'gridlock' avoidance was a hugely powerful factor in watering down the proposed freedom-of-information legislation to maximise Whitehall's continuing control over disclosure.

The Prime Minister's tetchily defiant speech on January 21, 2000, at a school in Forest Gate, East London – during which he declared that he would not be distracted by the 'forces of conservatism and reaction, left or right' – will be treated, I suspect, as a milestone in the progress of his premiership. And Blair's people, not too long before, had firmly linked his governing style with his determination not to be deflected. As one insider said of the Prime Minister: 'What he wants is results. He has a feel for the policies but not how the results come. He finds it hard to understand why things can't happen immediately. There is a frustration in waiting for the pay-off and he doesn't have time. He comes back to this when one or other of the policy areas gets hot: education, then transport and now health. He comes back to all this when the delivery focus changes. This is the real-time political management, which the administrators don't like. (They didn't like it under Margaret Thatcher either.)'

The great problem, however, is the messy and confusing gap between the old Cabinet system and the reality of policy decision-taking favoured by the Prime Minister. The nearest parallel, according to a shrewd observer, is business. Everybody knows that real decisions are taken in Blair's preferred way some distance from the Cabinet and its apparatus. But full Cabinet, and some of its committees, are used for the purposes of laying down an 'audit trail' in the manner of company boards. According to this view, what we are seeing is an attempt to marry Blair-style governance with the shell of the old and to link the Government's strategy with effective delivery through a sharpened and reformed administration system.

Two conclusions emerge from this analysis, and one running question. The first conclusion is that as the centuries turned there was still a long way to go before the new system, based on a blending of the traditional and the novel, was tested against reality. The second was the degree to which the new model depended on the Prime Minister. And linked to this was the continuing debate about prime ministerial power, the importance of being Tony. For driving this new hybrid system, it could be argued, both generated excessive prime ministerialism and depended upon it if momentum was to be sustained.

Such accusations of overmightiness at the centre have long annoyed Blair. Rebutting them at regular intervals has been a recurring feature of his premiership. By Blair's own testimony, you either have a strong and determined approach to the job or you have weakness, indecision and chaos, as if the operating of Cabinet and premiership were an either/or matter, a question of primary colours rather than more subtle and variable shades.

The weeks leading up to the third anniversary of the Blair Government's creation found the Prime Minister in [a] reflective mood. In an interview with Robert Harris he conceded that the 'reality' of the premiership was more intense and more relentless than he had anticipated. But, 'I have a very fixed view as to what I want to do for the country and I haven't shifted in my belief that I can do it. But keeping a grip of that big picture and following it through is the toughest part.'

Blair made plain to Harris that two of the big canvases he had in mind were the mending of the Liberal/Labour split on the centre-left during the First World War (of putting that right he said: 'I have never given up on that goal, and I still believe it can be achieved') and steering Britain into Euroland (though he would go no farther with Harris than saying that his 'objective' was for 'Britain to be a key and leading player in Europe').

Yet power is a wasting asset, as virtually all premiers have found – even those blessed with three-figure majorities in the House of Commons. Resentment of the 'centralised duopoly' of Blair and Brown has yet to crystallise into resistance in the Cabinet Room, though even now it is inconceivable that Blair could bounce a sceptical Cabinet into spending £750 million on a grand project such as the Millennium Dome. And as for a coalition with the Liberal Democrats, Blair would have to be prepared for the resignation of his Deputy Prime Minister.

It was Blair's Home Secretary, Jack Straw, who put the Blair style into perspective by conceding that 'our Prime Minister has adapted the mode' developed by Margaret Thatcher in the 1980s, whereby fewer decisions were made at full Cabinet level, with more devolved to Cabinet committees. And 'what Mrs Thatcher did was develop the idea of bilaterals with ministers', an approach extended by her successor-but-one in No 10.

Summing up the Blair style, Straw said: 'The Prime Minister is operating as chief executive of ... various subsidiary companies, and you are called in to account for yourself.' He added loyally: 'A good process.'

As for Blair's own assessment, he told Harris that he agreed that most political lives ended in failure. Why? 'It's because the public is always encouraged to be cynical about people. And, in the end, whatever the expectations are, you can't meet all of them.' Whatever else might be said of him, Blair is a command-and-control premier with a sense of political mortality.

Tony's signature: The Blair style of government since 1997

The Alistair Berkley Lecture, Robinson College, Cambridge, 14 November 2006

Sixty-seven years ago, a substantial number of the freshest and finest minds of this university sat some forty-six miles to the east of here in cramped and stuffy hutments inside Bletchley Park trying to penetrate the secret signals traffic of Hitler's soldiers, sailors, airmen, diplomats, and spies, which they eventually did to great and war-shortening success. They and the 'Y' (or listening service) that fed them became skilled at recognising the call-sign 'signature' of the particular operator of the Enigma machine on the U-boat at sea or the weather station on shore even before the message was decrypted.

After a few years in the historical trade, a similar phenomenon affects those of us who spend a good deal of our time in the archives. For example, towards the end of a long afternoon at the Public Record Office in Kew, you know it's a Churchill or a Macmillan minute before you see the initials 'WSC' or 'HM' at the bottom of the page, so fruitily individual were their styles. Prime ministers in particular develop too what Tony Blair's former head of delivery, Professor Sir Michael Barber, calls a 'policy signature' – key themes with which they are personally associated. I would extend the metaphor still further – especially for activist (or hyperactivist) premiers such as David Lloyd George, the wartime Churchill, Margaret Thatcher and Tony Blair – to the notion of a governing signature that reflects styles of operation as well as policy content.

Governing signatures can be very revealing of prime ministers who are fuelled by a large dose of personal destiny and in whom certainty and impatience jostle daily, if not hourly. For there is a 'destiny' spectrum among twentieth-century British premiers. At one end is Winston Churchill, who famously wrote of his assumption of the job on 10 May 1940 at a moment of extreme national peril that, as he eased his substantial frame into bed in the small hours of 11 May, he was 'conscious of a profound sense of relief. At last I had the authority to give directions over the whole scene. I felt as if I were walking with destiny, and that all my past life had been but a preparation for this hour and this trial'. Indeed it had.

At the other end of the spectrum sits the diminutive figure of my own particular political hero, Clem Attlee. Asked in the last year of his life to recall 26 July 1945, when, to his surprise, he found himself driven in the family car by his wife through the gates of Buckingham Palace to kiss hands with King George VI, he described his 'emotions' as 'Just to know that there were jobs that were to be done.' The increasingly desperate interviewer persisted:

'You didn't feel that destiny had overtaken you?'
'No. I had not much idea about destiny.'

A note of near hysteria enters at that this point:

'Have you ever felt in any way, Lord Attlee, as being, in fact, as you are, a man of destiny? Have you ever felt this kind of emotion which Winston Churchill has written about so much?'
'No, you see I didn't regard myself as a potential hero.'

Marvellous. The political genius of modest understatement – that rarest of traits.

Tony Blair is firmly at the 'destiny' end of the spectrum and has been from the first hours after the scale of his landslide victory became apparent on the night of 1–2 May 1997. His own account of his 'destiny' moment lacked a certain Churchillian fluency when he recalled it for a journalist a few months later. But, even though there was a slight Attleean dash of humility, the 'D' element was evident enough as he and his entourage flew down from Teesside Airport to Stansted in a chartered jet.

> There's a nice picture of us on the plane on the way down where she [Cherie] is really saying to me: 'Now be strong and realise what a great opportunity this is for you. Make the most of it.' But although it may sound absolutely ridiculous, all I could feel was a great sense of anti-climax. I felt that it was such an extraordinary thing to have happened to me. While others did the celebrating I really felt the need to tell myself how very fortunate I was, and, 'Don't you damn well blow it.'

The destiny element, and the determination not to 'blow' his legacy, is even more pronounced now in the twilight of his premiership.

At the end of July this year, with the war in Lebanon and northern Israel at its height, Mr Blair delivered one of the most fascinating and revealing speeches of his premiership to Rupert Murdoch, a gathering of News Corp executives, and assorted celebrities gathered at Pebble Beach in California. His theme was leadership and the inner convictions needed to sustain it. Turning to what he called 'the debate about terrorism or security,' he said: 'I have many opponents on the subject: but complete inner confidence in the analysis of the struggle we face.' And the implications of this total ring of self-confidence in these days of global anxiety and uncertainty? 'In these times, caution is error; to hesitate is to lose.' For his critics, this was primary-colours thinking verging on the millenarian.

As a seasoned Whitehall veteran, who had closely watched Mr Blair in action during most of his wars, put it privately shortly after the Pebble Beach oration: 'It's TB and the Holy Grail. He really does see himself as a latter-day crusader. It's dangerous.' Here the old sweat paused for thought and said: 'Thank God Bush and Blair weren't in charge during the Cuban Missile Crisis.'

Three days before the Pebble Beach speech, another Whitehall veteran, Sir Stephen Wall, who had worked for Blair as his European adviser when head of the Cabinet Office's European Secretariat 2000–4, took issue publicly with the Blair approach to the Middle East crisis and his excessive closeness to the Bush line, telling Channel 4 News that 'Tony Blair has supreme confidence in his own judgement.'

Blair, as a man apart and possessor of special insights that an often unappreciative world really needs, was there in technicolour in the concluding climax to his Pebble Beach declaration, laced with an unacknowledged touch of Kipling:

> For a leader, don't let your ego be carried away by praise or your spirit diminished by the criticism and look on each with a very searching eye. But for heaven's sake, above all else, lead.

Kipling's famous 'If –', you remember, contained these lines:

> If you can meet with Triumph and Disaster
> And treat those two impostors just the same;

This notion of destiny will run through the entire Blair premiership (however and whenever it ends) as it does from its opening bars through all four movements of Beethoven's Fifth Symphony. His time in Number 10 Downing Street cannot be understood without it, whether one is contemplating Tony as transformer of domestic public services or Blair the warrior/preacher abroad; 'for heaven's sake, above all else, lead' is the autobiographical key he has given to all his future interpreters.

Tony Blair's Pebble Beach ode to leadership also contained a delicious line for those with a taste for counterfactual history. 'I am sometimes taken to task,' he said, 'for being too ambitious in the radical nature of the policy changes I am seeking. I always have the opposite worry: not being radical enough.' What, one wonders, might he have wished to have done if he had felt completely untrammelled and free of that formidable, one-person resistance movement across the Cabinet table, in the person of the Chancellor of the Exchequer, Gordon Brown; or a party in Parliament several of whose members retained a certain tendresse for traditional Labour ideals; or a career Civil Service not so obsessed with a care for proper procedures?

How to make longer-term sense of this extraordinary figure – 'the great persuader', as his admirer and biographer, John Rentoul, calls him – and the nature of the legacy which so preoccupies him? This, naturally, is difficult to do in the compass of a single lecture and with no foreknowledge of the nature and timing of Mr Blair's political demise – and departures, as Macmillan's, Heath's, Wilson's, Callaghan's, and Thatcher's showed, very often leave a powerful aftertaste in the overall historical memory of their stewardships in Number 10. But here goes.

I'll begin with the Blair impact on the job itself. I was the recipient, at a private breakfast of top businessmen and senior civil servants I was chairing in March 1997, of the now famous line from a close Blair adviser that 'you may see a change from a feudal system of barons to a more Napoleonic system.' We were warned. Whatever the size of the majority in the forthcoming election (and there was nervousness within the Blair circle about the outcome until the final days of the campaign), it was not going to be Cabinet or Whitehall business as usual.

The perils of an excessively commanding premiership, compounded by a highly informal style of reaching many, if not all, decisions, has now become a cliché of contemporary politics. The mere use of the word 'sofa' is enough to trigger it. Last month David Cameron converted it into an election target for the Conservatives, telling his Party Conference in Bournemouth,

I'll tell you something important, something substantial, that we have to change. For too long, the big political decisions in this country have been made in the wrong place. Not round the Cabinet table, where they should be. But on the sofa in Tony Blair's office. No notes are taken. No-one knows who's accountable. No one takes the blame when things go wrong. That arrogant style of government must come to an end. I will restore the proper process of government. That means building a strong team and leading them. I want to be prime minister of this country. Not a president.

Douglas Hurd put it rather more elegantly that same week when comparing Blair to his predecessor-but-two, whose style he (Blair) so much admired and so carefully courted. 'Thatcher herself,' wrote Lord Hurd,

> kept some respect for the conventions of the constitution. She could be bossy in Cabinet and brutal to her individual colleagues, but she never disregarded Cabinet or the House of Commons to the extent now common. Sofa government would have been abhorrent to her; she believed in stiff chairs and the orderly conduct of business.

There is one huge, brooding qualifier to this picture of command-and-control from a sofa, which must be borne in mind at all times – the command chancellor, Gordon Brown, another destiny politician, albeit without Tony Blair's millenarian tendencies; Brown is more Parry's and Blake's 'Jerusalem' than Blair's Beethoven's Fifth.

The years since 1997 have seen the most bizarre job-share at the top, of a kind never experienced in Whitehall before. The Chancellor has enjoyed a kind of primacy on economic policy; the Prime Minister on foreign and defence policy and Northern Ireland. They dispute over some of the instruments of public-service reform and delivery and, when it's a live question, Britain and the Euro, where both think they are in the lead. With the two governing elephants bumping and grinding, little room has been left for the lesser Cabinet beasts. In fact, Cabinet government has been at its lowest ebb since Lloyd George at Versailles in the months following the Great War, when, as John Maynard Keynes put it in his classic essay 'Dr Melchior', there 'must be plenty of officials to hang about in case he might need them; but the real business ... was to be done by himself ... and the less the officials knew of what was going on, the freer his hands would be.' A historian of the years since 1997, as of 1918–19, needs to be more a scholar of courts than of Cabinets.

The lack of careful procedure and proper minuting blazoned forth from both the Hutton report on the circumstances surrounding the death of Dr David Kelly, the weapons expert, and the Butler report into the use of intelligence on the road to the Iraq War. And, although the Cabinet had several discussions about Iraq in 2002 and early 2003, the wherewithal of the collective decision-taking was lacking in certain key essentials, as we shall see in a moment. In my view, questions before a Cabinet come no higher than peace and war and collective failures here have a special culpability.

But at a lower, if continuously central level, economic decision-taking has suffered its own particular blight since 1997. The command Chancellor has, on occasion, been unwilling to share detail with the command Premier, let alone the Cabinet. According to Blair's economic adviser, Derek Scott, Brown kept the Prime Minister in ignorance of the strategy of his first budget until two days before it was delivered. And, very often, their bilateral exchanges on economic policy – which are far more important than any discussions at the Cabinet's economic affairs committee – take place without a private secretary to take minutes. Whitehall has somehow to decode what took place, producing, very often, a series of Chinese whispers augmented by leaks from the rival courts of Number 10 and Number 11 Downing Street. Even those who are fairly relaxed about procedural matters regard this as dysfunctional and unsatisfactory.

In the fading months of his premiership, Mr Blair began to make conspicuous, if belated amends. Battered by the reaction to his stance on the Israeli invasion of Lebanon in the summer of 2006 and the frenzied speculation about the manner and timing of his departure from the premiership (including some unusually direct criticism from his normally supine colleagues at the special 'Political Cabinet' on 20 September 2006), he announced his intention to deploy his Cabinet on six key reviews as the finger of political history beckoned him.

In fact, the return of Cabinet government was announced in two stages. The weekend before his fractious 'Political Cabinet' in September, the press carried the signs of a Number 10 briefing, beginning with *The Observer* on Sunday 17 September. Gaby Hinsliff's story neatly encapsulated the line that would be followed, with variations, across the national dailies on Monday morning:

> Tony Blair has ordered the return of cabinet-style government as he fights back from the attempted coup against him, reversing years of reliance on private deals with Gordon Brown and 'sofa politics' with his intimates.
>
> He is to give his entire team a much bigger say in future decisions after senior ministers privately complained of being left out of the loop and of fears that major decisions would be stitched up privately between the Prime Minister and Chancellor as part of the negotiations on the succession.

Not for another month, until the worst of what Nye Bevan might have called the 'emotional spasms' had run their course about the conduct of foreign policy over the summer and the very public outbreak of infighting about the leadership succession of early autumn had somewhat abated, did Blair get his Cabinet to endorse the six legacy-securing reviews on 19 October 2006.

The whole exercise was redolent of the Blair signature – the press briefed first in terms of a tough, defiant prime minister ensuring the fruits of his probable decade in power would not wither on the branch, while acting as Tony the persuader-healer of an anxious and divided Cabinet whose participation and inclusion would be guaranteed. The Prime Minister's official spokesman went to great and detailed lengths when briefing the lobby correspondents on what had transpired in the Cabinet Room. 'The Cabinet,' he said, 'had enthusiastically endorsed plans to take forward a formal Whitehall process which would see every aspect of Government policy come under scrutiny.' The journalists were told that the 'Chancellor had stressed how important he believed this process was and that it would help both the Government and the country address the unprecedented challenges facing the world in the coming years. The Deputy Prime Minister [John Prescott] had described it as an exciting project. John Reid [home secretary] had stressed its importance for Government renewal. Patricia Hewitt [health secretary] said it would strengthen the public's faith in their democracy.'

For all the zest with which they were launched, the true test of changing intentions and governing practice, however, will come in how the so-called 'Pathways to the Future' reviews into economic performance – security, crime, and justice; environment and energy; Britain's place in the world; public services; and the role of the state – are conducted. Having a Cabinet minister preside over each is a start in terms of the human geography of power. But how serious will be the intellectual R & D that goes into them be, especially as the clock is ticking for Mr Blair's tenure at Number 10? And, as Peter Riddell noted, 'the more public the reviews are, the less candid and far-reaching will be the analysis and conclusions. It was hard enough for officials, in private, in the late 1950s, to admit the full lessons of the Suez fiasco. Is Mr Blair really prepared in the dying days of his administration to admit publicly the failures of his Iraq policy?'

There have been proclamations of a return to Cabinet government before. For example, defenders of the Blair style have in the past pointed to the Cabinet presentations on their sections of the biennial comprehensive spending reviews by individual secretaries of state as demonstrating that there is life still in collective Cabinet discussion. But, as a very senior Whitehall figure put it, 'powerpoint is a narrative, not an analysis.'

The other serious reason for scepticism is a penchant, which the command Prime Minister and the command Chancellor share, for policy pre-emption (very much governing signature of both of them). 2006 saw classic examples from each of them in the nuclear field – civil in Blair's case; military in Brown's. In May, the Prime Minister pre-empted the government's energy review by two months by declaring that without 'the replacement of nuclear power stations, a big push on renewables and a step-change on energy efficiency', the government would 'be committing a serious dereliction of our duty to the future of this country.' Just over a month later, the Chancellor of the Exchequer, in his annual Mansion House speech, pre-empted the succession-to-Trident question by announcing that the government (Blair's and his, presumably) would demonstrate 'a sense of national purpose in protecting our security in this Parliament and the long term – strong in defence, in fighting terrorism, upholding NATO, supporting our armed forces at home and abroad, and retaining our independent nuclear deterrent.'

Both were extraordinary usurpations of subjects with such substantial policy and spending implications that they cried out for proper collective ministerial decision-taking rather than the politics of command. Even the Ministry of Defence's nuclear weapons specialists only knew of the Chancellor's intention, in Ernest Bevin's immortal words, to 'have a bloody Union Jack flying on top of it' until at least the 2050s the evening before. Why do the Cabinet put up with such disdainful humiliations?

The same thought occurred to one of their former colleagues. In a thoughtful piece about the 'fault lines' beneath the Labour government in the *New Statesman* of 4 September 2006, Charles Clarke wrote:

It is vital that our approach is systematic and thorough. Major policy issues, such as the place of nuclear energy in the drive to energy sustainability and the value to our overall security strategy of replacing Trident, need serious consideration. They cannot simply be dealt with as an aside at the CBI's annual dinner or a half-sentence at the Guildhall.

But, for all his candour, Mr Clarke did not mention the greatest and gravest example of policy pre-emption of all – Iraq.

A few weeks after Mr Blair returned from his visit to Mr Bush's Texas ranch near Crawford in April 2002, Whitehall insiders sensed a significant turn in the politico-military weather. The Prime Minister had persuaded the President to pursue a multilateral route on Iraq – seeking United Nations backing before using physical force against Iraq. But, should this route be blocked, the United Kingdom would back US military action, even if no other big international player did. This has since been reflected in all the most authoritative accounts of Anglo-American diplomacy on the road to Iraq.

This was a prime ministerial decision unannounced to the Cabinet, let alone Parliament and the public. It caused immense problems for military planning and procurement and for intelligence. For intelligence was to be used publicly and in advance to justify military action against the Saddam regime in a manner that had never been seen before and is most unlikely to be witnessed again. As the Butler report said of the government's dossier on Iraq's weapons of mass destruction of 24 September 2002,

   a. The JIC [Joint Intelligence Committee] had never previously produced a public document.
   b. No Government case for any international action had previously been made to the British public through explicitly drawing on a JIC publication.
   c. The authority of the British intelligence community, and of the JIC in particular, had never been used in such a public way.

This particular example of the Blair signature created immense problems for both his government and the reputation of the British intelligence community. As the former director-general of the Security Service, MI5, Dame Stella Rimington, said nearly four years later,

> I personally felt that putting intelligence into the public domain was not a good idea, that no good would come of it. If you're going to put intelligence into the public domain you've got to simplify it, and most intelligence reports I've read are full of caveats. People who receive them on a day-to-day basis know that, and understand that you may have an imperfect picture. So, when you come to decide that you're going to use intelligence to justify decisions you've already taken, I think you're moving down the wrong track. And I think that's what went wrong.

Intelligence has a special potency in Whitehall's information flows and needs the kind of fastidious handling that does not always come naturally to a political class that rises to the top by mobilising prejudice more successfully than its competitors. As Sir David Omand, the former co-ordinator of security and intelligence in the Cabinet Office, put it in October 2006: 'Knowledge is power, and secret knowledge is supercharged power.'

What about the wider briefing for the Cabinet on the road to Baghdad? Iraq was discussed at no less than twenty-four full Cabinet meetings. Lord Butler and his fellow privy counsellors reported that '[e]xcellent quality papers were written by officials, but these were not discussed in Cabinet or Cabinet committee' which meant that it was 'possible but ... obviously much more difficult' for Cabinet ministers outside Mr Blair's inner group to test out the evidence and the arguments presented to them by the Prime Minister in his 'unscripted' oral presentations. David Blunkett's taped diaries gave a real flavour of this when published in October 2006. On 7 March

2002, a few weeks before the Blair/Bush meeting at Crawford, Blunkett recorded that:

> At Cabinet we had a very good discussion about Iraq, which lasted for the best part of an hour, during which we all said our bit. I talked about social cohesion at home and the obvious issues that had arisen over 11 September [2001], where the real message was: Why aren't you doing something about the Middle East and the Palestine–Israeli conflict? Why are you just backing the Americans ... Apart from Jack Straw [foreign secretary] and Geoff Hoon [defence secretary] who had clearly got the message to be gung-ho, everyone else was drawing the conclusion that we needed to go into depth with this. In the end Tony said: 'Look, the management hasn't lost its marbles. We do know these things. We are not going to rush in.' But we all fear that they will.

Just linger a moment on those words – 'the management hasn't lost its marbles.' The Cabinet reduced to a group of non-executive directors feebly satisfied with oral briefings from the man in the know.

For me, the greatest collective dereliction of duty occurred just over a year later, on 17 March 2003, when the Cabinet did not test out the Attorney General's opinion on the legality of going to war in Iraq without a further UN resolution specifically authorising the use of force. We know from the Butler report that the full Cabinet were not shown the far fuller formal minute from the Attorney to the Prime Minister of 7 March 2003. As Lord Butler put it: 'The Attorney General set out his view of the legal position to the Cabinet on 17 March, by producing and speaking to the Written Answer he gave to Parliament on that date.'

By not insisting on the fullest briefing, and testing out the assumptions of the Attorney General's advice, Blair's ministers participated in the greatest single failure of collective Cabinet government since Sir Anthony Eden's ministers failed to press him on 23

October 1956, as the Suez Crisis neared its climax, when he told them 'from secret conversations which had been held in Paris with representatives of the Israeli government, it now appeared that the Israelis would not alone launch a full-scale attack against Egypt.' Policy pre-emption by premiers is only possible if their Cabinets allow them to get away with it.

Before I finish with the theme of Tony Blair as history, I must mention the big sub-themes I have not covered this evening. Public-service delivery is a huge and obvious one. It deserves not just a lecture but a book of its own. And I anticipate with the keenest of pleasure the study to be published next year by Sir Michael Barber, head of the Prime Minister's Delivery Unit 2001–5. The other is perhaps the greatest paradox of the Blair years – constitutional reform.

Future historians, I reckon, will treat the combination of devolution to Scotland and Wales, the Human Rights Act, and the Freedom of Information Act as the most remarkable remaking of the British constitution from within that our country has ever experienced in such a concentrated burst. Tony Blair rarely mentions it. Indeed, he sometimes appears to be running a campaign against his own administration's Human Rights Act. As for devolution to Scotland, in one glorious entry in Paddy Ashdown's diary the Prime Minister gives the impression of never having read the Scotland Act properly! Just listen to this conversation between the pair of them in May 1999. Ashdown reminds Blair that he (Blair) previously reckoned that provided Scotland could find the money from within its own budget, he wasn't 'fussed' about the Executive paying the tuition fees of university students. Was he now saying that was wrong?

> BLAIR: Yes, I was wrong when I said that. You can't have Scotland doing something different from the rest of Britain.
> ASHDOWN: Then you shouldn't have given the Scots devolution, including specifically, the power to be different on this issue ...

BLAIR (laughing): Yes, that's the problem. I am beginning to see all the defects in this devolution stuff.

That almost amounts to a legacy (in this case, a real and profound one) spurned.

The great French historian, Fernand Braudel, once wrote of the Greek city states that '[a]s always, to govern was to create resentment.' And, as Hugh Trevor-Roper noted nearly sixty years ago, even the most skilful and relentless political propaganda is subject to the law of diminishing returns. Eventual disbelief is often the fate of destiny politicians forever asserting an inner confidence in the wisdom of their insights, obsessed by the desire to dominate communications and what Jean Seaton called 'the politics of appearances' (both strong strokes in the Blair signature).

For command models grow the microbes which, in the end, cause them to crumble. And the factors which help those microbes develop are both human and procedural. Napoleons usually end up in some kind of exile. As Mark Twain liked to say, 'history may not repeat itself, but sometimes it rhymes.'

The undoing of prime ministers

On 25 October 2022, after a whirlwind forty-nine days in power, Liz Truss's premiership imploded in a spectacular and highly distressing manner. Even laying aside the fact she plunged the economy into swift near-peril, it was, to borrow from that acute political observer Lady Bracknell, a premiership and leadership campaign crowded with incident. During that brief time, she had managed to insult the French President Emmanuel Macron and to come up with a solution to the 'Scottish question' that is scarcely believable even now to recall – describing Scotland's First Minister Nicola Sturgeon as an 'attention-seeker', she declared that she would simply not talk to her. This, it turned out, was the only promise that she kept during her short time in power. Depicting Ms Sturgeon as attention-seeking might be described as a bit rich coming from Ms Truss.

It was her truncated and, it has to be admitted, pathetic premiership that got me thinking about the last days of the post-war prime ministers. So many have ended their time in Number 10 unhappily, almost as if their ambition sets them up for a very big fall; though even by normal standards Truss's demise was pretty spectacular. There was also an irony in her downfall. She came into office in September 2022 with an almost religious faith in the beauty, purity, and efficacy of markets. Within days – hours after her chancellor, Kwasi Kwarteng, unveiled their plan for growth that would burst the shackles of Treasury orthodoxy – the money markets and the central bankers took to their equivalent of the hills. Ever since her fall, she has suggested that the problem was that she was ahead of her time. Bizarrely, this reminded me of the way Marxists used to try to explain away the failure of communism by saying either 'nobody's tried it properly' or something along the lines of 'the masses have let us down yet again.' Unfortunately for her, she was the least successful of all the destiny prime ministers of the post-war years. Mind you, there were warning signs. To make the production and importation of cheese the subject of the most passionate speech of your political career is, to put it mildly, indicative of an unusual approach to political economy.

The length of Truss's premiership may have been novel, but the irony in her demise is not. In fact, I have come to the conclusion that if there is an 'iron law' of premiership, it's this: that they are undone by the very things they think they understand best.

Harold Wilson's special pitch, as a professional economist and statistician, was the engineering of a faster rate of growth through economic planning and shrewd state intervention. Yet during his first two governments, the country lived through a devaluation of the pound, a seemingly perpetual sterling and balance of payments crisis, and achieved a growth rate lower than that which Conservatives had managed during what Harold described as their thirteen 'wasted years' in office. Wilson, too, had an aversion in this instance to his analysis being challenged. For example, he prohibited any proper discussion of devaluation as an alternative to deflation until events forced upon him the much-resisted devaluation in 1967. The Treasury christened devaluation 'the Great Unmentionable' when the possibility floated through their corridors.

Wilson was, generally speaking, a proper collective Cabinet government man. But there were certain policies – the currency among them – he thought too sensitive for ventilation in the Cabinet Room. So he, too, suffered from a tendency to sustain his views, which rested on his professional skills and knowledge, against dissenters bearing an alternative policy that might have succeeded in avoiding deflation. His big idea – economic planning – contained in the National Plan of 1965 was blown away by the economic crisis of July 1966. The circumstances in which Wilson operated were stretching, certainly. But his great selling point during the 1964 general election of breaking the mould of relative stagnation and economic underperformance based on the 'white heat' of the technological revolution ended in cold, grey ashes. Wilson promised so much but was brought low on the very field of his primary expertise.

No senior Labour politician had a greater sensitivity towards the trade union movement than Jim Callaghan. As an ex-trade union official he was flesh of their flesh; the unions had given him his chance in life and he loved them. He'd gone to the stake for them over In Place of Strife in 1969 when he'd stood out against Barbara Castle and Harold Wilson's proposed reforms, designed to bring industrial peace through a reordering and remaking of collective bargaining processes in search of a harmony model that had eluded all prime ministers and chancellors since the initially successful days of incomes policy (when Attlee was in Number 10 and Stafford Cripps the chancellor next door). Yet his government broke on the rocks of nakedly applied trade union power in the early months of 1979.

Callaghan's tragedy was that his very formidable political skills were deployed in just holding the line against a rolling economic crisis without a majority in the Commons (apart from one year of Lib–Lab pact). Also, as he once told me, the premiership came to him late and as a sixty-four-year-old it took its toll. He developed the knack, for example, of going to sit on the government front bench of an afternoon, however unimportant the business might be, just to get a bit of a rest. The Labour Party he loved and led was moving, seemingly inexorably, into one of those internal civil wars at which it excels. I don't think he ever overcame the nature of his political demise – undone by the people and the institutions who had made him the very substantial figure he was and who, I used to think, he treated as a kind of extended family. I'm still saddened by the memory of what Callaghan said to his principal private secretary, Ken Stowe, in January 1979: 'I think I've let the country down.' He hadn't. For all the misjudgements he made with his over-optimistic incomes policy in 1978 – and by delaying going to the polls that autumn – it could be said that his beloved Labour movement had let him and his government down.

Margaret Thatcher arrived in Downing Street determined to avoid the fates of Wilson and Callaghan; she would not be broken by the immovable objects of economic circumstance or trade union power. Shortly after she became prime minister, John Ashworth, a friend of mine who was the chief scientist in the Cabinet Office's think tank, was presenting a 'tank' paper on unemployment. He sensed her hostility to its analysis and said, 'It's entirely based on the facts, Prime Minister.' She replied, 'The facts? The facts? I have been elected to change the facts.' It is hard to imagine any prime minister before or since who would have put it quite as bluntly as that. Indeed, when it came to many aspects of the 'post-war consensus', she did change the facts. She went beyond seriously curbing what many regarded as excessive trade union power to inject a powerful shot of liberal economics into the standard post-war model of a mixed economy/welfare state built largely on the analyses of William Beveridge and J. M. Keynes, the twin ventricles of the so-called post-war consensus.

However, the wrathful gods of politics, in the end, did not spare her either. Although no Conservative prime minister had a swifter or surer access to the mind of the aggrieved ratepayer, it was local government finance, in the shape of her hated poll tax, that holed her government below the waterline in 1989–90 before the deadly torpedo of the European question finally did for her as well. Her intellectually brilliant and personally forceful chancellor of the Exchequer, Nigel Lawson, detested the idea of a poll tax on every household as a concept, and warned consistently that it would face stiff resistance in the country. He wouldn't even turn up to the relevant Cabinet committee to discuss it. Yet, in her best Boudicca style, she drove her chariot of rates reform into what indeed did turn out to be a political maelstrom. She was convinced she understood local government like few others. Her father, the greatest single influence on her early life, was indeed a proud alderman. She particularly loathed local councils dominated by the hard Left. Her fabled handbag would be used on them ruthlessly. On such matters she would take instruction from no one.

Unusually for a prime minister – and unlike Wilson, Callaghan, and Thatcher – Anthony Eden had no deep knowledge of economic or domestic policy. However, he had – or so it was thought – the silkiest of touches on foreign affairs. He spoke Persian and knew the Middle East as intimately as any British foreign secretary could. He also, so people thought, knew where and how diplomacy had to be applied to avoid conflict. And he had a great track record; he'd resigned as foreign secretary in 1938 over appeasement and had had a very good war as foreign secretary once more. Yet he was blown away by the Suez Crisis and a serious misreading of the geopolitics of the Middle East and the US–UK relationship in general.

On the field of foreign affairs, he found it difficult to brook rival assessments of people, places, and episodes in instances where he'd already made up his mind. For example, in 1956 he took pains to make sure that Sir Harold Beeley, who was the great expert on this in the Foreign Office, was not in the inner loop on Suez. He ignored the Foreign Office legal adviser, Sir Gerald Fitzmaurice, who said that what Eden was planning to do was illegal, and he would not let Sir Edward Bridges, the permanent secretary to the Treasury and the head of the Civil Service, attend meetings of the Egypt Committee, the Cabinet's inner group on the crisis. In effect, Eden made sure that the people who knew best weren't involved. That was fatal for his career and, for a while, ruinous for his country. He resigned the premiership as a sick and broken man in early January 1957.

Blair doesn't quite fit the model of the prime minister undone by an area of personal expertise. The tarnishing of his legacy was more to do with his character. He seemed to believe that if he could negotiate, face-to-face, he could persuade almost anyone to his point of view or something close to it. This level of self-assurance and, to quite a high extent genuine personal charm, had undoubtedly helped secure what I think is the greatest single triumph of his long premierships – the Good Friday Agreement of 1998, which, though it did not end the latent civil war in Northern Ireland, lifted the curse of it for at least a generation and a half.

The problem arose when his appreciation of his own special gifts and insights led him astray on that unforgiving terrain in the Middle East, where oil meets sand and geopolitics seethe. For if the Good Friday Agreement was his finest hour, his conduct of the Iraq War with President George W. Bush was its lowest. He seemed to lack the humility needed when using force in the Middle East and indeed, in retirement after the Chilcot report had judged him and his government so vividly, he would talk about how little the UK and the United States knew about the societies which the war disturbed – to the point where the allies had no chance of post-war state-rebuilding, facing instead multiple horrors and bloodshed, of which ISIS was much the most appalling. He plainly believed that his special gifts could temper the Americans and also increase the chances of an easement of even the deepest and rawest conflicts in the Middle East.

Blair the Iraq War prime minister also had a lasting and, I would argue, damaging impact on domestic British politics. For without the rending of the Labour Party and the wider labour movement that the war caused, Jeremy Corbyn would have been inconceivable as leader of the Labour Party. Although Blair led the party to electoral victory in 2005 two years after the war, the seeds of the schism were already deeply planted – a schism that would keep Labour out of power for fourteen years. Tony Blair's tragedy is that Iraq dominates, more than any other single event, the way he and his governments are remembered. The considerable pile of social achievements and, in some cases, genuinely creative use of public spending are scarcely recalled compared to the invasion of Iraq and its dreadful aftermath. It could be argued, therefore, that Blair was brought low by those very gifts that his admirers thought genuinely exceptional.

It may seem eccentric to include Boris Johnson in the list of prime ministers undone by their greatest areas of expertise. For what were his personal gifts, the special aspects of his character, his deep wells of knowledge? Arguably, Johnson's true speciality was getting away with it, whatever 'it' happened to be. He didn't seem to believe that the rules applied to him. Some rumbled him very early on, including his house master at Eton, who wrote in a letter to Johnson's father, Stanley, in 1982: 'I think he honestly believes that it is churlish of us not to regard him as an exception, one who should be free of the network of obligation that binds everyone else.'

There were many aspects to Johnson's character and behaviour which made him, in my judgement, outstandingly unfit to be prime minister. One of which stemmed from his overwhelming determination to overcome all rivals to win and to hold the top office for himself and for a long time. He reminds me of a sentence Professor Chris Clark of the University of Cambridge wrote in a book review of his friend Jonathan Steinberg's life of Bismarck. 'Politics', Chris Clark said, 'ate up everything else inside him. It fed on and ultimately destroyed most of his friendships.' There was a difference, however, between these two men: Bismarck was a genius; Johnson is not.

For a while, Johnson appeared to get away with ignoring – almost taunting – the conventions on which the decencies of governing and political life depend. For example, the contents of the Ministerial Code – which is pretty well all that stands, on paper, between the decencies and the possible depredations of a rogue prime minister – he could brush aside as a mere convention, not a law which had to be obeyed.

In one of the richer, albeit darker, ironies of the Johnson years, given his rackety personal life, it was a sex scandal, but not one of his, that was the occasion of his ultimate demise. This scandal involved a Foreign Office minister turned deputy chief whip, Chris Pincher, the details of which, dear reader, I shall spare you. One could argue that Johnson's personal expertise on the sex-scandal front made him almost cocksure in his judgements on other people's peccadillos.

For him, alarm bells did not ring in response to Pincher's behaviour, even when they would have been pealing madly for others had they been in his position.

In a matter of a few days, fifty-three of his ministers told him he couldn't carry on, even those who had not seemed unduly worried by the conventions and probities of the Ministerial Code to which they were all expected to subscribe. He couldn't 'get away with it' any more.

I have no practical remedy to offer any future prime minister keen to avoid being biffed by my not-quite-iron law. Perhaps it would be futile; one of the problems with succeeding to the premiership is that it can all too often be treated as a very personal vindication of one's prejudices and insights, allied to a belief that the system of government itself cannot be so bad if it had the wisdom to pick you out and project you to the highest level. However, anyone aspiring to the top office might do well to hold in mind the mental equivalent of the monsignor walking in front of the pope on certain ceremonial occasions, flicking dust, metaphorically, in his eye and intoning '*Sic Transit Gloria Mundi*', or – to give it a demotic translation – 'Remember, matey, you too are mortal'.

Parliament and the state

The Speaker's Lecture, Houses of Parliament, 18 November 2014

It's a great pleasure and a real honour to be invited to give one of Mr Speaker's Lectures for 2014. I've been fascinated by Westminster since I came here as a sixth-former with a friend, Bob Gardiner, from our Gloucestershire grammar in Stroud, Marling School, to sit in the gallery for the very last day of the 1959 Parliament in July 1964 before catching the milk train, as we called them then, from Paddington back to the West Country. And the fascination will last, I'm certain, until I draw my very last breath.

How best to approach the history and the current condition of institutions and the relationships between them? How to answer the question: what is Parliament for?

For even the most knowledgeable, such questions are immensely difficult to answer in a sentence. Some can; most can't. A friend of mine who could was the Cambridge philosopher Renford Bambrough. As a young journalist on *The Times Higher Education Supplement*, I asked him: 'Renford, what are universities for?' Without pause he replied: 'Universities exist to take care of the curiosity of the species in the way the army exists to take care of its pugnacity'. When Mr Speaker asked me to deliver this evening's lecture I thought of Renford Bambrough.

What is Parliament for? The answer, Bambrough-style, I think is this:

Parliament exists to humanise the state and make it more bearable.

What I have in mind is General Charles de Gaulle's potent aside: 'The state is a cold monster'.

For me, one of Parliament's perpetual tasks is not only to curb the potential excesses of the state, but to warm it up a bit. To give it a dash of empathy. To remind the state in all its forms of the impact it has on people, on their life chances, and upon other institutions. More on that in a moment.

We all carry an individual map of Parliament in our heads – an accumulation of memory, impressions, episodes, and personalities. That map also embraces a cartography of expectations. When you look at the polling data on trust in members of Parliament, it is a lowering experience. The expenses scandal of 2009 scored a line across public perceptions, the scars of which are still vivid.

In all sorts of ways, the aftershocks of 2009 can still be felt not least in a mood of anti-politics, or mainstream politics as we have known it, which takes a myriad of forms. But the word 'shock' is intriguing. The fact that we remain shockable and are palpably disappointed when standards do not match up to our expectations is highly significant and, in a paradoxical fashion, heartening. For if, on hearing examples of personal behavioural slippage by politicians, we merely shrugged our shoulders and said 'Well, that's just the way they are', we would have passed through a one-way valve where cynicism had heavily trumped scepticism and we would be living in a different country. That we are still shockable is precious.

There is, however, much to be worried about. Neither Parliament, nor the state, nor those who people both institutions are currently enjoying the confidence of the nation or the hosannas of a grateful people. And we find ourselves in a vexing, buffeting, and stretching governing climate which is the product of multiple political weather systems, all of which require our political class – parliamentarians, ministers, and officials alike – to raise their individual and collective games.

At this point, however, I must come out as someone who lives at the romantic end of the spectrum. I am among those who work in the Palace of Westminster for whom its walls talk, who hear the echo of ancestral voices and the touch of ancestral practices which, as the generations passed, seared into the nation's consciousness the belief that it was Parliament where our conflicts and disagreements should be played out and, as far as possible, resolved. The national deal implicit in parliamentary government is 'raised voices, yes; raised fists, no'.

This is my rather feeble equivalent of one of my favourite Churchillian quotations. It's not the famous line in an otherwise lacklustre speech in the House of Commons on 11 November 1947 on the bill that eventually emerged as the Parliament Act 1949 – the passage we all know from the great man:

> No one pretends that democracy is perfect or all-wise. Indeed, it has been said that democracy is the worst form of Government except all those other forms that have been tried from time to time; but there is the broad feeling in our country that the people should rule, continuously rule, and that public opinion, expressed by all constitutional means, should shape, guide and control the actions of Ministers who are their servants and not their masters.

The Churchill words that really cause my atoms to tingle he uttered thirty years earlier at a particularly grim phrase of the Great War in March 1917. They are captured in the diary of MacCallum Scott, then a fellow Liberal MP. 'As we were leaving the House that night', Scott recalled,

> he [Churchill] called me into the Chamber to take a last look round. All was darkness except a ring of faint light all around the Gallery. We could dimly see the Table but walls and roof were invisible. 'Look at it', he said. 'This little place is what makes the difference between us and Germany. It is in virtue of this that we shall muddle through to success and for lack of this Germany's

brilliant efficiency leads her to final destruction. This little room is the shrine of the world's liberties.'

Glorious stuff. Powerful stuff.

Would anybody, could anybody – legislator or observer – think remotely like that today, even allowing for the uniqueness of the combination of imagination and wordpower that Winston Churchill possessed? Up to a point, yes.

Mr Speaker's invitation to talk this evening made me think about how I, as a historian of my own times (by which I mean Britain since World War II), would capture Parliament's indispensability as both humaniser, explainer, and scrutineer of the state and with both chambers, Commons and Lords – one, even in its rebuilt form after the war, still a 'little room', the Lords rather bigger and flashier – as the places where the great policy clashes are played out, the huge sequences of changes to our economy, our society, and our place in the world absorbed and, where possible, coped with. At the same time, the parliamentary weather is affected by the turbulence of the immediate, the here-and-now, the breaking story that disturbs the ganglia of Parliament, Whitehall, and the press alike.

In fact, Ladies and Gentlemen, I would argue that Parliament has twin functions which frequently rub up against each other:

- First, Parliament is the place where transient rows and passions play out in a very present-centred way.
- Secondly, Westminster is the place where parliamentarians constantly need to persuade the state to think about the long-term, the difficult, the important, and, sometimes, the unobvious – and generally of the need for the state to raise its game as a defender of the realm, its people, and its institutions. This second function is as stretching as it is significant. The great French historical sociologist, Raymond Aron, wrote of those 'who would accept the thankless task of reacting to events and discerning their meaning before their

consequences became apparent'. That speaks directly to the nature of parliamentary life.

Pondering these thoughts led me to re-read a gem of a book by Norman Shrapnel called *The Performers: Politics as Theatre*, published in 1978. Shrapnel was the *Guardian*'s gimlet-eyed parliamentary sketch writer for twenty years from the mid-1950s to the mid-1970s. He was, I think, the first of the gallery breed I read regularly. Shrapnel caught, in a single terrific sentence, the points I was just trying to make about Parliament's twin functions. 'So', he wrote of the two theatres of Westminster,

> what we have is a famous but ever-struggling national repertory company, busy dramatising an era, improvising its way through a mistily discernible plot lacking only (or so we must fervently hope) the final curtain.

Shrapnel characterised his post-war years as a parliamentary observer as 'an era of severe national hangover, of painful adjustment to new facts of life'.

Let's think about some of the great national dramas played out in Parliament – and grappled with by the state – since I emerged into austerity Britain at the end of March 1947:

- First, the fundamental nature of the domestic party competition stayed until recently remarkably stable (though we just might be in the middle of a turbulent sea-change; we'll find out whether we are or not in the small hours of 8 May if the parliamentary arithmetic of the general election shifts it beyond our two-and-a-quarter party system into something much more fragmented). The post-war steady state was, I think, the playing out and partially combining of two politico-economic philosophies which dominated both state and Parliament: liberal capitalism, in my judgement, the best engine of innovation and growth so far designed by man; and social democracy, the best system so far developed for curbing the excesses (though less so recently) of liberal capitalism, for distributing its benefits more equitably and creating the conditions of a fairer society. Sometimes the electorate has plumped for a greater shot of one rather than the other. The nature of the tussle between them has been, until now, the great weathermaker of our electoral politics and our Whitehall policy-making – and, as a country and a people, I think we have been the better for it.

- Secondly, as Norman Shrapnel indicated, Parliament has been the theatre in which our retreat from near top-of-the-range great powerdom played out. It was often uncomfortable, sometimes admirable; for example, in the way we (mostly) disposed of our territorial Empire. It has also been the theatre in which the anguish of Britain and Europe has been staged and what scenes await there in the coming months and years.
- Thirdly, Westminster has been the anvil of both argument and character, making and sometimes breaking those parliamentarians who would seek to lead their parties or head up great departments of state and Number 10 Downing Street itself. Parliament, in this aspect, is a combination of a political thermometer and a floating exchange rate of reputations. The state, Whitehall, of course, operates its own highly sensitive tariff of who's up and who's down, who can do the job and who can't. But that is back of house. Parliament is front of house, with the media as a constantly playing orchestra in the pit.

It may surprise you if I suggest that Parliament is getting better at its job in a number of ways, for all the current anguish about the reputation of parliamentarians.

May I offer just a few, though significant, examples in justification of this claim? Tony Benn used to recall for my students at Queen Mary something his father, who had served in Parliament from Asquith's time to Macmillan's, told him about Parliament and the state. 'Parliament', old Wedgie liked to say, 'exists to control the purse and the sword'. In the thirty-five years since the new department-shadowing House of Commons select committees came into being, I really do believe that executive policy and public money have become more effectively scrutinised with a width, depth, and consistency the previous select committee configurations had never managed. And since 2010, with the election of chairs and members of the select committees – instead of whip-dominated appointments – along the lines recommended by my friend Tony Wright, there has been another surge of accountability and scrutiny.

As a bit of a constitutional historian, I'm particularly pleased, too, at the way the post-1979 Commons select committees have enabled Parliament to have a real and sustained say in constitutional developments. I think of the Treasury and Civil Service sub-committees that made the running on the framing of the Civil Service Code in the mid-1990s under the leadership of Giles Radice and Austin Mitchell. I think more recently of the Political and Constitutional Reform Committee on the Cabinet Manual under the energetic leadership of Graham Allen. I hope and expect Parliament and its committees will rise to the level of constitutional events across the Kingdom as we deal with the consequences of the Scottish referendum result and in the further rise of the English Question.

As for controlling the sword, matters too have advanced. It was to Tony Blair's credit that he listened to Jack Straw and Robin Cook and gave the House of Commons a vote on peace and war in the run-up to the invasion of Iraq in 2003. I am sure that it is now a convention that, if time and circumstances allow, the Commons will have such a debate and vote on a substantive motion before substantial UK military operations overseas are authorised.

David Cameron deserves credit, too, as he has behaved as if the Chilcot Inquiry into the Iraq War had already reported. On Libya, last year's cruise-missile attack on Syria that never was, and this summer's deployment of RAF Tornados against ISIS in Iraq, there has been a vote (one of which stayed the hand of the Trafalgar-class submarine, HMS *Tireless*, in the Mediterranean) and a full legal opinion from the Attorney General made public. In the case of Libya and Syria, there was a proper assessment prepared by the Joint Intelligence Committee assessments staff in the Cabinet Office rather than an equivalent of the much-criticised hybrid intelligence dossier in the run-up to the Iraq War.

I was reminded earlier this month, when the House of Lords debated Lord Falconer's Assisted Dying Bill, of how good and admirable is the convention – I think I can call it that – between Parliament and the Executive, such that since the 1960s, reforms on capital punishment, homosexual relations between consenting adults, and abortion law, known as 'conscience bills', are exactly that: unwhipped exercises of individual conscience. That convention, as the same-sex marriage legislation of last year showed, is still in good repair. In the recent Lords debate on assisted dying, Lord Deben (perhaps still better known as John Selwyn Gummer) said, rightly, of Parliament that 'we represent society in having to take these very tough decisions'.

Back to the larger sweep. I have read the newspapers every morning since the Suez Crisis and the Hungarian Uprising of the autumn of 1956. Over those fifty-eight years, Parliament has provided a constant recitative to political and national life.

Only a few years ago, I discovered from documents declassified at The National Archives that there were plans drawn up in 1963 after the Cuban Missile Crisis to put Parliament into abeyance in the last hours of peace before a thermonuclear war between East and West in the Cold War tipped into Armageddon. But before Parliament was prorogued, the intention was to rush through an Emergency Powers (Defence) Bill to hand over powers to Cabinet ministers re-designated as regional commissioners in charge of the twelve mini-kingdoms into which the UK would be divided, with such huge powers over life, property, food, and finance, in the words of the secret contingency plan, 'as to amount to a voluntary abdication by Parliament of the whole of their functions for the period of the emergency'. And some recently declassified Home Office papers from the early 1980s (which I'm still reading) contain thoughts about how soon something resembling normal parliamentary and judicial proceedings might be resurrected out of the irradiated ruins of an H-bombed UK. Terrifying stuff. The cold print of the archives almost rises up and strikes you when you read those extraordinary files. Such a state, had it come to pass, would of its very nature have been the coldest of cold monsters.

I am, however, a convinced optimist about the continuation of the United Kingdom as a vital and viable parliamentary democracy. I have quaffed deep the perhaps mythical potion that our gifts for smart muddling through will always and everywhere see us through as one of those highly favoured nations whose democratic instincts give us a great and permanent competitive advantage as, in our own peculiar ways, a profoundly open society.

I am, ladies and gentlemen, one of those permanently in danger of falling into what David Runciman, in the best book on democracy I have read for ages, calls 'the confidence trap', published under that title in 2013. 'Democracies', he writes,

> are not good at spotting crises before they occur. They ignore the warning signs of impending trouble. At the same time, they overreact to the routine hiccups of political life, which adds to the air of distraction. Scandals grip democracies while systematic failures get overlooked. Democracies lack a sense of perspective. This produces repeated crises as mistakes mount up. But it also enables democracies to escape from crises, because no single mistake is ever conclusive. Democracies continue to adjust, adapt, and find a way through. This process is not pretty, and it creates a pervasive feeling of disappointment.

Spot on. How that fits our UK post-war experience.

There is, of course, as David Runciman makes plain, the possibility of a crisis that will overwhelm us. The Second World War was nearly lost at least twice between 1939 and 1945. And, as A. J. P. Taylor liked to point out, nuclear deterrence only needed to fail once during the Cold War and that would have been it. But optimist I shall remain.

Why? Because, through a combination of instinct and the experience of living in our islands since 1947, I profoundly share the belief expounded by that extraordinary parliamentarian Enoch Powell in a speech delivered in France – in Lyons – on 12 February 1971 on the theme of Britain and Europe. This is what he said – again, I won't attempt an imitation of that unforgettable West Midlands accent rising and falling, as if a classically trained air-raid siren:

> Take Parliament out of the history of England and that history itself becomes meaningless. Whole lifetimes of study cannot exhaust the reasons why this fact has come to be; but fact it is, so that the British nation could not imagine itself except with and through its Parliament.

My views have never entirely coincided with those of Enoch Powell. But helpless romantic that I am, I am with him on this one – on history, Parliament, and imagination. Mine is a sometimes irritated love of Parliament. But love it is. And it will not perish.

With my sisters Kathleen, Maureen, and Terry. I owe my earliest interest in history to Kathleen, who bought me R. J. Unstead's *Looking at History* for Christmas in 1958, and a great deal more to all three of them for looking after me all my life.

PART FOUR

ON CROWN SERVICE

The two words 'civil' and 'service', when put together, do not exactly set the pulse racing. If they are stimulating enough to arouse any image at all, it is likely to be of process-obsessed and procedure-bound men and women, performing worthy but unglamorous tasks with overlays of impenetrable bureaucracy. Why then should a young and keen journalist wish to devote the bulk of his working hours to reporting such a profession? If you have, as the UK has since the mid- to late-nineteenth-century reforms overseen by Gladstone, a permanent career civil service shifting silkily from one administration to the next, the influence, if not raw power, of such a body is bound to be very considerable indeed. It's important, therefore, to have some sense of who the players are, where and how they were educated, the method of their recruitment and the means by which they rise up the hierarchy.

There is also the drama provided by the perennially charged interplay between politicians and civil servants, with some less gifted ministers succumbing to the temptation to accuse their senior officials of attempting to block the more radical elements of their political programmes. The image of Jim Hacker and Sir Humphrey Appleby is scoured deep into our shared cultural memory. I can remember the late Hugo Young of the *Guardian* saying that many of the incoming Labour government in 1997, for example, treated *Yes, Minister* as if it were a documentary rather than a sitcom, coming into office determined that the Sir Humphreys were not going to sabotage *them*. I must admit that, from a professional perspective, it was quite useful to provide a shoulder to cry on for the aforementioned officials on the occasions when they felt somewhat besieged. The line between catharsis and outright leaking was not always entirely clear.

For all its external image, the Civil Service is not static or unchanging. It is interesting that the next phase of the sitcom coverage of Whitehall, *The Thick of It*, reflected the additional spice provided by the arrival of the special advisers in some numbers, particularly after 1997. Special advisers are temporary civil servants who owe their appointment to direct ministerial patronage. To parody, where Sir Humphrey was feline and cunningly indirect, the more rumbustious of the SPADs, as they quickly became known, are direct, speak in primary colours, and, as they are intended to be, are unashamedly party-political. This new strain in the governing mix produced considerable volatility as well as the very richest of pickings for satirists. Our government is still living in that ecology.

Some of what follows in this section are period pieces, in particular the profiles I wrote of the Cabinet Office and the Treasury for *The Times*. Both departments have now changed beyond all recognition, so this is not reflective of current Whitehall, though the bone structure of these two most powerful departments is, I hope, recognisable to those that now live in them. But I hope the reader will enjoy them as snapshots of institutional life at an interesting moment in their history, facing economic crisis and great pressure on the apparatus of government itself.

The big change since my curiosity was first piqued by the Civil Service in the mid-1970s is that, as a profession, it can no longer live off the record. This is partly because Parliament's select committees question many more civil servants in public. Plus, generally, a more open approach in society to institutions of all kinds, and, of course, the introduction of freedom of information. But, in my more self-indulgent moments, perhaps I can dare to think that the journalistic profession had a little part to play in edging ajar the great oak doors of discretion.

Why the best job in the Civil Service means carrying the prime minister's bag

The Times, *10 November 1976*

The geography of politics is one of the more fecund concepts thought of by political scientists in recent years. It is used not to describe diplomatic and military blocs or the politics of oil, but to illustrate the importance of physical proximity to decision makers for those who would exercise influence. To put it in Whitehall terms, a permanent secretary once declared he would gladly lose a senior member of his staff for every two yards of ground gained in the direction of the Prime Minister's study on the first floor of 10 Downing Street.

Judged by this criterion, the most influential job of all within the machinery of government is undoubtedly that of the Principal Private Secretary (PPS) to the Prime Minister. Nobody sees him more regularly or more often. Since the 1930s the post has usually been filled by a brilliant career civil servant in his mid-forties, seconded, more often than not, from the Treasury and serving for between two and five years.

There is an air of mystery about the job which is not merely a reflection of the confidentiality which inevitably accompanies intimacy of the kind that should develop between a Prime Minister and his chief of staff. It also springs from the infinite variety of relationships and work habits that grow up between the individuals concerned. No two combinations are alike.

Temperamentally, PPSs have ranged from overmightiness to humility. One incumbent has described himself as 'the highest paid bag-carrier and door-opener in the country' (the job currently carries a Civil Service Under Secretary's salary of £12,000). Others have never concealed their strategic position as one of the Prime Minister's most influential policy advisers. Even the most self-denigrating occupant of the seat can inspire jealousy from both ministers and civil servants more elevated than he in the hierarchy. A delicate balancing act is called for. All are acutely aware of the temptations and limitations of their power.

'It's very heady,' a former PPS recalled. 'There you are, sitting in the cockpit of the United Kingdom in an atmosphere that is friendly and close. You can say what you think. You don't lightly override the advice of your elders and betters. But you can if you want. You can tell the PM "this is nonsense" and deftly guide him to something better. But if you are demonstrably wrong, just once, you have had it.'

A good deal about the esoteric, chancy nature of being a Prime Minister's Principal Private Secretary is revealed in a book published today by Sir John Colville, Joint Principal Private Secretary to Sir Winston Churchill, with Sir David Pitblado, during his second and final premiership, 1951–55.

Colville was at No 10, in a more junior capacity as one of a supporting team of junior private secretaries, when Churchill replaced Chamberlain in 1940. The private office was transformed overnight from a secluded retreat to an overworked command-post bristling with the most advanced communications systems – a characteristic it has retained ever since even under more quietist Prime Ministers.

Though never since has there been anything to match the inspired chaos of the war years, the health of several private secretaries has been impaired by service in No 10 and one, tragically, died in harness. But reading Colville on the Churchillian routine, it is amazing that the casualty rate was not higher:

> There was nothing which could be described as orderly in Churchill's method of work. The car would be standing outside No 10, with its engine running, when there were only three

minutes to go before the Prime Minister's questions were due at the House, and no Prime Minister had emerged. He would still be in bed correcting a speech, when he ought to have been on the Front Bench preparing to deliver it. On Monday mornings, with the Cabinet due to meet in London at 11.00, he would still be at Chequers at 10.00 and the cars would be forced to tear up to London – police bells ringing, shooting red lights, going on the wrong side of islands, while Churchill sat unconcerned within. The windows were tight shut, he was smoking a cigar and he was dictating to a stifled, long-suffering stenographer who sometimes had to be revived with brandy on arrival.

So long as successive Prime Ministers resist the temptation to set up their own government department along the lines of the Washington White House with its 3,000 staff, the Principal Private Secretary and his team of four who cover home, foreign, and parliamentary affairs plus diary and general correspondence, will continue to live on the edge of exhaustion however stable the political scene or inactive the occupant of No 10.

The sheer mechanics of the job explain the strain and reveal part of the power that accompanies it. The PPS is the final conduit through which all paper passing upwards for Prime Ministerial approval is channelled – he is the keeper of the red boxes.

The PPS and his number two, the secretary provided by the Foreign and Commonwealth Office to handle their telegrams and to liaise between the Prime Minister and the Foreign Secretary, sit in a tall, well-proportioned room overlooking Horse Guards Parade adjacent to the Cabinet Room and linked to it by a double door. Three more private secretaries sit in a similar room next door.

Documents come up on a hoist from the 'Garden Room' in the basement where the secretarial staff is billeted. A duty clerk sifts the papers and places them, according to subject matter, in a series of bins known as 'live dips'. Material from the 'dips' which the Prime Minister needs to see is assembled in the Principal's room to ensure that he is aware of everything of importance that is going before his master in the traditional red box.

The PPS is at liberty to write his own suggestions or comments on minutes to the Prime Minister whatever their source. Normally, he is careful not to interfere with advice from the Secretary of the Cabinet or from the Prime Minister's own personal policy advisers in No 10.

If knowledge is power, then the PPS is in an enviable position. More than anyone else, he knows what is in the 'boss's' mind and the issues on which he must reach a decision. He sits in at the Prime Minister's meetings, listens in to all the Prime Ministers' official telephone conversations on a third line and is expected to do so, and notes down any points which may require following up. Would-be Woodwards and Bernsteins, sniffing the possibilities of a British Watergate, can turn off the adrenaline before it begins to flow. Such conversations are never taped, with the sole exception, it would seem, of diplomatic exchanges between heads of government: Readers of Mr Macmillan's memoirs will recall the verbatim reproduction of his conversation with President Eisenhower and appreciate that banality rather than revelation is the hallmark of such transactions.

Since Macmillan's time, the PPS has sat in at meetings of the full Cabinet and at most Cabinet committees, half hidden behind the Corinthian pillars in the Cabinet Room. Only the Cabinet Secretary and the Cabinet Office minute takers share this privilege. The No 10 Private Officer, therefore, has the great advantage of knowing what has been decided before the rest of Whitehall, which has to wait for the minutes to be typed and circulated.

On the Prime Minister's behalf, the PPS may, on occasion, have to deal directly with Cabinet ministers and permanent secretaries and exercise functions out of all proportion to his Under-Secretary rank. He is the doyen of the Whitehall private office network – the most advanced grapevine in the world, its operators say.

The private secretary's art is to know his minister's mind as well as he knows it himself, to get inside his skin. One former PPS described the ideal relationship as one where neither the Prime Minister nor the private secretary need to finish a sentence to be completely understood by the other. If this intimacy is successfully reproduced across Whitehall, conspiracy theorists might see the private office network as a hidden device for taking over ministers. But, as one of the more guileful of the No 10 practitioners put it, indicating to the Prime Minister that you are one jump ahead of him is another swift route to disaster.

Much of the PPS's time is taken up with the routine duties of an office manager, improving the procedures, refining the system and handling the staff. The high-pressure existence in No 10 often leads to frayed nerves and strained personal relationships. Again, a delicate touch is required.

Once a year, No 10 throws a summer party for all the major Whitehall private offices in the back garden which enables them to put faces to the voices they are used to dealing with day in, day out. 'Very good for business,' said one initiate. The Cabinet Office, their powerful neighbour linked to No 10 by an internal corridor, holds a similar party at Christmas.

Another source of the PPS's power is his role as keeper of the diary. Access to the Prime Minister is controlled essentially by him. A fine judgement is required to protect the 'boss' from wear and tear, carving out time for him to think from a crowded schedule, while avoiding the pitfalls of isolation from Cabinet colleagues, Parliament, party interest groups and the public.

An often forgotten but still significant constitutional practice is the Prime Minister's regular Tuesday evening meeting with his sovereign. This can require a good deal of preparation. Churchill, notoriously dilatory at reading telegrams and papers on subjects which bored him, was caught out by the Queen on two occasions during his last premiership, to his obvious chagrin. The poor PPS who had tried in vain to persuade the great man to read them in advance got an undeserved earful of inimitable rodomontade.

Mr Attlee, not the most avid conversationalist, was provided with a list of subject headings he might like to discuss with King George VI at the weekly audience. Early in Attlee's administration, the King's private secretary informed his counterpart in No 10 that the King had opined of his first minister: 'I gather they call him Clem. "Clam" would be more like it!'

With such a wide range of duties and so much time spent alone with the Prime Minister, no wonder the suspicions of overmightiness can develop in Whitehall about the role of the Principal Private Secretary. 'Every Principal Private Secretary must remember all the time that he is nothing in himself. He only has influence in that he reflects the Prime Minister', said one. Another PPS recalled a conversation with his outgoing predecessor: 'He said "you must give the PM all the advice he needs, but it is not necessarily your own. You must not set yourself up as a personal source." I never forgot that'. Most ex-PPSs prefer to describe the essence of their job as being an extra pair of ears, eyes and hands to help the Prime Minister in his ever-pressing duties.

Treasury men are particularly prone to suffer from the suspicion, usually unfairly, of being a plant in No 10 from the most overmighty department of them all. Sir Harold Wilson twice broke the pattern of Treasury men in the PPS's job. He inherited Sir Derek Mitchell, 1964–66, from Lord Home. But Sir Harold turned down two Treasury men, when it came to finding a successor to Mitchell, in favour of Mr Michael Halls, who had worked with him while Sir Harold was cutting his ministerial teeth at the Board of Trade in the late 1940s.

In 1974, Sir Harold inherited another Treasury man, Mr Robert Armstrong, from Mr Heath. Mr Armstrong served five years in No 10, longer than normal. His departure was affected by the timing of the 1975 referendum on British membership of the EEC, after which Sir Harold made some delayed changes in both the official and the ministerial spheres. Mr Armstrong was succeeded by the present incumbent, Mr Kenneth Stowe, who came to No 10 from the Department of Health and Social Security after a spell in the Cabinet Office.

Whatever the individual variations between the two men concerned, one crucial and singular element in the Principal Private Secretary's role must be recognized. *It is a political job.* Normally, career civil servants try to separate politics from administration and concentrate on the latter, leaving the former to ministers. That is the traditional essence of their calling. In No 10, it is simply not possible to do so.

The two strands are so mixed as to be inseparable. The office of Prime Minister stands at the summit of both politics and administration and the private secretary must reflect this if he is to work properly. Unlike other private offices, there is no government department on the other side of the door to inspire a dual loyalty to ministry as well as minister.

Former PPSs are candid about this: 'You have got to be a political animal. You have got to have the feel of what is politically sensitive. You cannot really do the job without that quality,' said one. Another described the tension between the two poles as turning the No 10 private office into 'a perpetual buffer state. To make the distinction between the official and the political is almost impossible and there is also this extraordinary spectrum from pure nannying at one end to high policy on the other'.

Some will be more political or more nanny-like than others. Perhaps political science can again be helpful in explaining the unique role of the private secretary in No 10 when it speaks of the civil servant as permanent politician. Better still is the summary of a former Prime Minister with a fondness for dogs: 'They can either be borzois or retrievers.'

The Cabinet Office: A magnificent piece of powerful bureaucratic machinery

The Times, *8 March 1976*

Public administration has never been a subject to excite much in the way of public fervour. A diligent observer of Whitehall in recent years could be forgiven for concluding that in so far as the structure of central government has attracted the interest of a wider public at all, it has become the subject of a protracted moan about 'cost-effectiveness', 'accountability', 'participation', 'openness' and all the other dreary catch-phrases that fade one into another. Those rare spirits who have a taste for drama, even romance in the conduct of high politics, find little to attract them in the worthy efforts of central government to adapt itself to the needs of the modern state. There are a few exceptions: the Foreign Office retains a certain glamour; the Treasury the kind of *elan* which comes from being the object of powerful, paradoxical feelings – admiration for its brainpower, contempt for its results – from a nation that has never quite made up its mind about the worth of clever people. But the most fascinating of them all is the Cabinet Office. Lying at the very hub of Whitehall, it is both the mainspring and the oil-can of the machinery of government. Tiny, powerful, shrouded in secrecy, run by a succession of dominating figures, relatively little is known about an institution which is the closest Britain has come to having a prime minister's department.

So firmly is the Cabinet Office embedded in the constellation of Whitehall departments that it is surprising to discover how recent an arrival it is, certainly when compared to the constitutional device of Cabinet government which stretches back in a clear line to the early eighteenth century. Founded with little fanfare nearly 60 years ago in December 1916 as an inspired piece of Lloyd Georgian 'ad hoccery', it represented an enduring reform which, in the words of Sir George Mallaby, brought a degree of 'indispensable articulation' to the machinery of government.

Modelled on the Committee of Imperial Defence, the office provided the Cabinet for the first time with an agenda and minutes of its conclusions. It was run by a remarkable marine called Maurice Hankey and 10 assistant secretaries. Viewed from the perspective of 1976, Hankey's outfit looks rudimentary, merely a collection of scribes with the chief scribe carrying great weight with the prime minister of the day for personal reasons. But at the time, the nascent Cabinet Office, a reform all except Asquith thought long overdue, transformed the handling of government business. Vansittart aptly described Hankey as: 'Secretary of everything that mattered ... he grew into a repository of information. He had an incredible memory ... an official brain which could reproduce on call the date, file, substance of every paper that ever flew into a pigeon-hole.'

After experiencing the very personal premiership of Lloyd George, not everyone remained quite so impressed. Bonar Law, coming in as Prime Minister in 1922, coupled the Cabinet Office in his mind with the 'garden suburb', the collection of huts on the back lawn on Number 10 which housed the private political office of the outgoing Lloyd George, as another manifestation of noisome personal aggrandisement. Law found a powerful ally in Hankey's wilful rival, Warren Fisher, Head of the Civil Service, who wanted to absorb the Cabinet Secretariat into the Treasury.

Hankey and his machine survived as an independent unit – but only just. From its wartime peak of 165 committees serviced by a staff of about 160, it shrivelled, under Law, to two standing committees – Imperial Defence and Home Affairs – with a staff of 28. Baldwin and MacDonald made some additions in the fields of civil research and economics but Herbert Morrison was fully justified in describing the apparatus as 'primitive' when he took office for the first time in the Labour Government of 1929.

The Second World War, once more, transformed the Cabinet Office as it did the entire structure of central government. First Anderson then Attlee as heads of the all-powerful Lord President's Committee acted virtually as 'Prime Minister for the Home Front' leaving Churchill to run the war with the chiefs of staff and the admirable General Ismay. The Cabinet Office came fully into its own as the supreme coordinating element in Whitehall, a pre-eminence it has never lost since.

Curious primitive touches still remained, however. Churchill was appalling at summing up Cabinet meetings and ministers quite often treated the minutes as recommendations rather than instructions. The office, at this time, was run by the inspirational, artistic Edwards Bridges. The present Prime Minister [Harold Wilson] was joint secretary to the manpower requirements committee and has sharp recollections of the period. He particularly remembers the day when Bridges asked him to write up the minutes of a Cabinet meeting which, Mr Wilson protested, he had not attended. Bridges handed him his own illegible notes and observed airily, 'Don't worry, it wouldn't be any better if you had been there'. The 24-year-old Mr Wilson duly obliged. He clearly relished his time in Richmond Terrace where the Office was then billeted, and often refers to it at present-day Cabinets. He was once asked did he ever regret not having taken up the offer of a permanent Civil Service job in the Cabinet Office after the war? 'Heavens no', replied Mr Wilson, with a faint trace of irony. 'I couldn't have stood the intrigue!'

In contrast to 1922, there was no question of dismantling the Cabinet Office at the end of the Second World War. Anderson wrote an internal report recommending its retention and development. Attlee accepted it and reorganised the secretariat and the standing committees in 1947. The only faint repetition of the interwar period came in the form of the slightly sour relationship that emerged between Bridges, who gave up the post of Cabinet

Secretary after the war to concentrate on running the Treasury and the Civil Service, and his successor, Norman Brook. There was a difference of temperament between the two men, the dry, fastidious Brook was a machine man *par excellence*. He drafted the definitive manual for Cabinet minute takers, exhorting them to be terse and eschew embellishment. There was more to it than that, however, and Brook was not alone in his growing scepticism of the Treasury and all its works. The political significance of the frequently quirky relationships between permanent secretaries in the 'top hamper' is too easily ignored. Dislocations at this level can have significant repercussions for the Government as well as for the Civil Service. When they go well, as they did with Brook's successor, Burke Trend, and William Armstrong, who was first at the Treasury and then the Civil Service Department – the two were close friends and sympathetic colleagues who held the central machine together for 10 years – it ceases to be a potentially disruptive factor. The present 'big three', Sir John Hunt, Sir Douglas Allen from the Civil Service Department and Sir Douglas Wass from the Treasury lunch together every Monday in the Cabinet Office Mess.

The Cabinet Office retained much of its Committee of Imperial Defence flavour into the postwar years. Suez was for its staff, as for others, a watershed. In 1966, symbolically it ceased to be responsible for organising and servicing the Commonwealth Prime Ministers' Conference. Increasingly, the office came to be preoccupied with the economy, the central issue of British politics. Whitehall has not failed to notice the accretion of power in this field to the Cabinet Office under Lord Trend and his successor Sir John Hunt. The increase in the office's staff numbers, very nearly half of whom are in the Central Statistical Office, from 407 to 681 between 1965 and the present day tells but part of the story.

The Cabinet Office rarely initiates policy, but a succession of the most trying issues that have taxed successive governments over the past 10 years have been handled there at their most crucial stages: Europe, Northern Ireland, counter-inflation policy, industrial policy and now devolution. The office is still, with permanent secretaries, deputy secretaries and under secretaries of the first rank, recruited on secondment from a wide variety of government departments, who are much more than mere minute-takers. Whether it requires fine-tuning or knocking heads together, this is where policy is invariably handled in its final stages.

These developments have been conscious and carried out with the approval of both Mr Wilson and Mr Heath, with varying degrees of acceptance on the part of departmental ministers. The Cabinet Office argument, which has held sway, concentrates on the need to strengthen the centre against the huge 'jumbo' departments like Environment, Health and Social Security and Defence, on the periphery. The office's view – to adopt the common metaphor which sees Whitehall as a village – is that it represents the only neutral house in the street where powerful, competing families can resolve their differences in a civilised manner, under the guidance of a benign, independent chairman.

Last year, by way of illustration, the draft of both the white papers on industry and incomes were eventually prepared by the Cabinet official committees under the chairmanship of a Cabinet Office deputy secretary. When the time comes in a few months for the final touches to be put on the devolution bill, that too will be tackled there. The Cabinet Offices' Constitution Unit which will handle it has the fascinating and, in Whitehall terms, unique task of unscrambling a tidy system, the reverse of normal Civil Service practice, which will require officials to break the habits of a lifetime. For once, too, the Cabinet Office will be the lead department on devolution.

Such developments in the hidden world of Cabinet Office interdepartmental committees are often concealed from even the best-informed outsider. After his first week as Director-General of the Central Policy Review Staff, the 'Think Tank' grafted on to the Cabinet Office by Mr Heath in 1970, Lord Rothschild was amazed to discover the undefeatable duumvirate of Trend and Armstrong which dominated Whitehall. 'Until this week', he confided to a friend, 'I never realised the country was run by two men whom I'd never heard of.' Within the Whitehall village, which, like all enclosed communities, devotes a great deal of time and energy to gossip and the attaching of labels to its *bella figura*, the aggrandisement of the Cabinet Office in the past 10 years has led to Lord Trend and Sir John Hunt being cast in the imperialist mould, though the two men are often contrasted; Trend as the intellectual, Hunt as the dynamo. 'Burke was feline, John is a Borzoi'; 'Trend was Byzantine, like Rothschild, Hunt is a sixteenth-century cardinal with a touch of the Borgias', are two of the more vivid characterizations.

The relationship between the Cabinet Office and the other government departments is delicate and fluctuating. There is clearly a Cabinet Office art that has grown up to cope with it. One of its most eminent practitioners in the past described it as removing the 'hidden boulders' that might otherwise disturb the smooth flow of Cabinet business. One of the most skilful of its current exponents outlines its requirements in this way:

> If there are signs that the department which is leading on a particular subject has got into a bit of a muddle or has got too close to the thing, you need a sharp eye and good nose for discovering just the right moment to ring up and say 'Why not have a meeting?' Very often this generates an almost spontaneous desire to pull the thing together even though the department concerned may have sweated blood in getting it this far. The managerial approach developed by John Hunt, particularly in economic affairs, means that the Cabinet Office tends to be in all the front-line fights. But we always have to carry the rest of Whitehall with us. If the departments ganged up on us, we would always be defeated.

It is not only in Whitehall that anxieties may have been aroused about the 'overmighty subject'. Ministers from both major parties have been heard to engage in anti-feudal muttering about the power of the Cabinet Office. Some Labour ministers returning to office in 1974 after three and a half years in the wilderness were taken aback by the growth of its stature and of its 118 official committees. The Prime Minister was not prone to this particular allergy but, as an old Cabinet Office traditionalist, he quickly put an end to the blurring of distinctions between official committees and ministerial committees that had occurred under Mr Heath.

Some of the more astute Whitehall-watchers were not so sanguine as their leader: 'Every other department is about something', one of them explained. 'The Treasury is about economics and finance, Environment is about housing and roads. The Cabinet Office is powerful because it is pure bureaucracy. It is a rapidly expanding power and reflects the times in which we live'.

Whitehall brief: How public servants keep it private

The Times, *22 September 1981*

Should you find yourself at a party in Esher, or some other area favoured by senior civil servants, and the conversation drifts toward what people do for a living, watch carefully for the Cabinet Office hands. They may not be quite the mundane state servants they seem.

Each year, the 568 officials who work for Sir Robert Armstrong, Secretary of the Cabinet, receive a note called 'Annual Reminder. Activities which may involve the Use of Official Information or Experience'. In a word, it says you must not say anything to anybody unless previously authorised to do so.

Attached to the reminder is a little gem, a collector's item for connoisseurs of British secrecy called *Talking about the Office*. It coaches its recipients in what cover stories to wheel out should they find themselves questioned about work by friends or contacts.

The Cabinet Office, it seems, is the Canterbury Cathedral of official secrecy. Even officials from such traditionally garrulous institutions as the Treasury or the Ministry of Defence must tread in reverential awe when recruited for a spell in 70 Whitehall for the warning 'may be particularly necessary for officers seconded from other departments if they were able to talk about their previous work fairly freely.'

Talking about the Office, itself a classified document, amounts to a sacred text in the literature of British administrative secrecy as it is the justification civil servants circulate among themselves for keeping their private world beyond the gaze of irritants like MPs, the public and the press. For that reason, it is worth quoting at some length:

> The work of the secretariat and much of the work of the Central Policy Review Staff are essentially confidential. This stems directly from the secrecy which properly surrounds Cabinet business and the advice given to ministers, and, by extension, the business of Cabinet committees.
>
> It has always been maintained by successive administrations that disclosure of the processes by which government decisions are reached weakens the collective responsibility of ministers which is what welds the separate functions of Government into a single administration.
>
> The first rule, therefore, is that even the existence of particular Cabinet committees should not be disclosed – still less their composition or terms of reference. That is so even though on occasion the Government finds it convenient to make a public reference to an individual committee.
>
> On social occasions Cabinet Office people must only describe their functions in general terms. Members of the Central Policy Review Staff should avoid mentioning projects on which they are working unless they have been made public. No details about the chain of command in the office should be given.

But it is the Joint Intelligence Committee and its supporting organisation which requires special treatment, even though its work is regularly mentioned in the press and it was included in the 'Consumer's Guide to Mrs Thatcher's Cabinet Committees' published in *The Times* on February 10.

According to the document 'It is not widely known publicly that the JIC is a Cabinet committee or that its assessment machinery is located here; and this should not be mentioned in conversation with outside contacts.'

It is different in other countries with political and administrative systems built on the Westminster–Whitehall model. For example, Mr Patrick Millen, Secretary of the Cabinet in New Zealand, sends details of Mr Robert Muldoon's Cabinet committees to *The Times* in the shape of parliamentary answers released in Wellington.

In Ottawa any visitor to the Privy Council Office can get a list of Cabinet groups including the membership of Mr Pierre Trudeau's Security and Intelligence Committee.

If the past is any guide, nothing short of a quiet revolution in Whitehall will shift Britain into line with Canada and New Zealand. In the meantime we shall have to rely on public-spirited 'moles' like the one who very kindly provided *The Times* with *Talking about the Office*.

No 10 in the Jay–Lynn eye: The megaphone theory of 'Yes Minister'

The Listener, *19 and 26 December 1985*

As we await the results of Jim Hacker's elevation to Prime Minister, Sir Humphrey's to Cabinet Secretary and Bernard's to Principal Private Secretary in *Yes Prime Minister*, Peter Hennessy has been seeking advice on their behalf from Lord Home, Lord Trend and Sir Derek Mitchell

Ten years ago, after a famous court case in which the Wilson government tried unsuccessfully to suppress them, the first volume of Dick Crossman's *Diaries of a Cabinet Minister* was published. Crossman, who had a passion to explain, wrote shortly before his death in 1974 that his 'ambition was to write a book which fulfilled for our generation the functions of Bagehot's *English Constitution* 100 years ago by disclosing the secret operations of government, which are concealed by the thick masses of foliage we call the myth of democracy.'

Crossman, though clearly an impossible colleague, brought a zest to politics which transcended what Orwell called the 'smelly little orthodoxies' (mainly because his own orthodoxies were as changeable as the weather), and soared above the drudgery and grind of running a department and endless hours in Cabinet committees. For him, it seems, even six years of Cabinet life under Harold Wilson were worth it, if by publishing his diaries he could do 'something towards lighting up the secret places of British politics and enabling any intelligent elector to have a picture of what went on behind the scenes'.

The diaries made fascinating reading for Whitehall buffs like me. And though widely criticised as inaccurate by those aggrieved by their portrait in his pages, the Crossman *Diaries* had an important cleansing effect. Never again would it be possible, with a straight face anyway, to publish works of public piety as a ministerial memoir with reality camouflaged in a dignified account of what is essentially a partisan and short-sighted shambles.

But in his wider ambition, the ebullient Dick, sadly, failed. In their pure form his works did not take off as vehicles of public enlightenment about those secret places. Mercifully for him and his crusade, two clever men with a flair for presentation read him and absorbed his legend and lore like a sponge. Antony Jay and Jonathan Lynn recognised the rich potential of Crossman's tales of the Whitehall woods and set about refashioning them into latter-day, up-market Ealing Comedy. You don't have to work at GCHQ to decipher the textual similarities between the Crossman *Diaries* and *Yes Minister*.

Take the first entry in Crossman *Volume One*: the account of his first day as Minister of Housing and Local Government in October 1964. For a start, it gave Jay and Lynn their title: '... they know how to handle me. Of course they don't behave *quite* like nurses because the Civil Service is profoundly deferential – "Yes, Minister! No, Minister! If you wish it, Minister!"'

And doesn't this passage seem vaguely reminiscent of Jim Hacker's first day in the Department of Administrative Affairs?

> I turned to my Private Secretary, George Moseley, and said 'Now you must teach me to handle all this correspondence.' And he sat opposite me with his owlish eyes and said to me, 'Well, Minister, you see there are three ways of handling it. A letter can either be answered by you personally in your own handwriting; or we can draft an official answer.' 'What's an official answer?' I asked. 'Well, it says that the Minister has received your letter and then the Department replies. Anyway, we draft all three variants,' said Mr Moseley, 'and if you just tell us which one you want.' 'How do

NO 10 IN THE JAY-LYNN EYE: THE MEGAPHONE THEORY OF 'YES MINISTER'

I do that?' I asked. 'Well, you put all your in-tray into your out-tray,' he said, 'and if you put it in without a mark on it then we deal with it and you need never see it again.'

Jay and Lynn served as Dick Crossman's megaphone. They brought the arcane world he depicted in his diaries to a huge audience from 1980 onwards. *Yes Minister* attracted nine million viewers on BBC1 at its peak. It changed, too, the craft in which I was then engaged – reporting Whitehall for a quality newspaper. It gave journalists like myself and Richard Norton-Taylor of the *Guardian* a megaphone as well. Our kind of journalism could be slotted into big audience radio and television programmes like *Today* or *Nationwide* at the drop of a verbal or visual cliche. Sir Humphrey, Jim and his Private Secretary, Bernard, had become household names in a way that Crossman, Moseley and their magnificent Permanent Secretary, Dame Evelyn Sharp, had not.

Now Jay and Lynn are clearing the foliage from another patch of arcana – No 10 and Cabinet government. Jim has been projected to the top of the greasy pole and Humphrey and Bernard have risen with him, Humphrey to the top Civil Service job of Cabinet Secretary and Bernard to the post of the nation's most influential minder, Principal Private Secretary to the Prime Minister. The cognoscenti, the real-life Jims, Humphreys and Bernards, cannot wait for *Yes Prime Minister*. They are totally hooked on the Jay–Lynn pastiche of their habitat.

For example, before a single episode of the forthcoming series has been screened, Lord Trend, Secretary of the Cabinet 1963–73, the man Crossman portrayed as a shadowy figure cooking the Cabinet Minutes and syringeing Wilson's more radical impulses, has been persuaded to rupture the total discretion which, with his tall figure and courteous manner, has long been his trademark. When I asked him to advise Humphrey on the art of the Cabinet Secretary, Burke Trend delivered a homily which will be the stuff of a thousand sixth-form and undergraduate politics essays:

'Humphrey,' said Lord Trend, 'has now got to be a different sort of animal. He's got to remember two things. (1) He's not the Prime Minister's exclusive servant. He's the servant of the full Cabinet. He's got to have no truck with the idea of a Prime Minister's Department, a 'Kitchen Cabinet' or a 'Garden Suburb'. I don't believe in them as a source of advice to the Prime Minister in the sense of being a rival to the Cabinet Office. There has got to be one centre round which the rest of the official machine can come together. (2) He's got to develop a rather different style. He's got to be a bit detached – not taking sides in departmental squabbles, ensuring they all get a fair hearing – and to deal with that endless upwards surge of business, driving it downwards where he can.'

Lord Trend is very precise. It used to be said in Whitehall that he could dictate White Papers from his head. His old chief, Lord Home, is a neat and tidy person as well. Remember his passion for flower-arranging during his spell in No 10? He adores *Yes Minister* but regards Jim Hacker as too much of a chump to be plausible. 'That awful fellow,' he says, 'I never saw a Minister who was as idiotic as that ... he oughtn't to be Prime Minister for more than half an hour.' Sir Derek Mitchell, who in 1963–4 was 'Bernard' to Lord Home's 'Jim' and Lord Trend's 'Humphrey' says he does remember one Minister–Permanent Secretary team from the Sixties who were pure Jim and Humphrey but discretion overcame him when invited to name them.

Sir Derek reckons his promotion will offer Bernard enviable new scope: 'In the past, he's been rather under the thumb of Humphrey. But as Cabinet Secretary Humphrey won't have the kind of access to the PM that the Principal Private Secretary has. Bernard is going to have opportunities from the early morning in the Prime Minister's Downing Street flat while Jim puts his teeth in until he gives him the last Red Box at night.' Lord Home tends to agree. He sees a Private Secretary as someone with whom 'you can let down your hair. They know how far they can go and Bernard goes a long way. Bernard is awfully good. You get that element of cheek in it. Derek

Mitchell was very efficient. I never understood a word about economics and his strength was the economy.'

Derek Mitchell is also deliciously enigmatic. He is adamant that Lord Home was nothing like Jim Hacker. 'No, of course he's not. He was Prime Minister as a result of a strong sense of duty. He never gave any sense of enjoying the power of the place.' Lord Home's year in Downing Street 'wasn't a farcical period', Sir Derek added, hinting, perhaps, that other premierships and other periods were.

As for the megaphone theory of *Yes Minister*, Sir Derek inclines to agree that it has changed the public's attitude to his old service. After a pause and a smile, he said in language courtly enough for a White Paper: 'It has probably done so to something like the extent that *Fawlty Towers* has given people a better appreciation of the British hotel industry.'

The Treasury: Bank manager and probation officer rolled into one

The Times, *28 March 1977*

British economic policy is made in a literally symmetrical fashion. The Treasury's four ministers, five permanent secretaries and seven deputy secretaries all sit two floors up above Parliament Square around an inner courtyard. The Circle, as it is called, is truly *the* commanding height of the British economy. A visitor in the labyrinth of corridors and staircases that make up Treasury Chambers can tell when he is there from the thick, shiny, red linoleum, the artery of inter-Treasury communication.

There have been countless newspaper articles on Britain's inadequate economic performance since 1945. Apart from the trail-blazing work of the inimitable Mr Samuel Brittan, however, relatively little attention has been devoted to Treasury men themselves, except for periodic attempts to show that they all read Greats at Christ Church and were unsuitable, therefore, to become anything but district commissioners in Kenya, a view as untrue as it was fatuous.

At the risk of seeming eccentric on Budget-eve it is instructive to put policy in second place for a moment and look instead at the kind of men who sit around the Circle, cerebrating and, from time to time, prodding a stubbornly sluggish economy. Do they occasionally despair, like the rest of us, about our ever getting it right? How much responsibility do they accept for the nation's economic decline? What are the limits they place on their advice to ministers? Do they trust their own forecasts of future economic performance? What kind of rows do they have with each other? How do they respond to public criticism and the suspicions of ministers?

The first impression from all but living with Treasury men in recent weeks is that they are far from monolithic in their views and backgrounds and almost as sceptical about their efforts as the more sensible of their critics. About economic forecasting, for example, their humility is positively Uriah Heepish. In this, they take their lead from the Chancellor of the Exchequer, Mr Healey, who has never concealed his view that economic predictions are about as reliable as long-range weather forecasts and that 'on the whole, running the economy is more like gardening than operating a computer'.

One of the forecasters' chief clients remarks: 'I don't believe young men get their figures right. I don't have much faith in computers.' The model-builders themselves spend a great deal of time reminding their superiors that their past predictions of the British economy have been between 2 and 4 per cent out on critical matters like the size of gross domestic product, the level of exports, imports and investment. The prime justification offered for forecasting by the economist with ultimate responsibility for the Treasury's huge, complicated model is that it stops eccentric decisions being taken on the basis of personal hunch by those at the top of the hierarchy and likens it to a flywheel which prevents policymakers from being thrown by the pressure of unexpected events.

It would seem that the art of the Treasury man is not to be a reader of cybernetic printouts. 'What you need here, as at the top of any large organisation, is people who are likely to make good judgments on impossibly contradictory sets of facts', said one. 'It's all to do with insights', said another. 'It's the relationships between sets of figures. You are really good in the Civil Service when you can do these things under pressure, relating them to wider horizons.'

The last image Treasury men wish to project is that of soulless 'number crunchers'. But they do talk a good deal about 'professionalism' and take great pains to dispel the aura of gifted amateurism. Members of the Government Economic Service are 'bedded out' to work alongside administrators in the policy divisions. They are encouraged to keep up with the latest thinking in their field, 'though I wouldn't want my young men to spend too much time on the lunatic fringe', said one of the Treasury's top five.

One economist, who has shuttled between the universities and the Treasury since the late 1940s, says the place is hardly recognizable when compared with postwar days: 'The difference at all levels in economic sophistication is quite tremendous. This is an intensely intellectual place. Everybody is interested in principles. We *are* economic thinkers.'

As Whitehall departments go, the Treasury is very free from hierarchy. It is all Christian names and young men being encouraged to speak, as Roy Jenkins once observed when comparing Great George Street with the Home Office, the other great department of state in which he had served as political head. Problem cracking in ad hoc teams, involving, very often, the Inland Revenue and the Bank of England as well, seems to be the style these days.

But on two facts Treasury men think as one: that 1976 was for them a pig of a year with their perpetual headaches made more acute by the country's desperately weak external position; and that they bent but did not break under the strain. Sir Harold Wilson has probably devalued the Dunkirk metaphor forever, but it is the best one to apply to HM Treasury last year.

A deputy secretary in one of its most exposed beachheads dealing with incomes policy, taxation and monetary matters, likes to talk about the past two years in terms of weaponry: 'First that pay/tax deal appeared on the horizon like a tank. Hardly had that one been dealt with than another tank arrived marked "Professor Milton Friedman." Both tanks – tax, pay and monetary policy – have been here ever since. Now "differentials" is the cry. Incomes policy is a frail craft. The Treasury has always given warning about the risk of putting extra luggage on it.'

But it is not just a matter of cheerfully muddling through and uniting in the face of external onslaughts. Treasury men on the second floor, who have been in the department since returning from the war, are good at thinking aloud about the intractable aspects of Britain's postwar economic performance and the degree to which they can 'turn it round' however skilled or consistent their advice to ministers.

The most donnish of the Treasury's 'Big Five' is highly philosophical about the limits to policy advice: 'There are very deep-seated problems that can only be affected at the margins by the policy instruments the government wields. It is arguable that with less "stop-go" and lower rates of personal income tax, we might have got a better performance. But I think it would have been pretty marginal. We have a body economic that has not functioned well. This may have something to do with the nature of our society, including the nature of the educational system, with the value we set by finance rather than industry and the public esteem we give our engineers. The City has preempted a lot of managerial talent as the colonial empire did and the Civil Service, to some extent, still does.

'These are not primarily government matters. Society has to change its attitudes but government can do a great deal by moral leadership. The question I continually ask myself is how much could government policy have wrought a fundamental change in Britain's economic position since the war in the way that the Commissariat du Plan helped to do in France? The industrial strategy is a response to these thoughts.'

Such reflections hardly square with the arrogance and hauteur traditionally attributed to Treasury men. But an outsider might suspect that they have been overdoing the gloom a bit of late, almost as a delayed reaction to the traumas of last year, especially when the most ebullient and irrepressible of their permanent secretaries, who gives the impression of having eaten a tin of razor blades and two ministers for breakfast, comes out with the remark that: 'I tell my young men you can win "only on the firm foundation of unyielding despair", as Bertrand Russell put it.'

The face the Treasury presents to the outside world is naturally very different from the way it runs itself internally. Sir Douglas Wass, its top permanent secretary, a quiet, Cambridge mathematician, who joined the Treasury after a war spent inventing new techniques of mine detection for the Admiralty, is a firm believer in collective leadership, a principle he enshrined in his 1975 reorganisation of the department.

The traditional problem of the Treasury Number One has been to unify and coordinate the powerful and often conflicting interests reflected in his policy divisions. The historically minded talk of feudal satrapies, an analogue that makes other Treasury men wince, but a good one. Sir Douglas (the Treasury a few years ago was brimming with men called Douglas and the *Financial Times* invented a collected personality for them which they called 'Sir Douglas Corridor') reconciles his barons every Thursday morning at his Policy Coordinating Committee, the PCC, nicknamed the 'Peoples' Congress' or 'Parochial Church Council' by its more waggish attenders.

Papers for the PCC are produced by a committee of staff officers of under-secretary rank, dubbed 'The Colonels' for obvious reasons, but properly known as the Macro-Economic Policy Group. They meet every Monday under the chairmanship of Mr John Isaac who runs Sir Douglas's Central Unit. The unit is his eyes and ears within the department. Admiring outsiders see his use of the unit and the 'Colonels' as the key to Sir Douglas's success in being *primus inter pares* in a department that has never been short of overmighty subjects. The central unit is also the key body in the preparation of large presentations like the annual Budget and occasional 'packages' of additional measures.

One of the first actions of Sir Douglas Wass on succeeding Sir Douglas Allen in 1974 was to reinforce Treasury practice whereby disagreements were to be ventilated and not suppressed. The PCC, therefore, is often the occasion for vigorous dialectics bluntly expressed, with Overseas Finance ('the winged messenger bringing gloomy reports', as its principal Mercury likes to put it) telling the

THE TREASURY: BANK MANAGER AND PROBATION OFFICER ROLLED INTO ONE

Public Services Sector just what Britain's foreign creditors will or will not take, and so on.

If the dispute is too deep to be resolved at the PCC, Sir Douglas Wass minutes the Chancellor, naming the disputants and elaborating their disagreements. The argument is then carried on before the Chancellor in his magnificent room overlooking King Charles Street. By all accounts, heterodoxy can break out in the august councils of the PCC. The alternative strategy of import controls and a siege economy was fought out there last year, particularly before the departure of Professor Lord Kaldor, Mr Healey's special adviser.

Where Treasury men, ministers and other parts of Whitehall disagree is over what happens to economic policy after the dialectical stage of the PCC has been passed. Some argue that the Treasury is just too good at keeping disputes within itself, disputes that are so fundamental to government strategy that they should be argued out not just in the PCC, which ministers do not attend, but in the Cabinet itself. This contention lies at the heart of the case for breaking up the Treasury into a spending ministry and a finance ministry, a split, its proponents believe, that would better reflect the more collective manner in which Labour Cabinets have come to take major economic decisions. It would appear from talking to some of the Treasury's 'top hamper' that the department exercises its own version of collective responsibility akin to that of the Cabinet: 'The PCC is a two-stage process with unbridled discussion and everybody saying what he likes. But when it gets to the crunch, you have in effect weighted voting. The second permanent secretaries and the deputy secretaries are there because they are presumed to have better overall judgement than the line man. There is an absolutely binding convention, which has never been breached, that argument is free up to the time the Chancellor makes up his mind. Then all the energy goes into securing what the Chancellor wants.'

Another PCC member explained that there was no alternative to this and that it operated on interdepartmental matters, like incomes policy as well. 'It's like the old Civil Service consensus technique – never stop trying to agree. It's our job to minimise difference. You can call it a fix, but I regard it as what we are paid for. It is our task to make collective responsibility work. If we didn't, there would be chaos or we would have to turn into politicoes. That would maximise differences all right.' Others, including, one suspects, the Chancellor, would contend that the Treasury no longer tries to keep the options unto itself while presenting a united front to the rest of Whitehall. Treasury discussion invariably leads to a set of alternative policy options which the Chancellor himself often displays in papers put before the Cabinet. It is then left to ministers to argue it out either at the fortnightly meeting of the Cabinet's Economic Strategy Committee, chaired by the Prime Minister, or at full Cabinet. Making a judgement on this matter is virtually impossible for an outsider but it is the key to the internal Whitehall debate about the future, power, size and shape of the Treasury. The Treasury's present set of ministers, the customers of the 'fliers' billeted around the Circle, say that, first and foremost, they want their civil servants to place all the facts before them. The Chief Secretary, Mr Joel Barnett, likes to be briefed, for example, on the case for more spending that will be put up against him by other departments during the annual cycle of the public expenditure survey.

The Chancellor insists on the issues being argued out in front of him – 'like the early Soviets in 1917', he says – before taking the decisions himself. Such an approach is vital in a ministry which Sir Stafford Cripps, the iron Chancellor of the austere 1940s, likened to a barrister's chambers with 'little task forces that only meet in the canteen', as one of today's insiders puts it.

Inevitably one aspect or another of Treasury work is always in contention. Not only is it the most political of departments with an interest in every aspect of government activity, as its former head, Sir Edward Bridges used to say, but its responsibility lies at the very heart of the country's past failures and future anxieties. This produces in successive generations of Treasury men an attitude of cheerful resignation to being abused for what they regard as their virtues.

Morale has improved of late, however. Cash limits have induced the feeling that spending is once more under control. The new financial information system for monitoring spending profiles each month to be applied to all government departments during the next financial year (run out of a turret full of computer experts above the Treasury rooftops under one of its most promising assistant secretaries) should take that process a step farther.

Provided ministers do not lose their resolve, the Treasury need not fear any more headlines of the 'Lost £5,000m' variety stimulated by the evidence of Mr Wynne Godley, one of its former forecasters, before the Commons Expenditure Committee.

The time-honoured criticism that Treasury men deal only with other government departments and never with that mythical entity, the 'real world' has partly been answered by the new Domestic Economy Sector which emerged from the 1975 reorganisation. Its control of the Industrial Strategy Staff Group places it at the centre of the Government's nuts-and-bolts attempt to regenerate industry from the ground up.

They do have an incentive to 'get it right' if they can. As one of the Treasury's public-expenditure men put it: 'Our work is an endless bloody grind. There is no glamour in it. If they are to have any motivation at all, my chaps have got to feel they are winning.' There is an element of defiance, too, particularly in Overseas Finance which bore the brunt of criticism during the collapse of the currency last year: 'From a professional standpoint, you can only do your best. If you are, blow the critics!'

Venerable institution though it is, with roots going back to William the Conqueror's Henry the Treasurer, the Treasury is a noticeably human organism, surprisingly, perhaps justifiably, self-critical of late. But scratch a Treasury man and the old Gladstonian sense of moral purpose comes shining through, not in the parsimonious, cheeseparing sense, but in a manner which portrays them as the nation's bank manager and probation officer rolled into one. In this mood, they quote Sir Bruce Fraser, a former colleague who told the old Estimates Committee they exist 'in order to curtail the natural consequences of human nature'. For all its pomposity, there is a kind of nobility about that.

The Good and the Great: The most elevated and distinguished casualties of the Thatcher years

The Listener, *7 February 1985*

Are they selfless servants of the public good, or an Establishment mafia? And do governments act on the results of their deliberations anyway? Peter Hennessy examines the declining reputation and influence of 'the auxiliary fire service of the ruling class'.

In the days before Mrs Thatcher was Prime Minister, the grand old institution of the Royal Commission and the Committee of Inquiry had a prominent place in the public life of the nation. These august bodies, authoritative and influential, were always manned by what is now the Lost Tribe of British Public Life, a decorous, distinguished collection of elders who went by the name of 'the Good and the Great'. For a large part of the postwar era their unofficial but universally acknowledged leader was Lord Franks of Headington, a figure of impressive austerity and great probity who ran the Ministry of Supply in World War Two, negotiated the North Atlantic Treaty as Ambassador to Washington, chaired Lloyds Bank, helped set up the National Economic Development Office, served as Provost of Worcester College, Oxford and chaired a host of official inquiries before retiring to an old farmhouse in North Oxford.

So might begin the chapter on the 'British Establishment' in a 21st-century history book on 20th-century Britain. 'The Good and the Great' were a marvellous Victorian invention. In the 19th century, Royal Commissions were high achievers. They created a substantial body of new evidence on public health and the condition of the poor. Governments acted on their findings. But Mrs Thatcher, an oft-proclaimed believer in 'Victorian values', cannot stand the G and G. For her, they symbolise the fudging and the compromise, the recycling of old orthodoxies, a key contributor to the cycle of failure which produced Britain's stunning economic decline. According to Clive Priestley, a former civil servant who worked closely with her, Mrs Thatcher has little time for 'the golden oldie type – and I dare say that would tend to cut out quite a number of those on the List of the Great and the Good'. In the judgement of Sir Anthony Parsons, the career diplomat who served in Downing Street as the Prime Minister's foreign affairs adviser, 'probably what she objects to about the classical Good and Great is that by their very nature – the fact that they all know each other, they are clubby people, they frequent the same environment – they do tend to reach moderate, balanced, medium conclusions about whatever matter they are dealing with'.

Good and greating was quite a brisk business in the first three decades of the postwar era. Whenever governments found themselves in a tight corner on some incendiary issue and wanted to douse the fire – it might be pay-beds, trade union reform or what to do about ministerial memoirs – the auxiliary fire service of the ruling class would be rushed to the scene. The flames would then subside, temporarily at least. Hostile questions in the House of Commons could be fielded with the words 'We are waiting for the report of Sir Alec Merrison/Lord Donovan/Lord Radcliffe', depending on the issue of the hour. The system had its benefits for the G and G as well – a nice red leather box like Ministers have (this was changed to a standard-issue black Civil Service briefcase in the late Seventies) with perhaps a trip to the Palace for a K when it was all over. All that has changed. The Good and the Great, loaded with honours, dripping with gravitas, oozing the accumulated experience of decades, have become the most elevated and distinguished casualties of the Thatcher years. Yet decay had set in some time before 1979. They were, by all accounts, an overripe target for the most anti-Establishment Prime Minister in living memory. David Owen, Foreign Secretary in the last Labour government, acquired a deep loathing of the G and G from his Whitehall experiences. He cannot abide the British Establishment: 'They are absolutely secure. They are the ones who were sent out to George or to settle up with Harry. They are everywhere. They are in the City, they are in industry, they are in the Civil Service ... you never really feel that they actually stand for anything. They are just part of the general British slide and decline.' However, Dr Owen is man enough to admit that, as Minister of Health in 1975, he rigged the membership of the Royal Commission on the National Health Service to get the result he wanted.

Oddly enough, the Good and the Great figure scarcely at all in the 'Decline of Britain' literature. Of all the great organisations contributing to what Mancur Olson called our 'institutional sclerosis', the furring of the national arteries which has prevented us from adapting and innovating as an economic power, the British Establishment has yet to find its chronicler. The reason is clear enough. Everybody knows it exists. But the BE is very difficult to pin down, or to measure. Virtually nobody will admit to belonging to it. Occasionally, history will throw up some Pooh-Bah of public life who is clearly *homo bonus et magnus*. A legendary example of the breed was Sir John Anderson, ennobled as Viscount Waverley. Waverley was a dry Scot who had run the Home Office in the 1920s and shown Baldwin how to break the General Strike. In the 1930s he had pacified Bengal and prepared a plan for civil defence in case Hitler turned nasty. When he did, Anderson served as Home Secretary, then Chancellor of the Exchequer. Churchill called him the 'automatic pilot'.

In the early 1950s, according to the story, the Russians sent a high-level delegation to Britain. They were conveyed from Tilbury to Westminster by launch and met by the Chairman of the Port of London Authority, Lord Waverley. An early engagement in their programme was with the Chairman of the UK Advisory Council on Atomic Energy and, to their mild surprise they found themselves shaking hands with Lord Waverley. That evening at a reception in Buckingham Palace they just happened to come across one of the Sovereign's most trusted Privy Counsellors, Lord Waverley. The next day, having expressed a particular interest in Britain's defences against coastal flooding, they found themselves in East Anglia with Lord Waverley, who was busy on an official inquiry into this very phenomenon. That night, as a farewell present, the Russians were taken to Covent Garden for a gala performance. There they were met by the Chairman of the Board of the Royal Opera House, Lord Waverley. The exhausted delegation cabled its report to Moscow: 'Comrade Stalin, Britain is not as we thought a democracy. It is an autocracy run by a man called Waverley.'

By their quangos and their committees shall ye know them.

One section of the British Establishment can be identified with some accuracy. It consists of Whitehall's committee-fodder, the men and women whose names are kept on the List of the Good and the Great to which Clive Priestley referred. This venerable artefact of the British system of government was once described by Lord Rothschild, former head of the Think Tank and the Chairman of the Royal Commission on Gambling, as the 'famous list of the Great and the Good, all of whose members, if I may be allowed to exaggerate, are aged 53, live in the South-East, have the right accent and belong to the Reform Club'. Lord Rothschild, when in charge of the Tank, persuaded his boss, Edward Heath, to let him run an investigation of the G and G. The senior civil servants set up a committee – and that was the end of that. But the issue did not go away. When Labour returned to office in 1974, Harold Wilson was convinced by the arguments of his senior Downing Street adviser, Bernard Donoughue, to get a wider, more representative slice of the nation on the List of the G and G.

Dr Donoughue is a match for Dr Owen in his contempt for what he calls 'the Establishment culture of sound and comfortable men'. He concentrated his fire on its most tangible manifestation, which Whitehall, in its prosaic fashion, calls the Central List. With

Wilson's backing, Dr Donoughue found an enthusiastic assistant in a career civil servant, Jonathan Charkham, who used to delight colleagues by describing his missions as 'finding chaps of both sexes for posts'. Donoughue and Charkham did a good job. As the breakdown of the 1983 List shows it is a distinct improvement on Lord Rothschild's cruel stereotype. The microcomputer of the Cabinet Office's Public Appointments Unit contains a better blend of women, people from the regions and the non-middle-aged, though the male/female divide is still pretty unbalanced. But in one crucial respect Dr Donoughue failed. His proposal to open the List properly by allowing people to nominate themselves or their friends was overruled by Ministers. 'They didn't want to give up a piece of power,' he says. Ironically the achievements of Dr Donoughue's proposed second stage of reform was sanctioned in 1980 – by a Conservative Minister. If you want to sign up, consult the chart.

It is doubly ironic that the right to self-nominate was introduced at the very moment the G and G were being put on ice. The Thatcher freeze was not lost on them. They are, almost by definition, sensitive and intelligent folk. In December 1982, some of their biggest names – Lord Rothschild, Lord McGregor (Royal Commission on the Press), Lord Benson (Royal Commission on Legal Services) – gathered in a Westminster basement, under the flag of the Royal Institute of Public Administration, for a collective whinge. There was talk of the 'deafening silence syndrome' which, even before the installation of Mrs Thatcher, had so often greeted their reports. The phrase coined by Professor Bernard Williams, 'pathways to the pigeon-hole', was on many a G and G lip. One almost felt sorry for them; old retainers eased out of the household in their twilight days.

But never underestimate the *ancien régime*. There'll always be an England while there's a Good and Great. General Galtieri, who is neither good nor great, changed their fortunes as he did much else in British political life. The Falklands War is the greatest trauma Mrs Thatcher has suffered during her premiership. The origins of

CABINET OFFICE

THE LIST OF THE GOOD AND THE GREAT

Total Number of Names	4,954
Men	4,092
Women	862
Those aged under 40	324
Men	299
Women	125

Geographical distribution

London and the South-East	2,425
Rest of the United Kingdom	2,529

Details of names on the list are secret.

If you would like to be considered for inclusion, write to:

> Mr Colin Peterson, CVO,
> Public Appointments Unit,
> Cabinet Office,
> 70, Whitehall,
> London SW1.

List of the Good and the Great.

the conflict had to be gone into, and the Prime Minister could not simply appoint a crony. The consent of the other party leaders had to be forthcoming. It was time to send once more for Lord Franks, the most golden of the oldies. On a Saturday morning in July 1982, Sir Robert Armstrong sat sipping coffee in North Oxford with his old friend. The G and G show was back on the road.

Lord Franks is good at running committees. He works them hard and fast. Franks Reports (Official Secrets, Tribunals and Oxford University are but three British institutions to have come under his gaze) meet their deadlines. He knows how to ease up when tension is building: 'Sometimes I've suggested they stop for five minutes and take a stroll round the corridors. If I can think of a joke I produce one, or I ask some member of the committee to tell a story about something relevant to what we are talking about – anything that comes to hand to break the clash.'

There is a serenity about Lord Franks which comes, one suspects, with an ascetic temperament, age (he's 80 this month) and his near-unique position in public life. A former civil servant said of him: 'If Britain was a republic, Oliver Franks would have to be president. No one else would do.'

So serene is Whitehall's Great Inquirer that he is prepared to admit the inadmissible: 'If anybody likes to label me in that way, I don't object because what it means is that I have done public duties from time to time – that is by definition ... being a member of the Establishment.'

Lord Franks remains unruffled, too, by suggestions, most notably from former Prime Minister, James Callaghan, that by exonerating the Thatcher administration from any blame for the Argentine invasion of the Falklands in his last paragraph, he had 'chucked a bucket of whitewash' over the whole report. The Falklands Committee had 'at times fierce' arguments, particularly over the interpretation of intelligence data, said Lord Franks. But 'I do not think a single member of my committee would have signed a report which they thought was fudging the issue.'

Wasn't it bound to be an 'Establishment job' if the inquisitors consisted of a former ambassador, a retired permanent secretary and four ex-Cabinet Ministers (Lords Watkinson and Barber for the Conservative, Lord Lever and Merlyn Rees for Labour)? 'The judgement that was involved,' Lord Franks explained, 'was a political judgement. Therefore it was reasonable that people experienced in political judgement should be on the committee ... I've never actually been on a committee when the members of it were so wholeheartedly devoted to trying to ascertain what they thought was the truth of the matter ... I was very impressed with the way in which party considerations did not enter into the deliberations.'

Oddly enough, bucket of whitewash or not, Franks on the Falklands did, at least temporarily, put the lid on the question of the Thatcher government's culpability in the 'signals' it did, or did not, send to the Argentine junta in the 1981 Defence Review, which announced the planned withdrawal of the ice-ship HMS *Endurance*. Since he reported in January 1983, public attention has been almost exclusively concentrated on an event which took place after the war started – the sinking of the Argentine Cruiser *General Belgrano*.

There has been precious little sight of the G and G either since 1983, with the notable exception of the Warnock Committee on Human Fertilisation and Embryology, dealing with the emotion-laden issue of surrogate motherhood. The philosopher Lady Warnock, who has just become Mistress of Girton College, Cambridge, is a vigorous defender of the Good and Great as a vehicle for public policy-making. Hers was a classic G and G operation in the Victorian mould. It broke new ground and created a corpus of evidence where none existed before. Lady Warnock admits she herself was somewhat muddled about the issue before her committee set to work. 'I have become a bit clearer-headed now, partly as a result of hearing the on the whole very ill-informed and violent discussions in Parliament ... One is always being told that the bad thing about Committees of Inquiry and Royal Commissions and so on is that they are all made up of the same sorts of middle-class people. The difficulty is, I think, to find any other sorts of people who have either the time or the will or the expertise to be members of these committees.' I put it to Lady Warnock that an unkind parody of her view would suggest she was depicting the Good and the Great as a mechanism carefully designed to get round the consequences of popular democracy. 'Why would that be an unkind thing to say?' she replied. 'I think it is absolutely accurate and very important.'

Are there any more issues on the political agenda crying out for a Royal Commission on the Victorian model? Plenty. Local government finance for one. After the Ponting trial the accountability and ethics of the Civil Service would seem a natural, not to mention Section 2 of the Official Secrets Act.

But wait a minute, wasn't that yet another Franks enterprise, circa 1972? Yes it was, and it trod the pathway to a Home Office pigeon-hole. What went wrong? 'Every government in power is very reluctant to give up any weapon of power, and control over communication is one weapon of power,' says Lord Franks. 'This holds for Conservatives. It holds for Labour. And while that persists, then I think that favourable conjuncture of events does not exist and that is why the report of the Official Secrets Committee has not been acted on yet.' A classic G and G appraisal. When you have answered the call from virtually every Prime Minister since Attlee, detachment and a sense of timelessness become second nature.

Lord Franks: The lord who sits in judgement

The Times, *17 January 1983*

There is more than a touch of the puritan about Lord Franks, which partly explains his reputation as the 'Lord Clean' of British public life. The day *The Times* leaked his appointment as chairman of the Falklands inquiry, a senior official, walking in the gardens of the Civil Service College at Sunningdale, was heard to remark: 'He's the reason I'm a monarchist.' Asked to explain this baffling statement he added: 'If Britain became a republic, Oliver Franks would have to be president. No one else would be acceptable.'

The last thing Lord Franks, OM, GCMG, KCB, CBE, PC, would aspire to be is a Lord Protector. But there is one line from the other Oliver (Cromwell) of which he would approve: 'If the fact be so, why should we sport with it?'

As to his general acceptability, the anonymous official was quite right. Lord Franks was the only name the leaders of Britain's political parties could agree on for the Falklands investigation when consulted by Mrs Margaret Thatcher last summer. A fellow member of the 'Good and Great', the stage army that provides the man and woman power for royal commissions and the like, recalled 'the universal sigh of relief' when the Prime Minister appointed him.

Lord Franks is clearly number one on the famous list, with a host of inquiries behind him into official secrets, and Oxford University to name but two great British inventions. But the Falklands was different. 'This time he was running a jury', said a fellow Privy Counsellor who sat in judgement with him.

Lord Franks is a tall, shy, somewhat forbidding figure for those who do not know him. He has great presence, a factor which hugely impressed several of the witnesses called before the Falklands jury. As one hard-boiled Whitehall figure put it: 'He is one of the few people of whom you can say you know he has an alpha-treble-plus mind. He asked all the simple, blindingly obvious questions that everybody missed – the hallmark of a truly great man.'

It seems strange to recall now that the only question mark over the suitability of the 77-year-old Lord Franks for the Falklands job was, in the words of one insider, 'the condition of his marbles'. On Saturday, July 3, Sir Robert Armstrong, the Cabinet Secretary, travelled to Oxford to test them. He found them in perfect rolling order. Lord Franks's precise grasp of truckloads of complicated documentation was something else that impressed those summoned to give testimony.

It was punishing work for the whole committee. Lord Franks asked his Privy Counsellors to break the back of Foreign Office, Ministry of Defence, Cabinet Office, Number 10 and intelligence archives by sitting reading six hours a day in the special cubicles through the bulk of August and September. For relaxation in the evenings Lord Franks reread Fernand Braudel on the sixteenth-century Mediterranean. 'I found it a very good antidote', he said in conversation last week.

When it came to light relief, there was also Lord Lever, a former Cabinet minister under Mr James Callaghan, the committee's licensed wag. A political colleague of Lever's began his statement to the Franks inquiry by acknowledging he had been 'a creature of Mr Callaghan's patronage'. 'Aren't we all?' quipped Lord Lever, helpfully.

There was a woman in the committee's life who brought a different kind of succour – Miss Anne Newman, of the Civil Service Catering Organisation. She placed a room off the Old Admiralty Building canteen at their disposal, filled it with cold cuts and generally mothered them; appropriately enough, the room was decorated with pictures of British warships. 'She looked after us superbly', said Lord Franks, 'We were very grateful'.

Once Miss Newman had left the Privy Counsellors to their viands and salad, Lord Lever would be off again, entertaining them with his delicious high-class political prattle. Lord Franks does not go in for gossip himself, But the others noticed how much he enjoyed listening to Lord Lever after a heavy morning of sombre reconstruction and interrogation.

Hitler brought Lord Franks into public life. On September 4, 1939. The day after war was declared, the 34-year-old Professor of Moral Philosophy at Glasgow University received a telegram sent by the Minister of Labour which read: 'Go to the Ministry of Supply' as if it came from a game of Monopoly. He caught the night train to Euston. Professor Franks entered Whitehall as a principal and finished up as a permanent secretary six years later. Or a 'temporary permanent secretary', as he likes to put it. For he was then offered 'the only job I'd ever faintly hoped for', the provostship of his old Oxford college, Queen's.

He was not left in peace for long. Attlee and Bevin had taken a shine to him during the war and invited him in the summer of 1947 to chair the physically and diplomatically demanding negotiations in a broiling Paris which led to the Marshall Plan. He returned to Oxford just before Christmas after a tour of the United States, explaining the need for a European recovery programme. While visiting his parents in the Mendips, his country called again, or rather his mother did after answering the telephone. 'Oliver', she said, 'a man called Attlee wishes to see you'.

This time he was wanted for the Washington embassy to drive through Bevin's stratagem for a North Atlantic Treaty Organisation, which he duly did. They made an odd pair, the ascetic ambassador and the earthy foreign secretary. Bevin once declined: 'You 'ad a university experience, Oliver. I was educated in the 'edgerows of experience'.

Washington at the height of the Cold War was Lord Franks's heroic period. Apart from atomic collaboration prohibited by the Congress when it passed the McMahon Act, his rapport with Dean Acheson, the US Secretary of State, probably represented the high-water mark of the Anglo-American special relationship. Acheson later described his 'unorthodox proposal. On an experimental basis I suggested that we talk regularly and in complete confidence about any international problems we saw arising.' They met at the cocktail hour, unbeknown to their superiors in Whitehall and the White House. The experiment lasted four years.

Below stairs, as it were, matters were not so cheerful. Maclean, Philby and Burgess were on the payroll at various stages in Lord Franks's embassy. Philby, an MI6 officer, he hardly knew. Of Maclean he said: 'I knew him to be efficient, doing his job well. All I ever felt about him was that he was slightly tense.

'Burgess was wished upon us from New York [pause] and was an unsatisfactory member of staff [a smile of pure understatement broke over Lord Franks's countenance at this point]. One day I got a very indignant letter from Lucius Battle, Governor of Virginia. Burgess had been trapped for speeding three times in one day. I sent him home by the next boat.'

In 1952–53, Lord Franks turned down more important jobs than most public figures are offered in a lifetime. Why was he in such demand? 'For a while one's name is known, and then they forget one'. But surely they had remembered and brought him back for the Falklands inquest? 'Surprisingly', he said. One of the jobs he was offered was the editorship of *The Times*. Why did he decline? 'I felt there was an element in it of an act of creation every day. I didn't believe my temperament was like that.'

He chose Lloyds Bank instead, and was its chairman from 1954 to 1962, until Oxford called him home once more. He preferred to become Provost of Worcester College rather than become Governor of the Bank of England as Mr Macmillan had wanted. Mr Macmillan had just pipped him for the Chancellorship of Oxford two years earlier. Lord Franks was in India and Pakistan throughout the contest on a World Bank mission. He wanted to talk to Nehru about development. All Nehru wanted to talk about was the prospects for the Oxford election.

In 1964 he was asked to chair an inquiry into the university which produced a flood of Franks Oxford stories, some of which may be apocryphal. This one is not. An eminent Oxford don tottering out after a session of questions put by Lord Franks, delivered the words: 'I now know what the day of judgement will be like. Though I expect God to be more human.' That sounds a bit harsh when applied to the Lord Franks of 1983, when he is a mellow rather than a severe eminence.

One of the best stories he laughed at, but said he was sure it had not happened, which is a pity, because it captures him. Allegedly, Lord Franks was at a garden party in Worcester College on a high summer's day with a distinguished American visitor. A member of Worcester, well sauced with Pimms, engaged them in brilliant conversation until the heat and the booze hit his system simultaneously and he fainted in mid-sentence at their feet. Turning to the startled American, Lord Franks, the supreme diplomat, is reported to have said: 'How pleasant to see the young fellows of Worcester making their points with such verve'.

A relatively recent task is the Political Honours Scrutiny Committee. That is how he knows Mrs Thatcher. 'She trusts him', said one Whitehall official, 'because he is politically inactive while being politically aware.' But he took the Liberal whip when given a life peerage? 'Proves my point', said the senior civil servant.

His remarkable span at the summit of British public life had seen an equally remarkable decline in Britain's fortunes. Did he feel it personally? He was worried about sounding pompous, but he pointed out that he had been born in the aftermath of the Victorian era when the Christian virtues conditioned the general attitudes of society. In recent times such certainty had been denied. 'But I have no doubt that Britain will decide which way it wants to go and will pursue it in due course. I actually believe in my country'. Were we beginning to find our way now? 'Maybe', he said with a Delphic smile.

New social foundations lack crucial conditions: an argument for the revival of 'Victorian' Royal Commissions

The Independent, *25 April 1988*

It may be early middle age eating into my grey matter, but of late I have had the feeling that in political terms, I am living in a cherished if slightly decayed Victorian city with a small army of demolition men and property developers already in the outskirts. These wreckers – powered by a 100-seat majority – are determined to surround me with tower blocks, shopping precincts and urban motorways which, once in place, will remain until my grandchildren, in turn, demolish them.

For it is now undeniable that the foundations of the post-war society in which I grew up are about to succumb, wholly or in part, to the JCB of what is loosely known as Thatcherism. The philosophical underpinning of these endangered foundations was the notion of top-flight public provision in health, education and welfare – funded on the basis of progressive taxation – as the bonding material of a common citizenship.

These are variously alleged to have made *me* feel dependent on the state (in reality I feel proud of and grateful for the post-war settlement) and to have sapped *our* will and capability to produce and compete with the rest of the world (the causes of that go far deeper than anything Attlee or Bevan did or did not do).

I might be consoled if I thought the new settlement rested on two factors which, to a large extent, buttressed the one being usurped: what Lord Haldane once called in the context of Cabinet and

Whitehall policy-making 'the duty of investigation and thought as a preliminary to action'; and the painstaking construction of a public consensus around the resulting proposals, which was crucial if they were to endure beyond the current political regime.

Gazing at the new foundations represented by the Community Charge, the Education Reform Bill (the idea of the curriculum apart), the new social security arrangements and the likely outcome of the review of the National Health Service funding, I am not convinced that either of these crucial conditions is present.

Even more unfashionable atavism overcomes me at this point. Was there a case in at least some of these policy fields for reviving a truly great Victorian value – the Royal Commissions comprising people of independent stature, not government place-men – to fulfil both criteria?

The Prime Minister cannot abide Royal Commissions and has appointed none. It is easy to see why. By 1979 they had become deeply discredited mainly because of their abuse by Lord Wilson of Rievaulx, who as PM, in Phillip Whitehead's brilliant phrase, 'bought the hours with beer and sandwiches at No 10 and the years with Royal Commissions'.

They became nothing more than political fixes, a means of kicking difficult issues into touch as in the case of the last Royal Commission on the NHS, which sat from 1976 to 1979. But they were not always like that and, if revived, do not have to be like that again. The Victorians used them to break new ground as a preliminary to action which was expected to follow and usually did. A corpus of evidence was acquired, questions were asked on the basis of it, and ringing recommendations promulgated to the political nation at large.

Beveridge was a Victorian. What was in effect his one-man Royal Commission (though technically it was no more than an interdepartmental review body) of 1941–42 was squarely in the Victorian tradition with its identification of Want, Ignorance, Squalor, Idleness and Disease, which were put in capital letters and denounced as the 'Five Giants on the Road to Recovery'. Anyone within Whitehall who drafted a White Paper like that these days would be rapidly on the road to early retirement.

In the twentieth century the process has not always been that straightforward. In the case of health, for example, the idea of a national service took off in Beatrice Webb's minority report to the Royal Commission on the Poor Law in 1909, became Labour party policy in 1934, was much discussed by the wartime coalition government, was embodied in an Act of Parliament in 1946, implemented in 1948 and rested on a consensus for a further 30 years.

On education there was a smattering of committees in the interwar years but the Royal Commission equivalent was 'Rab' Butler's endless wartime journeys cajoling the churches, the trade unions, the educationalists and a sceptical prime minister (Churchill) until his settlement found legislative form in the 1944 Act. Conservative ministers don't come like Rab any more.

A decade ago, the Royal Commission types themselves rose up in protest at the decay of their system. Lord Rothschild (the investigator of gambling), Lord Benson (legal services) and Professor Bernard Williams (pornography) all came up with ideas to prevent their output treading, in Professor Williams' words, a 'pathway to the pigeonhole'.

Their thoughts included placing an obligation on the government to respond to proposals within a relatively short space of time, reducing the size of commissions, raising their level of expertise and exercising restraint in their establishment to avoid cheapening their currency. It is high time these ideas were given another run and consideration given to reviving an older, calmer and more thoughtful way of proceeding. Victorian virtue demands no less.

After running the Snowdonia Marathon with the Attlee Memorial Runners in the autumn of 1985 to record a documentary for Radio 3, *Quasimodo in Trainers* (a reference to my less than graceful athletic style). I collapsed into the warmth of the family in the car park of the Llanberis Hotel. Photo taken by the late Gerallt Llewelyn.

Afterthoughts

Attempting a joint biography/autobiography plus collection of writings of this kind is, perhaps, an unusual literary enterprise. But, in a way, it does bring out the bricolage, the fragments of a life, as if displayed in a junk-shop window. If it seems random and bitty, that's because life is random and bitty. But for all that, there are consistencies in my unplanned sequence of jobs. I have held the same fascination for governing institutions and the people that staff them since my mid-teens, which may strike others as somewhat eccentric. Having investigated them as a journalist and chronicled them as a historian, I have managed, somehow, to join them, in the House of Lords. The sheer pleasure of writing has also been a constant. Since my mid-thirties, writing books has been a consistent pursuit, and the thrill of completing a new production never diminishes.

I no longer have the energy for deep excavations in the mineshafts of The National Archives, or the preparation needed for lengthy interviews like the *Reflections* series on Radio 4, which I so enjoyed making with Rob Shepherd. But there are consolations to be found in smaller forms and shorter pieces. It's been fun to revisit past journalism and lectures, as it has been to be on the other side of the interview sofa with my daughter, Polly, asking the questions. It may seem like cheating, but at least I know I am guaranteed a sympathetic ear and I can't claim that my daughter doesn't understand me. It's been stimulating, too, to compose some new pieces on the themes that emerged in the compiled book. Above all, Polly and I hope that the fun comes across to you, the reader.

Acknowledgements

We thank the team at Haus, Harry Hall, Ed Doxey, and Barbara Schwepcke, for taking on this slightly eccentric project. It would be impossible to thank all the people who helped me to have a life in writing, but let's go back to my great and cherished mentors Brian MacArthur, Louis Heren, and Charlie Douglas-Home. I'm very grateful to them and I miss them very much. Back in the present, thanks to Paul Coupar-Hennessy, Katrine and Andy Pebworth, Lisa McGrath, Richard Miles, Ruth Levis, Jake Wilson, Cecily Cromby, and Enid Hennessy for helping us reach the finishing line.

Also by Peter Hennessy

States of Emergency: British Governments and Strikebreaking since 1919 (1983) with Keith Jeffery

Sources Close to the Prime Minister: Inside the Hidden World of the News Manipulators (1984) with Michael Cockerell and David Walker

What the Papers Never Said (1985)

Cabinet (1986)

The Great and the Good: An Inquiry into the British Establishment (1986)

Ruling Performance: British Government from Attlee to Thatcher (1989) with Anthony Seldon

Whitehall (1989)

Never Again: Britain 1945–51 (1992)

The Hidden Wiring: Unearthing the British Constitution (1995)

Muddling Through: Power, Politics and the Quality of Government in Postwar Britain (1997)

The Blair Centre: A Question of Command and Control? (1999)

The Prime Minister: The Office and Its Holders since 1945 (2000)

The Secret State: Whitehall and the Cold War (2002)

Rulers and Servants of the State: The Blair Style of Government, 1997–2004 (2004)

Having It So Good: Britain in the Fifties (2006)

Cabinets and the Bomb (2007)

The New Protective State: Government, Intelligence and Terrorism (2007)

The Secret State: Preparing For the Worst 1945–2010 (2010)

Distilling the Frenzy: Writing the History of One's Own Times (2012)

Establishment and Meritocracy (2014)

Kingdom to Come: Thoughts on the Union Before and After the Scottish Referendum (2015)

Reflections: Conversations with Politicians Volume I (2016) with Robert Shepherd

The Silent Deep: The Royal Navy Submarine Service Since 1945 (2015) with James Jinks

Winds of Change: Britain in the Early Sixties (2019)

Reflections: Conversations with Politicians Volume II (2016) with Robert Shepherd

The Complete Reflections: Conversations with Politicians (2020) with Robert Shepherd

A Duty of Care: Britain Before and After Covid (2022)

The Bonfire of the Decencies: Repairing and Restoring the British Constitution (2022) with Andrew Blick

Land of Shame and Glory: Britain 2021–2022 (2023)